# Medieval Pirates

# Medieval Pirates

## Pirates, Raiders and Privateers 1204–1453

JILL EDDISON

'*Merchant and pirate were for a long period one and the same person.*'

Friedrich Nietzsche (1844–1900),
German classical scholar, philosopher and critic of culture

*Cover illustration*: Cogs in Action *c.* 1330. Cogs had a single square sail. Castles were added to give height. Here, the taller ship is winning the contest, while sailors falling overboard from the other indicate defeat. (BL Royal 10 E IV f.19. Published with permission of Bridgeman Art Library)

First published 2013

The History Press
The Mill, Brimscombe Port
Stroud, Gloucestershire, GL5 2QG
www.thehistorypress.co.uk

© Jill Eddison, 2013

British Library Cataloguing in Publication Data.
A catalogue record for this book is available from the British Library.

ISBN 978 0 7524 8103 6

Typesetting and origination by The History Press
Printed in Great Britain by TJ International Ltd, Padstow, Cornwall

# Contents

# Sources

irates left no official records. They were not in business to leave neat series of connected accounts for historians to assess several centuries later, and indeed it was probably that lack which explains why medieval pirates have escaped literary attention so far. As a result of the absence of systematic sources, the information for this book has had to be gathered from occasional, scattered, records found elsewhere. It has come from three distinct directions: the monastic chronicles; the official national records of government; and the large and varied bank of published, secondary, work.

The monastic chronicles are believed to have originated with Bede in the eighth century. The eleventh and twelfth centuries saw the foundation and flowering of an increasing number of religious houses, and by the thirteenth, chroniclers were busily recording not only the internal management of their own house and its estates, but were also interacting with local townsfolk and passing travellers to record the affairs of the wider world. They built up a picture of history, past and ongoing. They were, in fact, becoming the keepers of the nation's memory.

One of the best informed and most frequently quoted of the chroniclers was Matthew Paris (*c.* 1200–59), a monk who began by assisting Roger of Wendover, the chronicler of St Albans, from 1217 onwards, before succeeding him in 1236. He spent nearly all his life in that abbey, strategically well placed beside the Great North Road only 20 miles from London. Having a roving interest and remarkably broad understanding, he collected the latest news and opinions from travellers, messengers and from the royal court which was constantly on the move. He went further, and developed a personal relationship with both Henry III and his influential brother, Richard of Cornwall. Not one to conceal his own opinions, it is clear that Paris respected the king for his religion, but deprecated his inadequate political management: he openly criticised Henry's use of foreign relatives as his advisors. This exceptionally talented man illustrated his documents with easily recognisable pictures, and his maps (including one of Britain and another illustrating in a sequence of pictures the night-stops and the seas crossed on the route to the Holy Land) predated the advent of sophisticated, precise surveying techniques by some 300 years.

The Dissolution of the Monasteries in the late 1530s was a time of great upheaval which imperilled the survival of all these monastic documents. However, as the chronicles were recognised as such valuable collections of national history, and also because they were almost all conveniently written in books kept in libraries, separate from other documents, they were among the first to be rescued by the Tudor scholars. Matthew Parker, destined to be Elizabeth's Archbishop of Canterbury (in 1559–75), made sure that many of them were transferred to college libraries and there they have survived. Ultimately, beginning in 1857, government funding was directed to meticulous editing of these documents by Victorian scholars, an operation which continued for fifty years. In all, 100 chronicles were transcribed, calendared (summarised) and printed in 253 volumes, mostly remaining in Latin but accompanied by lengthy introductions in English. Those volumes are now generally available on the shelves of the larger libraries and archive offices.

While the chronicles are indispensable, often as the only records of early events, they do have their limitations. Matthew Paris and the others, like modern newsmen, delighted in drama, hence their stories are likely to be exaggerated or biased – and are by no means indisputable. Sometimes, where French and English accounts of the same occasion can be compared, they are scarcely recognisable. Some unsuccessful events were virtually ignored by the scribes on one or other side of the Channel. Memory is conveniently selective.

The Patent Rolls and the Close Rolls (and other series to a lesser extent), which were also calendared and printed, in English, towards the end of the nineteenth century, contain innumerable references to piracy, either complaints by foreign heads of state on behalf of their merchants in respect of losses to English pirates, or directions to various mariners not to 'intermeddle' with the ships of others. Here, the problem is that these edicts were instructions, and there is no guarantee or, usually, evidence that the recipients carried them out.

They may have simply amounted to wishful thinking. However, it was during a trawl through the Patent Rolls thirty years ago, following up another interest (historic sea floods) that this author was originally alerted to the intensity of complaints about piracy and their potential as a source of history.

In 1909 R.G. Marsden wrote on early prize jurisdiction, and in 1915 he published a pioneering collection of *Documents relating to Law and Custom of the Sea*. Three studies of the commercial life of south coast ports are also outstanding. Hugh Watkin's book on pre-Reformation *Dartmouth* was published in 1935, as one of a series of 'parochial histories' by the Devonshire Association. The title of the series belies the importance of this book. Watkin transcribed, compiled, précised (rather reluctantly, one feels) and indexed a large collection of records beginning in Saxon times, which had been jealously guarded as a record of the privileges and possessions of the borough and port over many centuries. Of particular value here are sixty pages of medieval naval and commercial records.

The other two books deal with different aspects of Southampton, always the most important port on the south coast. The first, *Italian Merchants and Shipping in Southampton, 1270–1600* by Alwyn Ruddock, was published in 1951. She deals with relations with the Italian traders, the source of the town's wealth in the time of its greatest historical prosperity – when the port was not only a gateway to the woollen wealth of Wessex and an entrepôt for the tin from the West Country, but also served as an outport of London. Ruddock therefore provides much detail of the exotic cargoes arriving at Southampton.

Before 1973 Colin Platt, later (1983–99) Professor of Archaeology at Southampton University, had spent four seasons as Director of Excavations in Southampton during a time when much good evidence was still exposed as a result of war-time bombing. His principal published work on the subject was a pioneering, multi-disciplinary study of *Medieval Southampton*. In this he combined the archaeological results and topographical observations with a much wider consideration of national and international history. He looked at the life of the town, the management and operation of the port and the men who made up its trading community, highlighting their close-knit personal relationships, the close connection with the continental ports, and the changing nature of trade over the centuries. In doing so, he brought to light the activities of some of the traders whose alternative career was piracy.

All these three authors mentioned pirates and some of the effects of their activities on the commercial world, but did so only occasionally, *en passant*. None of them attempted collation or analysis of the pirates or their activities. The people who did notice, and who researched some of those individuals in greater detail, were three American scholars. In 1912, Henry Lewin Cannon of Stanford University published a paper on Eustace the Monk in the context of the Battle of Sandwich in the *English Historical Review*. Henry S. Lucas of the University of Washington wrote up John Crabbe in *Speculum* in 1945. Stephen Pistono of the University of Wisconsin discussed the relationship of Henry IV with English privateers, principally John Hawley, in English journals in the 1970s.

The raw materials and the manufactured goods which formed the cargoes, the currency of the pirates, are essential to this story. It may, however, come as a surprise that the academic study of this, the economic aspect of history, began only towards the middle of the twentieth century. And, as a last point, it is also interesting to note that the pioneers of the study of much of the medieval trade, in wool and cloth, wine, and Spanish iron were lady scholars, of whom Professor Eleanor Carus-Wilson was the leader.

## AUTHOR'S NOTE

Medieval spellings, which were notoriously irregular, have been modernised and made consistent. Those place-names which cannot be traced are printed in italics.

The names Spain and Italy are used to identify their respective areas long before, in fact, such countries existed. Spain did not emerge as a unified country until 1492, following the recovery of the last part of the country from Muslim domination, the completion of the *Reconquista*. Italy did not become a united country until 1861, and even that date is disputed.

Sums of money are given as in the original documents, i.e.:

*l.* stands for *livres parisien*, and *lt.* for *livres tourois*, both ancient forms of French currency. English currency was expressed as *l. sterling* or, alternatively, as *pounds*. The latter was written £ s d. Every pound comprised 20*s* (*shillings*), and each shilling 12*d* (*pence*). Sometimes sums were quoted in *marks*, each of which was worth 13*s* 4*d*.

# Foreword

uthor Jill Eddison, who has made important contributions to our understanding of the history of the physical
landscape and the economy of that stretch of the English
coastline associated with Romney Marsh, brings us in this
book a highly original study of another specific aspect of
maritime history. No comparison to this book exists that tackles the study
of medieval piracy in this fashion. Its focus is principally, although not
exclusively, on the Channel from the early thirteenth to the mid-fifteenth
century, and as such deals with a period initiated by the loss of Normandy
in 1204 from what was a very substantial Anglo-Norman Angevin empire.
As a result, England was faced on the opposite side of the Channel by a
hostile France with which it engaged in recurrent phases of military conflict
that culminated in the Hundred Years War. The concluding date of the study
comes at the end of Henry VI's reign, when the Normandy coastline which
had been temporarily retrieved by Henry V was once again firmly in French
hands, as were most of the lands that had earlier formed substantial English
possessions across northern and western France. Eddison shows how the
lack of strong political controls on either coast bordering the Channel
made that waterway vulnerable to disorder, indeed at times anarchy, and
in particular privateering. She sets this vulnerability against a backcloth
in which she effectively draws out the allure to privateers of English trade
both through the eastern end of the Channel with Flanders and through

the Western Approaches with Gascony and northern Spain. She reminds us forcefully how sailing techniques and maritime technology exposed ships to great risks in open water, thereby inclining mariners to hug the coastline on their voyages and therefore exposing them to attack from privateers who could identify them from coastal vantage points and when they dropped anchor in bays or estuaries.

The distinctive strength of this book derives from the manner in which the author is able to show readily how frequently merchants, so intimately involved in seaborne trade, supplemented their income and that of their home ports by resorting to privateering. In so doing it is powerfully revealed how there was no clear demarcation between legitimate trade and illegal piracy. Indeed, too many persons in authority had an interest in the proceeds of piracy, since English and French monarchs were quick to use such individuals (some assessed in detail in this book, such as Eustace the Monk or John Hawley) to supply them with vessels for their fleets in times of warfare, which in effect gave them licence to engage in acts of illicit plunder and thefts at sea, and in opportunistic raids on both home and enemy ports. Only in the reign of Henry V, who for a brief period had control of both Channel coastlines as far west as Cornwall and Brittany, was some semblance of order achieved that significantly reduced the scale of privateering and its impact on Channel shipping and ports.

This book will be of great value to any reader, specialist or general, who has an interest in the history of Anglo-French relations, but also who wishes to know how a wide-ranging scholar is able to weave together a knowledge of maritime geography and environments with that of international trade and state development to create a very novel account of the inherent instability of maritime life through the Channel and the Western Approaches over two and a half medieval centuries. As a bonus, in a final chapter Eddison makes some highly perceptive comparisons between piracy in the medieval Channel and that occurring in the contemporary Indian Ocean.

Richard Smith
Cambridge
August 2013

# Preface

irates have plundered shipping from time immemorial, ever since man first went to sea, and they still hit the headlines today. Historically, they have gripped the imagination, and so they have featured prominently in literature – in mythology, in fiction, in fact. Numerous books and films have dealt with their exploits off the coasts of the Americas, off the Barbary Coast of North Africa and in the South China Sea. But, remarkably, almost all of those are set far from home, and in the Elizabethan era or later. Earlier generations of pirates, those who operated in European waters during the medieval period, have scarcely been mentioned.

This book takes up that new subject, medieval piracy. It focuses principally on the English Channel, but since many of the ships which sailed that waterway and even more, the cargoes they carried, came from much further away, this story inevitably ranges widely too. As well as the trade and, essentially, the politics of England and France, it involves Flanders and Scotland in one direction, and Gascony, Iberia and some of the Mediterranean states in the other.

The period covered is just 250 years. The story begins in AD 1204, with the opening of a new chapter in history. In that year Normandy, which had been allied to England since 1066, fell to the expanding French monarchy. Thus the Channel became a wide and lawless frontier zone between two conflicting powers, conditions under which piracy was bound to flourish.

Fortuitously, the beginning of the thirteenth century was also the time from which historical documents begin to survive, and to produce evidence of that piracy.

The story ends in 1453, at the conclusion of another chapter of history, the Hundred Years War. That was the year in which, having recently left Normandy, England lost Bordeaux, the last of her French possessions except Calais. English maritime strength was temporarily sapped (except, perhaps, in the south-west) and the country was becoming immersed in civil war. By coincidence, in the same year the advancing Ottoman Turks put an end to the Genoese monopoly of the alum trade, and thus made a significant change in maritime trade.

By that time too, the seafaring world was expanding its sights. It had already begun to look to Iceland and explore further west and south. As we leave it, maritime history was entering a new phase, and European pirates were on the brink of extending their operations across a much wider world. A new, very different chapter was beginning.

# Acknowledgements

r Joan Thirsk and Dr, later Professor, Richard Smith, did much to encourage and promote my interest in medieval history. Dr Mark Bailey provided further insight into the period and into its sources at summer courses at Madingley Hall, Cambridge. Dr Mark Gardiner, medieval archaeologist from whom I had already learnt a great deal, discussed this project in advance and made valuable comments on an early draft of this book.

The basic research was carried out in the Canterbury Cathedral Archives and in the Templeman Library at the University of Kent at Canterbury. Occasionally I also visited the East Sussex Record Office. In all of them, I was grateful for the efficiency and cheerfulness of the staff. Charlotte Deane, who also helped as a picture researcher, kindly provided reference material which was available in London but not in Kent. Towards the end, my cousin, Captain David Balston, Royal Navy Rtd, alerted me to the challenges of present-day piracy, and provided a lot of detailed information.

In addition, the ten years covered by this project saw great technological changes and expansion of horizons for research. In 2003 Dr G.R. Boynton of the Libraries at the University of Iowa pioneered the way by making the Calendar of the Patent Rolls available on the web, free of charge. More recently the Dictionary of National Biography and much other material also became available there, so that some research could be carried out at home.

Joanna Hitchcock, friend from our student days and former director of the University of Texas Press, has, as ever, provided enthusiastic support and offered much very helpful advice. The late Dottie Gray spurred me on through the early years. More recently, Jane Lushington read painstakingly through each chapter in turn and provided valuable comments.

Ever since we acquired our first personal computer some thirty years ago, my son James Eddison has updated the equipment and guided my use of various systems. Patiently, he saw all the material into the Dropbox which took it to The History Press. Lastly, he compiled the index. Minh Tran also took a hand, upgrading my equipment. Throughout this time my husband David has kept the home fires burning, giving me the freedom to follow other interests.

Without the help, support and expertise of all these people, in all their varied fields, the material could not have been assembled, nor the book written, and it certainly could have not reached the publisher. I am profoundly grateful to them all. The interpretation of the story is, however, entirely my own.

Jill Eddison
June 2013

Fair digital copies of my manuscript maps were made by Philip Stickler in the Cartography Unit, Department of Geography, University of Cambridge.

# 1

# A Lawless Domain

*The sea was a lawless domain beyond the borders of*
*civilised society and the seaport a real frontier town.*[1]

iracy was endemic in the Middle Ages. Men stole each other's ships; they looted each other's cargoes at sea or in port; they demanded ransoms from those captives likely to be able to pay and they threw useless crew members overboard into the sea. Life was cheap and often short. In an age when men easily and quickly resorted to violence, these were universal, accepted facts of life.

This book explores the role of piracy in its widest sense, unofficial or semi-official activity in a fast-moving, volatile political world. It centres particularly on the English Channel, an exceptionally interesting stretch of water which served two different and frequently conflicting functions. On the one hand the Channel was a highly important seaway, a rich commercial artery, an essential link in the trade which formed the foundation for the rising economy of the western world. On the other hand, it was also a political frontier between two evolving, ambitious and belligerent monarchies, England and France. Throughout this period those two countries were hostile to each other. Short bouts of declared war in the thirteenth century led on to longer spells of warfare punctuated by periods of truce, lasting from 1337 to 1453, and described (much later) by historians as the 'Hundred Years' War'.

While the commercial world needed stability in order to function satisfac-
torily and to the benefit of nearly everyone, the political world, represented
by the whims of a very small number of rulers, was far from stable. And
political, dynastic and military considerations almost always prevailed.
On the grounds of both expense and war-weariness of the troops, however, it
was beyond the means of any monarch to continue declared, open warfare
for more than a few years. It was much cheaper, and incidentally almost
invariably more swift and effective, to operate unofficially. One means of
doing so was to encourage piracy.

Piracy took many forms – which merged into each other, so there are
no firm dividing lines. Trade, including fishing, was always competitive
and, for commercial reasons or simply to satisfy personal greed, it easily
and frequently escalated into violent appropriation of other people's goods.
Ships risked being pilfered when they put into ports for supplies of water or
victuals, or when they were seeking shelter from storms, and passing vessels
risked being captured and ransacked.

Competition easily developed into feuds. Adjacent ports, often on the
same estuary, like those on the Exe below Exeter or like Sandwich and Stonor
on the Kentish Stour, fought each other over installation of weirs which
obstructed shipping, over rights to bring in cargoes, to levy customs, to take
the dues on ferries across their estuary. There, and on a wider scale, long-
running vendettas raged between groups of ports, sometimes against their
fellow countrymen but often against foreigners. The rivalry between the
Cinque Ports and Yarmouth, based on shared facilities at the annual nine-
week herring fair, amounted to a petty war whose history went back to the
Saxon period, lasted for centuries and influenced international politics.

Raids on opponents' ports, sometimes based on feuds, sometimes politically motivated, were an extension of the same activity. The basic pattern
of a raid was remarkably simple. Armed invaders sailed into a port on a
high tide, plundered any goods they found, ransacked houses and warehouses, set fire to what they left behind, and departed on the high tide of
the next day, before effective defence could be mounted. The success of
these hit-and-run episodes depended on surprise attack spreading instant
alarm among the local inhabitants: there was seldom any resistance. Those
individuals who were fit enough made themselves scarce; the weaker
members – the old, the women and children – remained behind and were
killed or maltreated. A succession of raids could be extremely effective as
a tool to achieve political ends, as the French showed in the fourteenth
century: by disabling the south-coast ports they wiped out much of the
commercial capability of England.

The latter half of the fourteenth century saw the evolution of a new form of organisation. The scale of maritime trade had increased but, because of excessive wartime expenditure, the resources available to the monarchs were seriously reduced. They therefore resorted to commissioning certain leading merchants to assemble their own fleets and go to sea to harry 'the king's enemies'. Given this official authority to attack their rivals, and with the promise of keeping most, sometimes all, of the prizes they captured, the merchants were happy to oblige. On these conditions they became known to the English as privateers, while to the French and Spanish they were corsairs.

It is evident that piracy was used as much as a political tool as a means of achieving personal profit or settling personal scores. Rivalry was easily and frequently exploited and stoked up by political leaders for their own ends – but always carried the risk of the violence backfiring and becoming beyond control. It was also a very short step for the mariners to set off independently, entirely in their own interests.

A political map of western Europe in 1204, had there been one, would have been very different from that of today. England, the major part of this offshore island, was already a single kingdom although her Celtic boundaries were by no means fixed: both the principality of Wales and the kingdom of Scotland were still independent and one or the other was almost continuously troublesome. Edward I (1272–1307) officially subdued Wales, although later on rebel armies were still able to issue forth from their sanctuary in the mountains of Snowdonia to trouble him and his successors. At much the

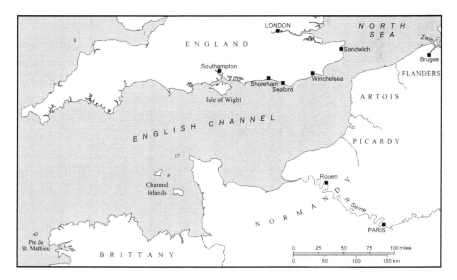

The English Channel, 1204.

same time as Wales was officially subjugated, relations with Scotland deteriorated abruptly after the last strong king, Alexander III, died as a result of falling off his horse in the dark in 1286.

In contrast to the more or less consolidated English kingdom, in 1200 the French king ruled only a small area, consisting of the *Ile de France*, which surrounded his stronghold in Paris. Beyond that, the rest of present-day France was a patchwork of large quasi-independent states, each of which was led by its own duke or count. These included Brittany, which commanded a long and important coastline, and retained its independence beyond the end of this period. Most importantly, the King of England was feudal overlord of about half of the area of modern France, including the entire coastline from the River Somme south to the Spanish border. But in 1200 the pendulum of power was already swinging: Henry II's Anglo-Norman-Angevin empire was about to break up. By 1224 a large part of that English-dominated land, including that bordering the Channel, had been regained by France, although England continued to hold Aquitaine, her land in the south.

To the north of France lay the County of Flanders whose name, *Vlaanderen*, derived from Middle Dutch, meaning 'flooded land'. It consisted of the very low-lying ground, on the border between land and sea, which now includes the area of France from Calais northwards, with much of Belgium and the south of Holland. In 1200 this area was already established as a centre of the woollen industry, and was the economic powerhouse of northern Europe.

Each of these three states, England, France and Flanders, was manoeuvring to increase its territory and to maintain or expand its commerce at the expense of the others. Friction was frequent. Relations between France and Flanders, for instance, were never good. France was intensely jealous of the industrial strength of her northern neighbour. She also coveted the *Zwin*, a sheltered inlet of the North Sea which provided an extensive anchorage near Bruges and Sluys, which has long since silted up and disappeared but was then an exceptional asset. It was essential as a harbour, used not only for commercial shipping but also for assembling fleets for various French attempts to invade England. Conversely, it was a threat to France, because it was one of few places where England was able to land troops in large numbers before they made their way south. Franco-Flemish animosity was therefore continuous and France made several attempts to invade and conquer Flanders, all of them unsuccessful and counterproductive. The most she achieved were minor advances and the destruction of the industrial centres which she had sought to control.

In contrast, at the beginning of our period Flanders had a very strong, long-established commercial connection with England and, presumably on account of that, their political relations were much better than those between Flanders and France. But from 1265 onwards difficulties with Countess Margaret of Flanders gave rise to nearly continuous embargoes and confiscations, and led on to intense Anglo-Flemish piracy and reprisals in the North Sea. By the end of that century Flanders was supporting Scotland in her wars against England.[2]

Because France was perpetually opposed to England, she too naturally took the opportunity of supporting Scotland. She also supported Wales on various occasions when that principality was rebelling against heavy-handed English rule. By the fifteenth century the Dukes of Burgundy, who controlled a large part of present-day eastern France, were also the Counts of Flanders, and their claim to the French throne resulted in a lengthy war.

The states which lay to the south also had an interest in the English Channel. Aquitaine had a strong political and commercial relationship with England, an arrangement which went back to 1152, when the future Henry II of England had married Eleanor of Aquitaine. But in due course, building up from the mid-thirteenth century, it was the status of English ownership of Gascony which was to become one of the main bones of contention between England and France.

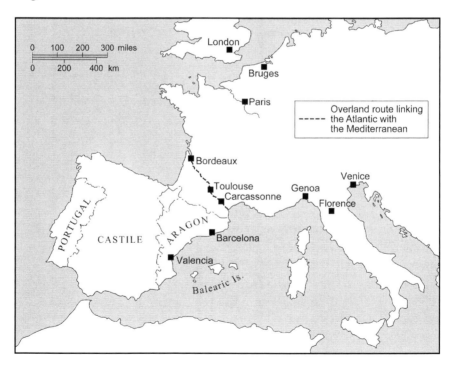

Trade with the South, 1250. Until 1278 trade with the Mediterranean was either carried over the Alps or went partially overland, via Bordeaux and Carcassonne.

During the first half of the thirteenth century, independent merchants from Castile were beginning to establish trading connections with the north.[3] The area of present-day Spain, like that of France, consisted of a number of smaller states. Then, in the 1230s and 1240s, Alfonso VIII of Castile extended his boundaries to include a broad north-south swathe of the Iberian peninsula, between Portugal on the west side and Aragon on the east. These boundaries, which remained constant until the marriage of Isabella of Castile and Ferdinand of Aragon in 1469, after the end of our period, gave Castilian merchants access to the sea in three directions, to the Bay of Biscay in the north, to the Atlantic at Seville and Huelva in the south-west, and to the Mediterranean in the south-east, including Cartagena.

Relations with England were generally friendly, but only after his internal reorganisation was the King of Castile ready to consider formal arrangements for external trade. Then, on 1 March 1254, a treaty was signed with England, and the future Edward I of England married Eleanor of Castile, sister of the king. This heralded thirty years of prosperous Anglo-Castilian trade.[4]

The trading giants in the Mediterranean were the Genoese and the Venetians, but 1204 was too early for direct maritime contact with them, because it was considered that the inward (eastward) current which flows continuously through the Straits of Gibraltar, combined with prevailing winds blowing in the same direction, made it impracticable for the craft of the day to make the outward passage. Goods travelling to and from the Mediterranean had to be transferred to flat-bottomed boats and taken along inland waterways, and carried some of the way overland by mules, via Bordeaux and Carcassonne. But, in time, commercial developments within the Mediterranean stimulated pioneering attempts to travel westward, and the earliest record of a cargo shipped from the Mediterranean to England by that route was one of alum from Asia Minor, brought by a group of Genoese merchants in 1278.[5] This was followed, spasmodically at first, by a growing number of ships from Genoa, Venice, the Balearic Islands and Valencia. As well as physical hazards on the long voyage up the Atlantic coast of Europe and up the English Channel, those ships had to contend with French pirates based at La Rochelle and on the islands in the Bay of Biscay and with multi-national pirates off Brittany.

Sooner or later these southern states were drawn into the Anglo-French conflict in a variety of ways – when their commerce was caught up in the piracy in the Channel, when their men and ships were employed as mercenaries chartered by one of the main contenders, or as the result of political alliances. Altogether, international relations were always volatile and frequently changing.

Internally, too, the governments of both England and France were often unstable, and weak government afforded enhanced opportunities for piracy. Powerful and power-hungry great lords, known respectively as barons and vassals, were always waiting in the wings. Both countries suffered spasmodically from weak leaders, domestic disturbances, civil wars and the occasional *coup d'état*. The English deposed two of their kings in the fourteenth century. It was always tempting, and possible, to exploit the internal weakness of opposing governments. Thus for numerous powerful and interacting reasons, the political background was unpredictable and continuously changing, and a general pattern emerges showing that greater instability on land was always accompanied by an increased level of piracy at sea.

The ports are central to this story, and it is impossible to overemphasise their importance, especially to England, an island nation which depended on the sea for all communications with the outside world, not least for its commerce and its wealth. The smooth and continuous operation of the ports was essential to economic prosperity. When the ports flourished, so did the commercial life of the country. And for that very reason they were frontier towns, who bore the brunt when foreigners attacked, as (Great) Yarmouth complained in anguish in the disastrous circumstances of 1386. Just as in 1940 the Luftwaffe went for the ports and railway junctions, the means of communication, so in the medieval period the French attacked the English ports, especially after the political tide had turned in their favour in the decades after 1360. When the ports succumbed, trade diminished and royal revenues fell with the consequence that the whole economy, the whole country, suffered.

To understand the special nature of these coastal communities, and how they operated, it is necessary to look back to their origins and evolution. Almost all of them started life as small settlements focussing on the twin activities of fishing, providing a vital source of protein, and boat-building. Of necessity, they all grew up in sheltered positions where they were protected from the rough water of the open sea. Hence each one was either situated on a river estuary, where they had the additional advantage of good communication further up river into the hinterland, or behind a substantial barrier of shingle and sand. (The barriers were ephemeral and liable to succumb to erosion, so that the geography of many of the medieval ports is now unrecognisable.) The communities in the ports were exceptionally close-knit, because of their commercial interdependence and because of the dangers which they faced together at sea. The seafarers depended on each other for their lives as well as their livelihoods. The vessels they built had

to be safe enough for them, their families and neighbours to use as they
went about their daily occupations. On both sides of the Channel, everyone
involved, the owner of the ship, the master who took it to sea, everyone
who provided supplies of any kind, down to the ordinary sailors, benefitted
from a 'share' in the profits of the day's catch, or cargo, in proportion to
their investment in the enterprise. This custom extended to include sharing
out the proceeds of piracy.[6]

Well before the dawn of the thirteenth century, every port must have
become involved in trade to a greater or lesser extent. A few, in especially
favoured locations, had evolved into impressive towns, complex trading
centres which required sophisticated management. London stood out in a
class of its own. Southampton, Winchelsea and Sandwich were the largest on
the south coast, with Shoreham and Seaford in the second rank. Throughout
the period covered by this book, the ports were led by small groups of entrepreneurs – people with courage and initiative, who had management and
business skills as well as seafaring expertise. They were the merchants, who
had the interests of their communities – and of themselves – at heart. Most
importantly, they had never been part of the feudal system and so had never
been subject to the kind of regulations which controlled the rest of society.
They travelled, spreading trade, prosperity and culture across Europe. A class
apart, they, exceptionally, were able to operate independently of authority
except, up to a point, that of the king.

Society within the ports was essentially competitive and structures were
fluid. At Winchelsea, the Alards achieved early prominence which lasted
well into the fourteenth century. The early leaders at Southampton were
the St Laurences, the Flemings, the Bulehouses, the Fortins and, somewhat
later, a redoubtable lady called Claramunda, though many of those families
were replaced by others within a generation or two. In Southampton those
leading families formed, with a few others, a small, close-knit group, which
was strengthened by joint commercial interests and by intermarriage. They
managed the port and collected the fee-farm (rent) for the king. They organised his trade. They supervised the upkeep of the castle which functioned as
a warehouse for his wine and wool and provided security for his treasury
as well as being his occasional residence. They collected his customs. For
performing all of those tasks they received payment from the king, thus
building up their own personal wealth. From their ranks too, the mayor,
the bailiff (the chief executive officer) and other officials of the municipality
were elected annually. This independent municipal management resulted in
intense local pride and self-confidence, which in turn fostered rivalry and
encouraged disputes with other ports.

Those families were also busy trading on their own account, dealing in the export of wool and the import of wine, together with many other commodities. They were, in short, wealthy men who invested their money in at least part-ownership of ships and some of them owned several houses not only in Southampton but also in Portsmouth, Winchester and elsewhere in the locality. Some, like Walter le Fleming (fl.1210–58) and Claramunda (fl.1250–60), are also known to have been benefactors of charitable institutions in Southampton and of Quarr Abbey on the Isle of Wight.[7]

Movement of shipping in the ports, including the arrival and departure of sea-going ships and ferrying by lighters of cargoes out to vessels anchored in the main channels, was all subject to the tides: activity in many ports would have been restricted to a few hours on either side of high water. And then, when the rigging of ships was infinitely more simple and limiting than that of the sailing vessels of today, the annual programme of commercial shipping was often confounded by adverse weather.

The weather also controlled or overruled numerous political plans. The prevailing south-westerly winds blew ships onto the coast of Flanders and of France north of the Seine. Time after time, continental attempts to invade England were frustrated not by the English, but by the weather. Fleets which had been assembled at great expense in the great inlet at Sluys (the *Zwin*), or occasionally at Calais, Boulogne, Le Crotoy or in the ports near the mouth of the Seine, were thwarted in their plans for crossing the Channel. Some were delayed, confined by the wind to those continental harbours; others could only wait until they ran out of money and so never got started; others did indeed set out, only to be blown off course, so that when they did arrive it was not at their intended destination. Little was predictable. It is safe to say that for a number of reasons the English were never well prepared to defend themselves against invasion fleets, so the winds were a helpful defence, although they did add to the difficulty of knowing where the enemy might strike. Conversely, the same south-west winds were a great benefit to the English when their fleets set out in the opposite direction. It seems certain, for instance, that Edward III had the wind as well as the sun behind him when, having sailed over from the estuary of the Orwell, he won his celebrated victory at Sluys on that summer afternoon in 1340.

In the other direction, voyages to and from the Bay of Biscay, to Gascony and beyond, towards Spain and the Mediterranean were dominated by the same south-west winds. When the Italian merchants initially came up the Channel, primarily in search of English wool, they did so in midsummer, and by August they had left again, keen to be clear of the Atlantic before autumn gales set in and drove them onto the rocky shores of Brittany or northern Spain.

South-bound English expeditions, whether military, political or commercial, were also dominated by the weather. For instance, when in August 1372 Edward III intended to take a force to relieve the acute military situation in Poitou, he was confronted by persistent contrary winds. First, he was pinned into the Downs at Sandwich. Then, after three weeks spent attempting to sail south-west, he had only reached Winchelsea, some 50 miles down the coast, and in October he was forced to abandon the voyage altogether. (By then it was anyway too late in the season and the ships he had commandeered were urgently needed for the annual voyage south to Bordeaux for the wine: had he persisted, he would have faced rebellion by the merchants.)[8] In 1402 Henry IV ordered a high-level delegation to fetch his future wife, Joan of Navarre, to England. They left on about 27 November, but after eleven days being buffeted by the sea and coming within sight of the Brittany coast, contrary winds were evidently either going to force them round into the 'Spanish Sea' (the Bay of Biscay), or to return to England. They chose the latter. Joan eventually embarked at Camaret near Brest on 13 January 1403, intending to land at Southampton, but after five boisterous days at sea she was obliged to land at Falmouth.[9] In December 1414 five of the king's ships which set out from London to collect the reek wines from Bordeaux got no further than the 'Foreland de Wyght': they had to return to Winchelsea and ultimately to London without getting anywhere near Bordeaux.[10] Those are just a few representative examples of problems frequently faced by the ships' masters.

Building ships was an expensive business and the wooden ships of this period required frequent maintenance even during the course of their voyages, a glimpse of which was provided by the standard-bearer of Diaz de Gamez, a Spanish corsair cruising in the Channel in 1405–06.[11] Having taken care of that, sending them to sea carried serious risks of piracy and shipwreck, as well as dangers emanating from war. On the other hand, the rewards of a successful trading voyage were very considerable, given skill and a measure of good luck with the weather. The merchants were able to reduce their risk to a certain extent by sharing the ownership of their vessels and distributing their goods between different ships going to the same destination. As long as their ships were working, the merchants prospered. But when the ships were not able to trade normally, the merchants suffered serious losses and complained bitterly.

One reason for their complaints was the king's right to commandeer merchant shipping. This was several centuries before there was an effective royal navy, a permanent reserve of ships for the king's use. Some of the medieval kings of England, notably John and Henry V, did possess more than a few ships of their own, but even those were not nearly enough to fulfil all their needs. To equip themselves with vessels to provide troop-ships, supply vessels, men-of-war, or ships to carry their messengers or their own wine and other commodities, they had perforce to look to the merchants and hire or, more often, commandeer commercial craft. More often than not, therefore, what were described nominally as 'the king's ships' belonged, in fact, to merchants. The French kings were, in comparison, somewhat better equipped because in the late 1280s Philip IV, le Bel, established a royal dockyard, *Le Clos de Galées*, beside the Seine just below Rouen. Nevertheless neither country had enough vessels for their military needs, and from time to time both had to hire, at considerable expense, ships and crews from the south, usually from Castile or Genoa.

The merchants supplemented their income – and that of their ports – by piracy, and in the medieval period there was no dividing line between what we would now identify as legitimate trade and what we would see as illegal piracy. No law existed to define or deal adequately with maritime violence, and indeed it would have been impossible to enforce any such law. Up until the later thirteenth century, foreigners who suffered from depredations by English seafarers could only apply to the English king in his council for redress. But they were then referred, through itinerant justices, to the common law, which contained no provision to deal with their cases and therefore proved of little use to them. Early in the fourteenth century the king and council began to appoint commissioners or arbitrators, individuals from the particular locality, to deal with each case as it arose. From 1360 offences committed at sea were dealt with by the new Court of the Admiralty. The admiral was usually a high-ranking nobleman whose business, owing to his other preoccupations, was normally carried out by deputies or lieutenants. When it proved impossible to obtain satisfaction from them, perhaps because of corruption, the petitioner could appeal to the chancellor. An important statute of 1353 gave the owners of unlawfully captured cargo the right to recover it if they gave proof of their ownership, either by their marks on the cargo or by documents, or by evidence of other reliable merchants. This was quoted in several fifteenth-century West Country cases, but often did not produce the desired redress: argument and evasion still prevailed.[12]

The object of all their enquiries was to establish what had happened, to enquire into the legitimacy of the claim and obtain restitution of stolen ships and goods, or their value, rather than to prosecute the pirates. There was no suggestion of criminality. The only exception to that came under the extraordinarily firm, organised, hand of Henry V. In 1414 his Statute of the Truces declared that acts of piracy which involved breaching a truce were high treason, punishable by death. But in the longer term this met with violent opposition, and in 1436 and again in 1442 the Act was suspended.[13]

Innumerable ordinary sailors met their deaths at the hands of their maritime opponents, mostly by being tipped overboard. The merchant-pirates themselves were more likely to survive, simply because they might be worth a ransom. But very few pirates, if any, were publicly punished in this period.

In addition, and just as importantly, piracy had the support of strong vested interests. People of every degree from the king downwards stood to gain from its proceeds, so there was no inclination or incentive to suppress it. From the time of King John (1199–1216) all the kings of England (with the notable exception of Henry V) tolerated piracy, provided that they received a share of the spoils.[14] The percentage the privateers were (officially) allowed to keep depended generally on the urgency of the political situation. The more acute the situation, the more they were allowed to keep, generally building up until the privateers in the time of Henry IV kept their entire prizes.

The fate, the practical handling, of the stolen goods once they arrived in port is obscure, but important to this story. Some were divided up and immediately distributed to numerous people in the port or its locality, which made it very difficult for officials to trace them even a few days after the event. Some of the wine was presumably drunk, and some captured food-stuffs would also have been consumed on the spot. The remainder of the wine, the spices and other goods were then sold on to traders working their way inland. It travelled along with goods which had arrived by more orthodox means and, following the accustomed trade routes, it reached the halls, the kitchens and the tables of the nobility and of the sheriffs, the senior officers of the law. The fine cloth and other luxuries reached the same destinations, and the means by which the goods had been obtained mattered not. Thus the network, the basis of power of the merchant-pirates, was spread far and wide; innumerable people were implicated, and absolutely no social stigma was attached to the means by which the goods had been obtained.

The majority of the sea-going pirates with whom this book is concerned were therefore well-heeled and well-connected merchants in control of their own ships and crews, and often in control of their ports as well. In addition to them, a very small number of other adventurous, independent, individuals joined in and 'worked the system'. Without apparently possessing their own ships but evidently with established reputations for their seamanship, audacity and, sometimes, diplomacy they managed to sell their services. Men of the calibre of Eustace the Monk in the early thirteenth century and John Crabbe a hundred years later were taken on by national leaders at times of particular crisis and supplied with ships to deal with problems. These independent operators were, however, notoriously fickle and were liable to change sides as opportunity offered. In doing so they made many personal enemies.

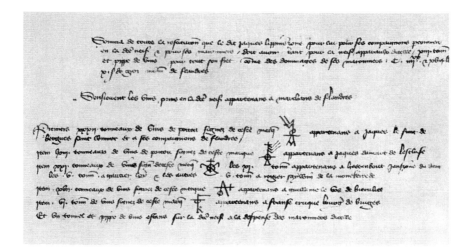

A claim for wine stolen by pirates, itemised and including merchants' marks.

As a result, Eustace was captured and beheaded on board his own ship at the end of the Battle of Sandwich in 1217. In contrast John Crabbe, albeit at different times deeply unpopular with both Scots and English, managed to end his days as a royal advisor living in Somerton Castle, Lincolnshire, the medieval equivalent of a grace-and-favour residence. Henry Pay of Poole, the notorious pirate who was active at the beginning of the fifteenth century, was another of the same ilk: there is plenty of evidence that he used other people's ships, and no certainty that he possessed any of his own. He made himself so deeply unpopular with the Castilians that they raided Poole in revenge for his activities, although they only found, and killed, his brother. Like Crabbe, later in his life Henry Pay seems to have entered royal service, and served as water bailiff of Calais. He died on 26 March 1419, and was buried at Faversham, which suggests that he had eventually settled down at the eastern end of the Channel, a long way from his roots, where perhaps he was none too popular. Finally, the end of this story witnesses the beginning of another era, when the seafarers of Devon and Cornwall were becoming professional plunderers who brought their booty back to their home ports, or to established markets, including one on the Isle of Wight.

None of the pirates had any sense of national loyalty, except on the rare occasions when that coincided with their own personal purposes. On the other hand, many of them were concerned with the economic well-being of their own ports. At a time of confrontational politics and rich commercial prizes, piracy was guaranteed to flourish.

# 2

# The Passing Trade

he Channel was arguably the busiest trading artery of the medieval world. The cargoes carried up, down and across that great waterway formed the basis for our civilisation. They also became the source of invaluable taxation for England and the bargaining counters of competing political powers. They were the livelihood of merchants from a number of countries and, in addition, they were the prizes for pirates. Overall, the volume and the nature of this seaborne trade altered considerably during this period; nonetheless it was dominated from beginning to end by two great staples: wool and wine. Nearly every commercial vessel that plied the Channel could be guaranteed to be carrying one or other of these, and sometimes both.

The medieval economy was founded on the wool trade, on the production of various kinds of cloth from raw wool, in one or other of two industrial centres: Flanders, which was close to the southern North Sea, and the area round Florence in northern Italy. Inherent in this trade was massive seaborne transport. First, the wool and most of the other raw materials, the dyes and the mordants (which fixed the colours to the materials), needed to be shipped to the industrial centres and, eventually, the manufactured products had to be conveyed to the purchasers, wherever they were in the world. Long distances were usually involved.

It was the exceptionally fine quality of the long wool produced by her sheep which placed England firmly on this economic map. Throughout the first half of this period Europe relied on a steady supply of English wool, and England in turn relied to a large extent on that wool for her wealth. So dependent were Flanders and Italy on this supply that, when faced with a heavy burden of debt in 1275, Edward I was able to institute the first regular national system of taxation on foreign trade, in what had previously been virtually a free trade area. This tax, known as the Great, or Ancient, Custom was payable by both English and foreign merchants on the export of wool, woolfells (the skin of the animal with the wool still attached) and hides. It brought in to the exchequer a sum of around £10,000 a year, and on the strength of that assured, constant, income the kings were also able in due course to take out large loans from Italian bankers.

By 1303 the king's need had increased to such an extent that a second tax was imposed on all the goods imported or exported by foreign merchants, which included an additional tax on wool. It was known as the New, or Petty Custom. Specific duties were imposed on wool, hides, wax, wine and cloth. Eventually in 1347, in response to the changing pattern of trade as the export of cloth manufactured in England began to build up, a third tax, the Cloth Custom was imposed.[15]

To ensure payment of these taxes, royal officials were appointed to every port for the specific task of taking details of the name of every ship entering or leaving its home port, its master and every item of cargo, together with the name of the merchant responsible and the amount of duty payable. These detailed records were kept in the ports, and unfortunately most of them have since been lost. However, short summaries were sent to the Exchequer and those have survived in the Public Record Office, as the Enrolled Customs Accounts, and it is they which enabled twentieth-century scholars to build up an overall picture of English medieval trade. Altogether, the wars of three kings, Edward I, II and III, who reigned one after the other from 1272 to 1377, were financed by the taxes and loans secured on this wool, and a lasting symbol of that source of national wealth was the woolsack, on which the Lord Chancellor, the chief law officer of England, was traditionally seated for many centuries.[16]

Although it is known that cloth manufacture flourished in English towns and served the home market at the end of the twelfth and beginning of the thirteenth centuries, it is the overseas export of the wool which concerns us.[17] Even before the Norman Conquest bales of fine wool from sheep on the wolds of Lincolnshire and Yorkshire had begun crossing the North Sea to Flanders. And, since the sea route to the Mediterranean had yet to be opened up, some of that wool was sent on over the Alpine passes, strapped to baggage mules, to northern Italy. In 1200 the Flemish industry centred on Arras, St Omer and Douai, all reached by canals, but by 1300 the great triumvirate of Bruges, Ghent and Ypres, also accessible by inland waterways, had taken over. Bruges, so favourably placed at the head of the *Zwin*, the large inlet of the North Sea, became the leader.

This concentrated urban population could not possibly be self-sufficient, so it generated its own supporting overseas trade. At the same time as the cloth was shipped out, fish was brought in from the North Sea, corn, candles and furs from further north, and cheese and meat from Normandy. If these maritime supplies were cut off, the results were massive unemployment and starvation. During the war of 1297, for instance, hordes of starving Flemish weavers roamed the countryside looking for food, and during the Great Famine of 1315–17 both the Count of Flanders and the Admiral of Calais employed groups of pirates to scour the '*Narrow Seas*' (the Straits of Dover) for vital food supplies being brought in from the south to feed the starving people in northern Europe.

However, these weaknesses surfaced only temporarily, and Flanders retained its lead as premier (northern) producer of cloth until, as the result of the combined effects of serious internal dissention and of war, it declined in the middle of the fourteenth century. After a pause caused by the Black Death and ensuing epidemics, England, which was fortunately self-sufficient in raw wool as well as in food and water-power, took over as the industrial centre of the north. Whereas her wool exports had increased until 1305, exports of English cloth increased from a small number in 1347, to 40,000 cloths in 1400 and a peak of 60,000 around 1447. Thus, towards the end of the fourteenth century, along with the raw wool still being exported from London, and particularly from Southampton, went the cloth which was being manufactured in increasing quantities beside the swift-flowing streams of the Cotswolds and Wessex, especially in the area between Winchester and Bristol. In the meantime Castile, a land of great transhumant sheep ranches, was serving as a second producer of fine, if different, wool. Theirs was merino, fine white and curly, which in the mid-thirteenth century was already being exported from the ports of northern Spain to Flanders and England.[18]

Besides wool and cloth, the other English product for which there was guaranteed, widespread overseas demand was tin. This valuable mineral, found near the granite masses which form the core of Devon and Cornwall, had in all probability been exploited in antiquity, though no archaeological confirmation of that has been found. Whether that suggestion is true or not, by the medieval period this area had assumed great importance as the only significant source of tin in the western world, and so it remained until the later fifteenth century, when mines in Saxony and Bohemia became important suppliers.

Tin was as fundamental to the economy of Europe as it was to the finances of England. An indispensable material, it had many and varied uses, usually in combination with other more readily available metals. Alloyed with copper, it formed bronze, the only metal which was strong, durable and resistant to corrosion (it does not rust). Alloyed with iron, tin was used as solder. In various forms, it was used in roofing, glazing and plumbing (providing drainpipes) for the great stone castles and cathedrals. In an alloy which consisted of about three parts of copper to one of tin, it was also used by the church for bells, which as alarm signals or as the means of summoning public interest had much greater importance than they have today. Of particular interest to the political masters, tin also featured in the manufacture of armaments and, by the second half of the fifteenth century, was being used for gun metal. Its other importance was as an essential constituent of pewter, which was made by alloying tin with small quantities of lead or copper. This became increasingly important throughout the medieval period, to a large extent because it replaced pottery (which had the disadvantage that it was always subject to breakage) for serving food and drink. Tavern pots, for instance, were made from it. In the early thirteenth century it began to be used by the Church for flagons and chalices, while by the end of that century it was becoming popular for domestic use as well. Spoons and platters, dishes and salt-cellars of various sizes were all made of it. In the fourteenth century, manufacture of pewter became widespread and there were pewterers in a number of the larger English towns: they were recorded in Cornwall and Devon too, in Lostwithiel (in 1327), Exeter (1370) and Truro (1379). It is evident, however, that a large proportion of the mined tin was shipped away.

The importance and value of this metal was recognised at an early date: a tax known as the coinage had already been imposed by the 1150s. King John gave a charter to the 'tinners' of Devon and Cornwall in 1201. The increase in the scale of that mining can be traced through the number of miners involved in Cornwall: it is estimated that in 1300 they numbered 2,000, whereas by 1400 that had risen to 5,000. Production was closely monitored, and every 'piece', every smelted block, had to be taken and measured and taxed at one of nine centres spaced out down Devon and Cornwall. These were Chagford, Ashburton, Tavistock and (from 1328) Plympton, all near Dartmoor in Devon, and Lostwithiel, Bodmin, Liskeard, Truro and Helston in Cornwall. By 1200 Bodmin had emerged as the administrative centre and Lostwithiel as the leading port.

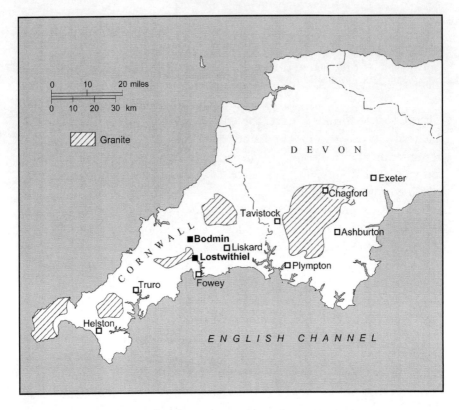

Export of tin from Cornwall and Devon.

In the thirteenth century shipping of tin was largely in the hands of foreign merchants. Men from Flanders came to take the tin over to the markets in the Low Countries, from where it was distributed widely across northern, central and eastern Europe. Others from Rouen and Abbeville took it across to France, but probably the greatest quantity was taken by merchants from the south, from La Rochelle, Bordeaux, Bayonne and the north coast of Spain. From Bordeaux some of it continued on a long journey, first overland by river craft and packhorses through the Carcassonne Gap to the Mediterranean, then onward in Italian galleys to the ports and markets of Alexandria, the Levant, Asia Minor and the Black Sea, until ultimately it reached the Middle East and Central Asia on the back of camels. During the fourteenth century a change took place. Once the Italians had opened up the Straits of Gibraltar, they gradually took over the export of the tin, and certainly from the time of Richard II (1377–99) onwards, the English were shipping it along the coast to the entrepôt of Southampton where it was loaded onto the great Italian vessels.[19]

Tin was so important that at an early date the miners had been given extensive rights and privileges. They were authorised to cut wood and dig peat, both of which provided fuel for smelting, and they were permitted to divert watercourses and make their own roads, all on condition that they did not stray into gardens or orchards (areas where food was produced), into churchyards or onto the public highways. In the process of digging out, washing and smelting the tin, they moved large quantities of loose soil and rock, evidently laying waste to considerable areas and throwing up masses of rubble into unstable spoil heaps. In time, this disturbance caused its own tribulations. In 1355 it was reported that Lostwithiel was losing its trade, its lifeline. Apparently, great quantities of rubble produced by stream-workings on the slopes of Bodmin Moor had been washed down the river, perhaps in flash floods, and deposited at the port, the point at which the river met the high tides, making it unnavigable for the merchant ships. The industry and the river had combined to snuff out the prosperity they had previously brought to the town. Today, the river bed there is filled up with gravel, used by children as a summer playground, and the waterfront is used only by very small motor boats. The tides retreated and the valley downstream silted up (Col. Plate 1).

Fowey, previously only a small fishing hamlet perched uncomfortably on a very steep slope, but advantageously in a sheltered position near the mouth of the river, took over from Lostwithiel as the centre of shipping, though Lostwithiel continued as a base, an up-river retreat of Cornish pirates. Universally highly valued, both tin and pewter must always have been valuable trophies for pirates along the various trade routes. For example, in 1364 a ship owned by a consortium of London pewterers and carrying 40 tons of tin was seized by the French.

As a sideline, along with their trade in tin, the men of Devon and Cornwall developed their own independent two-way trade with south-west France. Cured fish, butter, cheese, salted hogs and, in due course, cloth, so much in demand in Gascony, was sent out with the tin. On their return voyage the ships carried salt for curing the next catch of fish and pitch for caulking the ships, together with wine, iron, woad, garlic, dried fruits and sometimes corn.

If wool was England's principal export, wine was her major import, being the day-to-day drink of the higher echelons of society. It was consumed in vast quantities by the royal household and the nobility, in monastic establishments and by leading merchants, especially at the great festivals of Christmas and Easter. In the telling words of Salzman, 'There was probably no import with which the medieval Englishman would have dispensed with so unwillingly as wine.'[20]

The Normans had established the habit of wine-drinking in England in the eleventh century, their sources being in northern France, the Seine valley, Burgundy and the Loire. But then political changes, the loss of Normandy in 1204 and of La Rochelle in 1224, restricted access to those white wines and stimulated the trade in the red wine of Gascony, which had already begun well back in the previous century, possibly as a result of the political connection forged by the marriage of Henry II to Eleanor of Aquitaine in 1154. In response to this demand for wine, the domestic economy of Gascony underwent a revolution. Arable, pasture and waste land were all converted to vineyards, on such a large scale as to make the region dependent on imported food. So, to satisfy that need, the ships which sailed south from several south- and east-coast ports of England to collect the wine were loaded with fish, meat, dairy products and cereals, as well as cloth and hides. In the fourteenth century a Bordeaux merchant sounded a note of caution. Observing the dangerous implications of this Gascon monoculture, he asked, 'How could our poor people subsist when they could not sell their wines or procure English merchandise?'[21] When, indeed, communication by sea was interrupted by warfare or piracy, the result was great hardship.

However, for the first thirty-five years of the fourteenth century the Anglo-Gascon wine trade remained generally buoyant and stable. In the years 1305–09, for instance, records survive to show that up to 100,000 tuns (a tun was a wine cask holding 252 gallons) were exported annually to northern countries from the ports on the Garonne estuary. At least 20,000 tuns of that came to England. The wine produced in the valleys of the Lot, the Tarn and the Garonne was shipped out through Bordeaux; that from the Dordogne from Libourne; and ports further down the estuary dealt with that from the neighbouring Bordelais. In addition, Bayonne shipped wine from the vineyards further south, nearer the Pyrenees.

The wine ships returned north twice a year. As soon as the freshly picked grapes had fermented and the scum had been cleared off, the casks were sealed and the new wines were sent off, aimed to arrive in time for Christmas. The trip to England took roughly two months and, for example, the customs returns for Winchelsea in 1266 show that a fleet of a dozen ships of Bayonne and her Castilian neighbours, San Sebastian and Fuenterrabia, arrived in Christmas week with 465 casks of wine. Later on in the winter, in January or February, the wine which had not been sent off so hastily and had time to settle, was 'racked' off the lees and then sent north, arriving in time for the great festival of Easter. This, the reek wine, was clearer and more mature and could have been expected to have been of higher quality than the earlier wine, though any shipment might be adversely affected by storms encountered

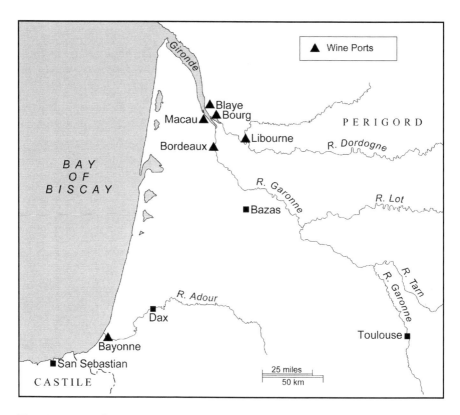

The wine ports of Gascony, 1300. (Based on James, ed. Veale, map 2)

on the voyage. Some of these ocean-going ships unloaded their wine at Southampton, Winchelsea or Sandwich. Others went on to London, or went north to Hull or Berwick[22] (Col. Plate 2).

This predictable twice-yearly traffic must have been a bonus for pirates, who made simple preparations, lying in wait for the expected ships, targeting particularly any which by choice or by accident were sailing alone, not in a convoy. It is evident, for example, that at the great peak of piracy in the year 1403, the two most spectacular group-piracies took place in the spring and in late October.[23]

Other bulk imports coming north included essentials for the woollen industry. Neither Flanders nor England possessed sufficient quantity of dyes. The most important of these was woad, which provided the blues and was the basis for greens and violets. This plant, wound into large balls and packed into casks for transit, was initially imported from the Somme valley. When Anglo-French relations deteriorated and access to the Somme was reduced in the first half of the thirteenth century, production switched to the Toulouse area, and woad eventually became second only to wine as an export from Bordeaux. In the fifteenth century the volume reaching Southampton was so great that it constituted almost the entire cargo of some of the Genoese carracks. Later, when the tide of war turned in favour of the French and access to Bordeaux became difficult, woad was brought from Italy, from Piedmont and Tuscany. Other dyes were much smaller in volume but higher in value. The most prestigious was grain, the scarlet dye derived from the dead bodies of the tiny insect kermes which lived on the evergreen oaks of the Mediterranean. Brasil, the cheaper red dye used for leather, originated in the East Indies. Yellow colour was provided by weld or saffron. The latter, which was derived from parts of the dried stamen of a particular crocus cultivated in the semi-arid lands of the Mediterranean, was also valued for medicinal purposes and for flavouring food, and was particularly expensive.[24]

But it was the need for alum, the mineral which fixed the colours in the cloth, which seems to have had a strong influence in promoting an important alteration in the trade route, and probably even had an indirect hand in changing the design of the ships. Before the last quarter of the thirteenth century, supplies of alum came from various Mediterranean sources and had to be brought overland via the Carcassonne Gap and Bordeaux, from where it was shipped north. But 1278 was the year in which the Zaccaria, an enterprising Genoese family who included in their number the one-time Genoese ambassador to Byzantium, gained control of the great mines producing high-quality alum at Harakissar (now Foça) on the Gulf of Smyrna in modern Turkey. It was the need to bring this in bulk to the flourishing cloth industry in the north and to avoid all the expense and delays of trans-shipment involved in the Carcassonne route which seems to have stimulated the crucial revolution in the trade route, and ships began making their way west out of the Mediterranean.[25]

Before this time, pioneers had already been experimenting with this difficult passage, but it was in 1278 that the first recorded consignment of alum arrived in England by the new route. The high-grade *alym roche*, which came in semi-translucent blocks, usually white, sometimes grading towards green or red, was one of the most valued (and certainly one of the most attractive) commodities which came up the Channel. The Genoese continued to hold a virtual monopoly of this supply until the mines were overrun by the Ottoman Turks in 1455.

Iron was another indispensable commodity. As far as low-grade material was concerned, England had her own deposits which were sufficient in quality and quantity to meet basic needs, the scythes, ploughshares, horseshoes and nails for agriculture, and spades, pickaxes and hammers for quarrying and mining. But higher-grade, phosphor-free ore which bent but did not break was needed for the tie-bars used in the construction of the cathedrals and castles, for decorative work inside those buildings, and of particular interest here for the nails and pins, the anchors and chains needed by shipbuilders. Put another way, high-grade iron ore was important to the richer and more influential groups in English society. And the most convenient source of it, as far as southern England was concerned, was near Bilbao on the north coast of Castile. The deposits there were massive; they were easy to extract because they occurred on or near the surface; and as they were near the coast, transport to England was easy and relatively cheap.

In the early years of the thirteenth century there are scattered references to Spanish traders in English ports: they were evidently beginning to extend their trading links, though there is no written record of them bringing iron at this early date. Those traders were, possibly, somewhat in advance of political developments for, during the first half of that century, the kings of Castile were busily occupied in expanding their territory by taking over other Iberian provinces. Only by 1252 had they achieved the boundaries which remained constant until the end of our period. Those boundaries included a broad north-south swathe, with command of the ports along the north coast together with those in the south-west near Seville and Cartagena on the Mediterranean. But they excluded Granada in the south and Aragon, which held much of the Mediterranean coast. In March 1254 a treaty was signed between Castile and England, and later that year Henry III's son, the future Edward I of England, married Eleanor of Castile, which heralded thirty years of good trading relations between the two countries.[26] Portugal always remained independent.

While England and Castile enjoyed good relations, the same could not by any means always be said of the Basque sailors and their near-neighbours, the Gascons of Bayonne. They had a love-hate relationship. The two groups shared similar situations. Both were isolated, remote from the centres of their ruling states. When it was convenient, they shared transport, using each other's ships to carry their goods. But relations between the two easily became competitive, and could quickly deteriorate, especially at times when England was, or recently had been, at war with France.[27]

The first surviving record of a shipment of Castilian iron being landed in England was at Winchelsea in 1266, while the first written record of the use of Spanish iron in Canterbury Cathedral concerns the remarkable gates through Prior Eastry's quire screen between the Bell Harry Tower and the chancel, which date from 1304 and are still in use today.[28] It is not known when or where this particular consignment was imported, but later on, Castilian iron was imported principally through Sandwich and Southampton. The Hundred Years War, combining warfare with chivalry, provided a great stimulation to the demand for Spanish iron for arms, and for the armour which was being manufactured in Castile. The cargo of a Spanish ship which was wrecked in the winter of 1357 off the Isle of Selsey in Sussex was presumably typical of the time. It included seventy-one tuns of wine, chests, plates of iron, swords and other goods, as well as some partially manufactured and some finished iron goods.[29] By the late fourteenth and in the fifteenth centuries, iron had become one of the country's major imports, and much of it was being shipped direct to London, the weight making it difficult to transport over land. For example, in the two years 1390–92, nearly three-quarters of the transactions of Gilbert Maghfeld, a prominent London merchant, were in iron.[30] In other words, by that date it was one of the most important cargoes coming up the Channel.

Salt, the last of the bulky imports to be considered here, was an age-old necessity of humanity. It was used to flavour and to preserve food, not least fish, an extremely perishable commodity which in a strongly Catholic world provided essential protein for all sections of society. It was said, indeed, that it was only the herrings which prevented many of the poorer people from starving. But the herrings needed to be preserved very rapidly after they were caught. In the early Middle Ages, Domesday Book (1086) shows that salt was being extracted from seawater on a large scale on the salt marshes which fringed southern England. However, in these northern latitudes, the process of concentration was labour-intensive and tedious, involving the use of large quantities of fuel to evaporate the brine, and the works were very vulnerable to sea-floods. Altogether, salt-production in the north was a marginal business.

In marked contrast, the shallow sandy salt-water lagoons on the coast south of Brittany were more extensive, more stable and enjoyed hot summer weather where a combination of sun and wind guaranteed complete recovery of the salt by natural evaporation. So it is hardly surprising to note that from the beginning of the thirteenth century, at the latest, English merchants were bringing back sacks of salt from the Baie de Bourgneuf, universally known as 'The Bay', south of the Loire (Col. Plates 3 and 4).

Rising population and a higher standard of living increased demand in the fourteenth and fifteenth centuries, while at the same time salt production in the north was reduced. But political conditions had to be satisfied, and it was only after 1364, following a period of foreign occupation and local warfare, that John of Montfort was recognised as Duke of Brittany by both England

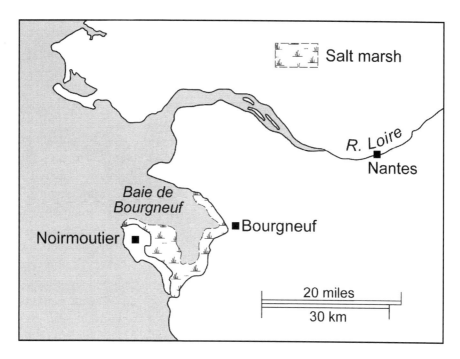

The Baie de Bourgneuf, principal source of the salt trade.

and France, and the south could begin to fully meet the need of the north for salt. Even then, in view of the continuing threat of piracy, the salt ships had to take the precaution of travelling in convoys, the most famous of which was the 'Bay Fleet' organised by the Hanse, a dominant consortium of merchants from the Baltic and the Low Countries, which dealt with the Baltic trade in fish and grain and some Gascon wine, as well as the salt. Their ships were assembled in the *Zwin* and set off between December and March on their southward voyage, in order to bring the salt north in time for the opening of the Scania (Swedish) herring market on 25 July.[31]

Other raw materials and manufactured goods, smaller in volume but higher in value, were usually included with the bulk shipments of woad, alum, wine or iron, but unfortunately are not often mentioned in the summarised calendars of the demands for compensation. The variety and quantity of these increased as incomes grew and the taste of the well-to-do for luxuries increased, especially as southern England profited from its cloth. By the fifteenth century, the Italian carracks and galleys arriving in Southampton Water with the prime objective of collecting wool were also feeding a growing demand for luxuries, some of which had already crossed the greater part of two continents on their way to the well-off people in

England especially, perhaps, the wool merchants of the Cotswolds and Wessex. These cargoes included exotic Eastern spices (almost always carried by the Venetians), oriental silks and carpets, African cotton, ivory and sugar, and even monkeys and parrots destined to be household pets. From the eastern Mediterranean came sweet wines, and from Lucca and Florence sumptuous velvet, satin and cloth of gold. On the way past southern Italy, Sicily, or from the Balearic Islands, Spain and Portugal the Italians collected figs and raisins (important sweeteners used in northern kitchens), citrus fruits, almonds and olive oil, saffron, sulphur, brimstone, mercury (quicksilver) and carpets. Cordwain, intricate leather-work, came originally from Cordova but was later worked in Italy. Wax came from Spain and Portugal, to provide the candles so important for lighting, and it was also used for seals and in the lost-wax process, in which metals were fashioned for statues, statuettes and for jewellery.

From Southampton the Italians went on to Bruges and then returned to Southampton to leave a variety of manufactured goods from the markets of Flanders. These included lengths of linen, bales of fine cloth, magnificent hangings and coverlets, felt hats, hoods and gloves, leather belts and shoes, and fur garments for which the fur had originated in Russia or the Baltic countries. There were also endless supplies of pots and pans and other household utensils. They then departed for home, aiming to have left the Atlantic before the autumnal storms closed in on them – though later on, by the 1420s, some were choosing to over-winter in Southampton Water. [32]

# 3

# Ships, Shipping and Trade Routes

 he importance of shipping to the medieval world cannot be overstated, and ships are central to this story. In 1200, two different cultures of shipbuilding existed in Europe, producing two very different types of ships. Separated by geography, they had developed in response to two contrasting environments: one in Atlantic waters, the other in the Mediterranean. By 1450, after a space of only 250 years, these two basic designs had been merged, and the result was a ship which was capable of sailing out, away from European shores, across the oceans of the world.[33] In other words, the period covered by this book saw vital changes in the culture of ship design, and they took place more rapidly than those in any other similar time-span before the twentieth century.

That very general outline is undisputed but questions of detail, as to where, how and exactly when those changes occurred, are much more problematical and remain matters of conjecture and debate. The reason is lack of evidence. Archaeological evidence for this period is extremely limited. Visual representation of vessels on pew ends or graffiti are the work of artists and their shape and other details were dictated by the medium on which they appeared. The town seals of ports are likely to give more accurate information, though limited by the space available, and even they do not offer any precise dates. Written evidence is sparse, and chronicles and official documents may use the same names for different ships at different dates, or in different places. What follows here is only a general outline, offered with full acknowledgement that there must have been local variations, in space and time. But what does shine through is that the two most important steps in the evolution of ship design in this period must have taken place in the Mediterranean, and that the first occurred in response to economic demand.

In northern and Atlantic waters, vessels needed to be able to withstand great storms and survive mountainous, continuous, rolling waves. The ships of 1200 were successors of those of Viking and Norman times which had been double-ended, meaning that there was little or no difference in the shape of the hull between one end and the other. Their rudder was adaptable, being moved as required to the relevant steer-board (the origin of the word starboard) side. By the beginning of the thirteenth century, the rudder was fixed in a permanent position, attached centrally to a vertical stern-post. The type of ship which had emerged was known as the cog, with variations known as the nef or hulk. It had high sides and was notably wide in relation to its length. This design proved so satisfactory that it was to remain unaltered as the standard commercial bulk-carrier on the Atlantic run from Portugal northwards for 200 years. It was strong, stable and seaworthy, and in addition, it could readily be adapted for that other medieval activity, warfare.

The cog was a one-masted vessel which derived its power from a single square sail suspended from a horizontal yard arm. In technical terms, the hull was clinker-built, which meant that it was built upwards from the keel in a sequence of overlapping planks, each of which was riveted with clench nails to the plank below. A timber frame which included beams across the vessel was added, secondarily. The result was an exceptionally strong, high-sided, flat-bottomed, ship. The stem and stern posts were straight and steep-sloping.

This strong, stable structure made it capable, in due course, of supporting additional wooden superstructures known as 'castles', mental extensions of warfare on the land which were built up from the deck. One, the forecastle, was fitted onto the bow, and another, the aftercastle, onto the stern. A third structure, the topcastle, smaller than the others, was placed up the mast, from which extra height arrows, quick-lime and other projectiles could be hurled down on an enemy (see cover and Winchelsea seal on p. 74). Originally the castles were temporary, removable, structures, fitted under royal orders for each campaign as it occurred. But by the fifteenth century they had become permanent fixtures, a fact which explains the better-known outline, high at both ends, of Tudor ships in the sixteenth century. The name forecastle (or fo'c'stle) lives on today, being the part of the bow of a vessel where the crew is quartered and stores can be stowed.

The second important adaptation was made for carrying horses, an essential part of medieval warfare. Wooden gangways were provided for their embarkation and hurdles supported them during the voyage. These were, of course, also temporary structures, which were ordered and installed for every voyage as needed, and then taken away as appropriate.[34]

The cog was a multi-purpose vessel, which no doubt accounted for its longevity. A wide ship with high sides, it had a large capacity and so was particularly suitable as a commercial bulk-carrier. (The high sides also served as a deterrent, making it difficult for pirates attempting to come on board.) It also served as a ferry, taking pilgrims across to the continent, and members of the Anglo-Norman nobility and their followers to and fro to their estates across the Channel and further afield, principally to Gascony.

The cog had many advantages. Set against those, of course, it also had limitations. Tacking against the wind was very difficult, and it was neither fast-moving, nor could it be manoeuvred in confined spaces. Therefore, particularly for war-like short-distance coastal work on both sides of the Channel, most English kings of this period kept a number of galleys, vessels powered by oarsmen.

The commercial world was also involved in a conflict of interest with the monarchy. In general, these ships belonged to the merchants, whose livelihood depended on them reaching a successful conclusion to every voyage. On the other hand, the king had the right to commandeer any ships at any time for military purposes, to transport his armies with their horses and the other equipment of war, which varied from hundreds of thousands of arrows to unwieldy siege engines, on their frequent overseas campaigns. Or he might need them for defence of the English coast. There were frequent occasions when this conflict of interest between the ship-owning merchants and the government surfaced, and merchants became adept at finding reasons why their ships were not available at the time when royal demands went out. Civilian need was continuous, albeit largely seasonal, whereas military demands, which had overriding priority, were only spasmodic.

In the Mediterranean, conditions are very different. The waters are comparatively protected, so there are no great periodic waves. On the other hand, sudden squalls and relatively short-lived storms result in difficult choppy seas. In 1200 the traditional ships, the galleys (this was the Mediterranean galley, not to be confused with the northern galley) were successors of the ships of the Romans and were similar to the feluccas which can be seen on the Nile today. They were notably different from the cogs of the Atlantic in appearance and operation, in the construction of their hulls, in their steering and rigging, and in their propulsion.

The hull was carvel-built, which meant that the ship relied for its strength on a skeleton of strong timber. A series of ribs were fitted onto the keel, and only when that skeleton was firmly in place was it covered with a light skin of planks, the upper edge of each one abutting the lower edge of the one placed above it, which produced a smooth, flush surface. The rudder was installed on the side, near the stern. The rigging normally consisted of two masts, a large one in the prow and a much smaller one aft of that. Each of the masts supported a single triangular (lateen) sail, one corner of which was attached to the deck forward of the mast. These ships were powered by oars as well as the sails. One variation of this was the dromon, the oared fighting ship of the Eastern Roman Empire, in one of which Richard I of England had fought on his way to the Third Crusade in 1191.[35]

However, the Mediterranean galley was essentially limited to sheltered 'inland' seas, primarily the Mediterranean, the Black Sea and the Red Sea. The rigging was very demanding: it needed to be handled by a large crew, and was extremely difficult to manage in heavy seas. The distance this galley could cover was limited to how far each man could row, unless they were to incur the extra expense of carrying an additional crew. In addition, the sides of these vessels were low, which made them vulnerable to being swamped in rough water and also, when it came to repelling boarders, the low sides contrasted unfavourably with the higher ones of the cog. Although very suitable both for commercial purposes and for fighting against similar ships within the Mediterranean, these light-weight vessels, lying low in the water,

Modern portrayal of a medieval Mediterranean galley. Graffiti carved on rock at Aigues-Mortes, Provence.

would not have been able to cope with the rigorous conditions in the Atlantic. In the twelfth century, Atlantic-style ships had already been seen in the Mediterranean, making their way from west to east through the Straits of Gibraltar on their way to the Crusades. Their style must have been noted. But shipbuilders were a conservative breed, understandably favouring the safety of a traditional design. Thus, in 1200 the two shipbuilding traditions were as far apart as they had ever been.

But in the meantime, commerce between Flanders, England and northern Italy had been building up. For a century or more Italian merchants had been a familiar sight selecting the annual wool crop in England, and the Genoese had been continuing to convey quantities of that wool, together with cloth from Flanders, to Florence. But they travelled by the land route over the Alps, in the face of multiple difficulties caused by poor roads, landslides and avalanches, the dangers of brigands, and the possibility of getting caught up in local wars. The incentive to establish an alternative route became increasingly strong.

The stage was set for the first of the two great advances in ship design. What was needed was a ship capable of making the sea voyage through the Straits of Gibraltar and north up the Atlantic coast. What emerged was a hybrid ship. The carvel-built hull of the Mediterranean craft was retained, but the two masts were gradually reduced to one, the lateen sails changed to a single square sail, and the single stern rudder was adopted, all features of the cog of the north. There is no specific information about where this innovation took place, but there is strong circumstantial evidence to suggest that it happened in the shipyards of Genoa. The Genoese seem to have needed it above all others, and it was they who took the lead in using the new ship. Indeed, they must have been experimenting for a considerable time, because one of their vessels was recorded in La Rochelle, well up the Atlantic coastline, as early as 1232, although evidence for a breakthrough of commercial significance to the north does not appear until the last quarter of the century.

Unfortunately, nothing is known about the evolution of shipbuilding in Genoa, or about the management of Genoese fleets, because that was in the hands of individual capitalist families who were very secretive, operating fiercely independently of government interference or supervision. The captains of their ships were merchants. They managed each voyage individually, making *ad hoc* decisions about which ports they would visit on that occasion. It is remarkable that when petitions were drawn up protesting about the depredations of English pirates, they came, not in the name of the state, but from merchants of the Genoese group who were living in London

A carrack-like ship, carved on a pew end in the chapel of St Nicholas, King's Lynn, now in the National Maritime Museum, Greenwich. Possibly similar to the carracks captured in the Seine in 1416 and 1417. (National Maritime Museum)

or, in the 1450s, in the name of the individual merchants whose property was involved. The Genoese acquired the reputation of being a quiet, rather dour group, though it is possible that this stemmed from their remoteness owing to lack of record-keeping.

It is, however, well-known that it was the Genoese family of Spinola who hired three ocean-going ships, the *Sanctus Johannes*, the *Sanctus Anthonius*, and the *Alegrancia*, and brought the first cargo of alum through the Straits of Gibraltar to reach England by the sea route. Genoese entrepreneurs returned in several of the ensuing summers, though not by any means every year, and merchants from other western Mediterranean ports arrived swiftly in their wake. One Majorcan galley loaded 267 sacks of wool and bundles of woolfells in London in 1281, and another was in Sandwich, also loading wool, in 1287. In 1311 a merchant galley from Catalonia, presumably from Barcelona, was at Southampton unloading a cargo of almonds, leather, quicksilver and iron, all the produce of Spain.[36] These were the pioneers, taking advantage of the new design of ships capable of using the new trade route. That route, avoiding both the perils of the Alpine crossing and the double trans-shipping involved in the Channel crossing, and the inevitable delays and expense of the Carcassonne route, was an outstandingly important legacy of the late thirteenth century.

The transition was completed by the arrival of specialised galleys from Venice. There, a very different vessel had been constructed to cope with the sea journey to the north. They retained more features of the Mediterranean galley, keeping specifically two or three masts and the distinctive lateen sails on a vessel which was also powered by oars. The Venetian ships came up the Channel somewhat later than those of the other Mediterranean city states, their departure having been delayed first by a war against the Genoese (which they lost) and then by fighting a campaign on land against the Papacy. It was therefore not until 1314 or 1315 that the first fleet left Venice to sail north to Flanders. Their style, with brightly painted vessels and highly coloured lateen sails, could scarcely have been more different from that of the stolid Genoese. Nothing like this had ever been seen before in the northern ports and, as we shall see, when they eventually sailed up Southampton Water in 1319, they received a very mixed reception.[37] They became known on this route, famously, as the Flanders Galleys.

In marked contrast, too, to the individualistic Genoese, Venetian commercial activity was closely promoted and controlled by the state. Hence all the details were carefully documented and our knowledge of them is all the greater. Every fleet was state-organised, and presided over by a Venetian nobleman who had been elected by the senate, and he travelled in a style designed to impress (and intimidate?) all those with whom he came in contact. He was accompanied on board his flagship by a large retinue which included his personal priest, two physicians and four musicians as well as personal servants. Each galley in the fleet was also commanded by a Venetian nobleman, and each vessel carried 170 oarsmen and 30 bowmen, all chosen by public contest. Then there were navigating officers, a purser, a caulker, carpenters, cooks and so on, all the details inscribed on a magnificently illustrated commission, several of which have survived.

Commission appointing the captain of the (Venetian) Flanders Galleys, 1472.

By coincidence, at much the same time as the first important advance in ship design was happening in the Mediterranean, another notable development in shipbuilding took place in the last quarter of the thirteenth century at the eastern end of the English Channel, this one in the interest of warfare. In the 1280s, in the context of increasingly bellicose rivalry between England and France, Philip (IV) le Bel needed a reliable supply of good fighting ships. He established the *Clos de Galées*, a large-scale naval dockyard designed specifically to build swift-moving southern-style galleys on the south bank of the Seine at Rouen, a situation safely protected well inland. Since local shipbuilders lacked the necessary skills, he brought in Mediterranean shipwrights, at considerable expense, first to build the shipyard, and then, year by year, to build and maintain the galleys.[38] Those vessels were to prove especially valuable to the French for their short-distance assaults on the south coast of England from 1360 onwards, and the *Clos* remained in service, controlled by the Genoese, until destroyed by the French themselves in the face of Henry V's advancing army in 1418. Although the southern galleys must have been a familiar sight to summer visitors to the Channel in the fourteenth century, Rouen was the only place where they were ever built north of the Mediterranean.

Warfare apart, throughout the fourteenth century the main carriers of bulk cargoes were the great galleys, often referred to simply as great ships, and sometimes, confusingly, as cogs. Many were sailed by the Genoese, others by Spaniards or the Portuguese. Then, towards the end of that century, the second and last major medieval innovation to the design of the sailing ship gradually took place, presumably stimulated by a combination of increasing commercial demand and the permanent necessity of protecting the ships and their cargoes from marauders in a disorderly period. The new ship, with three masts and three sails, two square and one lateen which gave it the best possible mobility, was known as the carrack or alternatively the caravel. The tarit seems to have been the name applied to a somewhat smaller version. By 1450, the end of the period covered by this book, the carrack had developed into a fully rigged ship with three or four masts and five or six sails, the design which was to last until the end of the age of sail. It was this, combined with advances in the science of navigation, which made possible the exploration, expansion and exploitation of every part of the globe over the next four centuries. In fact, this new design was so successful, and so permanent, that a master who could handle one of these vessels of 1450 would have needed little help in sailing a ship at the Battle of Trafalgar in 1805.[39]

The records of piracy show, remarkably consistently, that in the fifteenth century ships in the Channel consisted of two types: on one hand, the large carracks and Venetian-style galleys, visitors from Mediterranean latitudes, and on the other, more locally derived vessels known as barges and balingers, which were smaller and fast-moving ships equipped with both oars and sails. The rigging varied, as the three masts were progressively adopted. Although these balingers were smaller and of local derivation, some of these did, on occasion, venture as far south as Cape St Vincent, the southern extremity of Portugal.[40]

Throughout the period covered by this book, the course taken by all the ships was a gift to potential pirates. The masters steered, as far as possible, within sight of land, for several reasons. Without possessing accurate navigational instruments, they needed to use familiar landmarks in order to determine their position. They also needed to put into ports frequently for supplies of drinking water and other provisions, for repairs to their ships or rigging, and to be able to seek shelter quickly whenever threatened by storms. Then, when these sea-going ships eventually reached their destinations, they normally anchored offshore, out in the main channels, and lighters came out to carry their cargoes, cask by cask, bale by bale, piece by piece, to and from the shore. The lengthy process of loading and unloading, with cargoes deposited on the hard above high-tide level, must have offered easy prey, and a great deal of piracy and pilfering, including wholesale removal of ships, evidently took place within the tidal estuaries which served as harbours.[41] And, as the records of the great French raid on Southampton in 1338 show, looting was by no means restricted to foreigners. At Sandwich the ships were particularly vulnerable: they anchored and were unloaded off-shore, where the sandbanks known as the Downs provided excellent shelter from the sea and the weather – though none at all from foreign pirates.

The men of the south-west, in Devon and Cornwall, had their own refined method of acquiring passing goods and merchandise. When ships sought shelter and anchored in those deep-water estuaries, they were likely to have their anchor cables cut by pirates, so that the winds of the storm, or simply the rising tide, drove them onto rocks where they could be relieved of their cargo by land-based wreckers. However, little credibility can be attached to the well-circulated fables about ships being enticed onto the rocks by showing false lights. What medieval light would have survived a storm, and what mariner would have been able to see it or, even less likely, been able to direct his vessel towards it?[42]

In order to reduce their losses on their voyages, the merchants spread their consignments across several vessels. The other, practical, way of trying to avoid losses, originally recorded in the wine trade and subsequently used frequently elsewhere according to the demands of war, politics and piracy, was to sail in convoy (*con-voi*, sailing together). In addition to which, the sailors were often provided with arms, or armed soldiers were put on board, all of which added considerably to the cost of the cargo.

When the Anglo-French war broke out in 1324, and more seriously at the beginning of the Hundred Years War, royal action was rapidly taken to protect the wine ships, and in 1337 they were only permitted to sail if they were in convoy. Through the more dangerous spells during the reigns of Edward III (1327–77) and Richard II (1377–99), a rigid convoy system was again operated. Then, during the exceptionally unruly period dominated by privateers during the reign of Henry IV (1399–1413), royal intervention ceased altogether and was replaced by a system of mutual support organised by the merchants themselves – which added to the already considerable power of some of the merchant/privateers. During the reign of Henry V conditions in the Channel were infinitely more peaceful: royal intervention was not needed, but it seems that the merchants continued to organise the convoys themselves. After 1449, during the final phase of the Hundred Years War, shipping once more became chaotic, and when Bordeaux fell to the French in 1453, the whole system of wine fleets came to an end as far as English fleets were concerned. But English merchants and small Breton ships took over, sailing independently, and the historic trade continued, albeit in chaotic conditions of warfare and piracy.[43]

It is evident, however, that delays waiting for convoys to assemble caused annoyance and expense for both the masters and the merchants, and in the commercial interest of speed, some still preferred to take the risk and sail alone. Others, which started out in convoy, fell behind or became separated by storms. Any ships which sailed singly, for whatever reason, were those most at risk from pirates.

Besides defending themselves physically, masters were able to make use of one of two legal steps to insure against possible losses. The first, and simplest, apparently dates from Hubert de Burgh, when he was acting as regent for the young Henry III. He initiated a system whereby they could obtain a 'safe conduct' from the ruler(s) through whose waters they proposed to sail, and each of those rulers would authorise the proposed voyage and guarantee the master, crew and cargo safe passage. This was, in effect, a form of early passport. The earliest record of this, allowing the bearer to enter and leave England, and to trade freely by land or water *except in time of war* without being molested by pirates, appears in the Great Charter of Henry III, in 1225.[44]

However, the limitations of these written documents are illustrated by numerous cases: they were often disregarded, torn up and thrown into the sea by the pirates, along with all but the more important people on board. But proof of the one-time existence of a safe conduct did at least make it possible to make a complaint to the king, or other authority, in the hope that, sometimes for reasons of political expediency, he would order his subjects to restore the lost possessions, or their value, to the owners. How often this produced the required result is doubtful, but on the other hand the enrolled complaints do provide valuable material for the historian.

A second and perhaps more effective means of recovery of the value of the stolen goods, which emerged in the late thirteenth century and came to be employed frequently when other methods had failed, was known as a 'letter of marque and reprisal'. In the case of a reprisal, the king whose merchant had suffered the loss gave orders to the officials in his ports to seize goods of any merchant from the country of the offenders, up to the value of the lost goods and for a set period of time. A letter of marque went one step further and authorised the aggrieved merchant to take matters into his own hands and try to punish the offender. Needless to say, both reprisals and letters of marque led to counter-reprisals, which stoked up to a personal war between merchants and often drew in others who had not offended, including those of neutral countries. The system was both complex in form and long-winded to administer. Its application was confused by the fast-changing nature of international relations, especially as truces were rapidly made and even more swiftly broken, and may or may not have been established or renewed. The lack of up-to-date information available to those abroad or at sea provided another ready excuse. Offenders were always ready to claim ignorance. It usually took weeks, sometimes months, for commissions to be sent out asking the necessary questions about the situation at the time of the offence, and even longer to bring the legal process to a conclusion. During that time, the stolen goods could, of course, have been distributed far and wide. Overall, initiative, speed and time were on the side of pirates.

A final word concerns two traditions which date from the early years of the Gascon wine trade. One was the means of measuring the cargo-carrying capacity, and hence the approximate size, of ships. The term tonnage, in use today, originated in the tuns, the wine casks, each of which held 252 gallons.

The other was a legal code known as the Laws of Oleron, which apparently evolved in the twelfth century to deal with all kinds of disputes which might arise in the course of, or in connection with, a commercial voyage. The master, often the owner or part-owner of the ship, was responsible for all operation and administration. The ship, its ropes and all other equipment had to be in good repair: it had to be properly navigated, and reach its destination safely within approved time limits. He might take a pilot on board for all or part of the voyage, and a pilot who made an error was subjected to heavy penalties. The master also had to provide, control and look after his crew. They were to be included in consultations about the weather, and when the ship could safely put to sea, and they were to expect fair discipline, acceptable food and wages, and due care if sick or wounded. A sick man was to be put ashore as soon as possible, with the provision of adequate care. The master was also responsible for safe loading and carriage of the cargo, and he was to negotiate with the merchants or their representatives before jettisoning any of the cargo if that became necessary in a storm. Since the problems and the terminology of navigation were universal, the language was intelligible to the crew whatever their nationality, and this code soon became recognised from the Baltic to the Mediterranean. Under it, the medieval mariner seems to have been, though he did not know it, much better looked after than his counterparts were under less well-regulated conditions in the Tudor century.[45]

# 4

# The English Channel: A New Frontier

n 1204 England lost Normandy to France, and thereby the Channel became a frontier between two competitive, bellicose monarchies. This marked the beginning of a new era, not only in the history of the Channel, but for trade with Poitou, Aquitaine, and places further south.

The situation in 1200 had built up as a result of events which had taken place in the 1150s, in 1066 and even earlier. The name Normandy was derived from Rollo, a Norse (otherwise Viking) raider who settled down and established a colony in the fertile valley of the River Seine in AD 911. By 1066 that colony had expanded and attained approximately the present borders of Haute Normandie combined with Basse Normandie, the land on either side of the Seine. It included all the coastline from Eu, north of Dieppe, west to Mont St Michel, together with the Channel Islands.

After the Battle of Hastings Duke William set about securing a very strong Norman presence in England, his new country. The land was parcelled up and placed in the hands of Norman overlords. Castles and cathedrals were built. For those in the south, they used, to a considerable extent, Caen stone imported from Normandy: several of these vast symbols of Norman authority remain standing today. The great monastic houses in Normandy established daughter houses in England. The official language of England became Norman-French, and was to remain so for some 300 years. The links William forged between England and Normandy were therefore close and long-lasting, and they were not only political, but also seigniorial, ecclesi-astical, cultural and commercial. Cross-Channel traffic increased as people went frequently to and fro to their different properties, and commerce built up. As a result, the ports on the Channel coast of south-east England enjoyed unprecedented, and increasing, prosperity.

Some ninety years later, following the tumult and disorganisation of the English civil war between two of the Conqueror's grandchildren, Matilda and Stephen, it was eventually agreed that Stephen should reign for his lifetime, and should be succeeded by Matilda's son, who in due course became Henry II. In the meantime Matilda, her husband Geoffrey of Anjou, and their son had settled in France, where the youthful prince indulged in empire-building. In 1150 he was given Normandy by his mother and the following year his father died, leaving him the provinces of Anjou, Maine and Touraine, which were on a par with Normandy in terms of agricultural riches. In 1152, at the age of 18, Henry married Eleanor of Aquitaine, a fiery spirit twelve years his senior whose marriage to the saintly Louis VII of France had been annulled only six weeks previously. By means of this diplomatic union Henry gained control of a further large area which is now south-west France, north and south of the River Garonne and down to the Pyrenees. Thus when Stephen died two years later and Henry succeeded him as Henry II (1154–1189), he ruled not only England but also a large part of present-day France.

When John (1199–1216), the youngest son of Henry II, inherited this Anglo-Angevin-Aquitaine empire from his brother Richard I (1189–99) it was still intact – but only just. Stretching nearly 2,000 miles from the River Tweed in the north to the Spanish border in the south, it was physically, economically, and demographically very diverse, and vast. It had survived for over forty years, but only because it was not challenged by any strong external opposition. By 1200, however, the balance of power was shifting and the empire was under threat from a new force.

In 1180 Philip (II) Augustus, young, energetic and very competent, had become king of France, which at that point consisted of only a small land-locked area round Paris. He reorganised his capital, built a wall around the city, promoted the growth of the middle class, and brought financial stability to the country. From that basis he began to expand his territory. In 1191 he seized Artois, and soon afterwards arranged the marriage of his sister to the Count of Ponthieu (one of several counties which made up Picardy), and thus gained control of a stretch of coastline opposite England. He then fought a sequence of successful campaigns against King John which culminated in 1204 in England's loss of Normandy, the richest of the French provinces and also the one in which most of the Anglo-Norman lords in England had a strong interest.

The Anglo-Norman-Angevin empire
of Henry II (1154–89), as it remained
in 1200.

After 1224, French control of their
coastline menaced shipping.

By these three moves Philip Augustus had not only gained control of his
first length of the French seaboard, stretching from Calais to St Malo, but
had also secured the vital routeway of the Seine which connected Paris
with the sea. Philip Augustus died in July 1223, and his son Louis VIII
continued his succession of conquests, capturing the port of La Rochelle the
following year. This was a conclusive move, which significantly altered the
balance of power for, while it strengthened France, it weakened England.
He had managed to sever the empire of Henry II, which was already much
reduced, into two distant parts. Aquitaine became separated from England
by nearly 1,000 miles of stormy seas which, with French access to the
Bay of Biscay, had serious implications for the trade route between north
and south.

The loss of Normandy was an event of the greatest significance for the
political and strategic history of the Channel. It signalled the beginning of
Anglo-French hostilities which were to continue spasmodically through the

period covered by this book – and long into the future beyond that. The two countries faced each other across a wide sea where no laws applied to reduce piracy, and indeed no laws could have been enforced. At the same time, the Channel was one of the principal commercial highways of the medieval world, and therefore all the other kingdoms and principalities with commercial interests in the great seaway became politically involved, not least Flanders, the rich industrial heart of north-west Europe, and the kingdom of Castile, the forerunner of the great sea power Spain, which was rich in its own right in raw materials, especially high-quality iron.

It is important to note, too, that in the medieval period large-scale battles between opposing fleets at sea were a rarity. There were three main reasons for this. The limitations of their rigging meant that the ships themselves were difficult to manoeuvre. Secondly, tidal flows in the Channel are strong and change continuously, adding to the problems of lining up potential adversaries. Lastly, the weather is notoriously inconsistent and unreliable. As the chroniclers frequently reminded their readers, a fair dawn with a favourable wind might be followed by a 'tempest', which may be interpreted as a strong wind in a different direction, in the afternoon. Therefore, major confrontations out in the Channel were never planned or contemplated. Most of the few encounters which have gone down in medieval history as naval battles took place in the sheltered area of a port on one side of the Channel or the other. (The only possible exception to this was the battle which took place against Castilian carracks in the sea off Winchelsea as they headed for home in 1350, but that was certainly unplanned and very likely took place in the lee of the Fairlight cliffs rather than out in the Channel.) The great set-piece battles of naval history belong to a much later era.

In the natural no-man's-land of the Channel, piracy and raiding proved far more appropriate and effective tools with which to undermine opposition, and certain areas were of special strategic importance. The first and most obvious was the Straits of Dover, where the waterway narrows down to little more than 20 miles across and where all shipping has to run the gauntlet in full view from the cliffs on both sides. Control of the ports and anchorages in this area was therefore crucial to both England and France. Near at hand, two great anchorages, one on either side of the Channel, were of fundamental importance in the medieval period. Both disappeared from the landscape centuries ago, as a result of rapid natural changes of low-lying coastlines.

In Flanders the *Zwin* was a tidal inlet which, destined to have untold political and commercial importance, had apparently opened up in the great sea flood of 1134. The tides probably once reached south to Bruges, and the channel widened in the north to give extensive shelter from the sea behind some islands. However, the channel soon began to silt up, and in response to the increasing needs of shipping, Damme and Sluys developed as important outports, nearer the sea and more accessible for sea-going ships than Bruges itself.

On the English coast, the Camber (*la chambre*, an enclosure) opened up similarly, but probably rather later. The emergence of Winchelsea and La Rye from obscurity in mid-twelfth century suggests that they were based on a marine inlet which already existed, but there is no doubt that it was greatly expanded when the sea broke down a shingle barrier and flooded up channels during storms in the second half of the thirteenth century.[46] Both the *Zwin* and the Camber, so important in the medieval period, silted up around the end of that period and have long since disappeared. The sea retreated, abandoning several medieval ports on both sides of the Channel, with little or no trace of their once-important waterways.

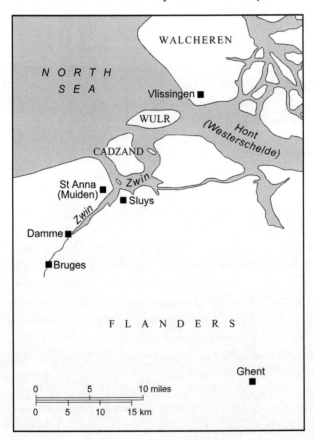

The medieval *Zwin* – a sheltered anchorage, vitally important for commercial and military interests. (A conjectural map based on Vos and van Heeringen, 1997)

Secondly, control of the islands near both shores was critical, and sometimes difficult to maintain. The Channel Islands are much closer to France
than England, with Alderney and Jersey lying within sight of the French
mainland. But, perhaps surprisingly, they remained in English hands for
nearly all of the time after 1204 and were used as bases by raiding parties
setting off for either Normandy or Brittany. They were also an important
victualling stop-over point for ships sailing up or down the French side of the
Channel, and they proved to be excellent bases for pirates lying in wait for
those ships. On the English side of the Channel, the Solent, sheltered in the
lee of the Isle of Wight, provided an excellent and very extensive anchorage
close to the ports of Southampton (sometimes, and for various reasons, used
as an outport for London) and Portsmouth. It was there that armies could
assemble, that vessels could lie up when delayed by adverse winds before
starting their voyages, and it was the sheltered anchorage where the great
convoys of ships assembled before starting off their voyage westwards
down the Channel to collect wine and salt during the dangerous years of the
Hundred Years War. The island itself is conveniently large, measuring over
20 miles from west to east, and 12 miles from north to south, and served
several useful purposes. It was an attractive bridgehead for potential foreign
invaders, and at various times it was also a retreat for outlaws, and a base for
pirates as a market centre for their goods.

The third critical area of the Channel was the western tip of Brittany, and
the Pointe de St Mathieu in particular, off which trading vessels congregated,
pausing on their way north or south to take on board water, to revictual and
usually to wait for a change of wind. It was therefore an obvious place for
pirates also to congregate and lie in wait: they might be sailors of Brittany, of
relatively local origin, but very often they included troublemakers who came
from much further away (Col. Plates 5 and 6).

When the Channel became a frontier, the ports became frontier towns,
the focus of intense political as well as commercial interest. The French
reacted quickly by walling their coastal towns most at risk. For example,
the walls of Boulogne and Montreuil (the latter long since deserted by the
sea) are mighty defences which survive from the early thirteenth century.
Calais was fortified by Philip Hurepal, son of Philip Augustus, in 1224. Two
major castles in the Channel Islands, Castle Cornet, guarding the harbour of
St Peter Port on Guernsey, and Gorey Castle on Jersey were English defences
dating from the time of King John (1199–1216) (Col. Plates 7 and 8).

On the English side of the Channel, however, with the notable exception of Dover Castle, the pressure to spend money on defensive works was
spasmodic, and the reaction was much more laid back. It is indeed worth

considering how possible it ever was to defend the English coast against invaders. Looking back to the third century AD, some ten vast, sturdy forts 'of the Saxon Shore' had indeed been built in an attempt to cope with invaders arriving from northern Europe but, in the absence of conclusive evidence, seem to have had little effect. In the medieval period, many more wide tidal estuaries were still open than exist today. These offered suitable landing sites for invaders, but altogether they created a deeply indented coastline, making movement of troops along the coast impracticable. It would never have been possible to achieve an effective, integrated system of national defence, even if the administrative structure had existed.

Moreover as it was, responsibility for defence of the ports lay in the hands of the prosperous and influential merchants, who were expected to pay for the works. They depended for their livelihood on commerce, and to them easy access between their large cellars and warehouses and the waterfront was an overruling priority. Any defensive wall would be a serious impediment to movement of goods to and from their ships. It would also result in serious deterioration in the value of their properties which they feared would degenerate into 'gardens', in modern terms waste land affected by planning blight. Therefore there was strong local opposition to building walls and notable lethargy in spending funds on them. For example, in the face of threatened French raids from 1336 onwards, the burgesses of Southampton evaded the issue.[47] Castles were, in fact, used for purposes other than defence: considerable expenditure is recorded on that at Southampton, but it was used as an occasional royal residence, as a store for the kings' wine and wool, as the site for a stone-built (fire-proof) royal treasury, and as a short-term prison. In October 1338 the French and Genoese were to prove that neither the town wall, such as it was, nor the castle at Southampton was in any condition to give the inhabitants confidence in the protection it afforded.

The loss of Normandy, which made the Channel into a new political frontier, combined with general political instability and uncertainty to produce just the conditions which favoured adventurous, entrepreneurial sailors in their enterprising activities. These men were useful to the various authorities because they were able to react spontaneously and exploit political situations immediately, as they unfolded. The other side of the coin was that they lost no opportunities to make profits on their own behalf. The earliest of these to be recorded was Eustace the Monk, a nobleman from Boulogne, who first appears in 1205. He is a somewhat legendary figure who filled the roles of both pirate and mercenary. His story is derived from a combination of some ten of the medieval chronicles, which included a 'romance', or biography, which was written in the Picardy dialect, but even that not until 1284, some seventy years after his death. The chronicles are notorious for dramatisation and exaggeration, and no doubt the stories became embellished in the telling as they were handed down from one generation to another. They contain many contradictions. As with other colourful, larger-than-life historical characters, including the medieval outlaw Robin Hood, in the story of Eustace fiction became well embedded in fact. The following account, based on three secondary sources which were themselves based on the chronicles, is what seems most plausible.[48]

Eustace was born into a noble family near Boulogne, probably around 1170. It is said by the *Romance* (and only, it seems, by that one source) that in his youth he visited Toledo in central Spain, which had been under Moorish domination for some three centuries until 1085. There, he studied the Black Art so successfully that he was without equal in the whole of France. Be that as it may, he is said to have appeared in a variety of disguises and terrified his opponents who knew of his reputation for his 'power to become invisible' as well as for his violence. Early in his life he also spent some time as a monk in the abbey of Samer, near Boulogne, in spite of the fact that one record describes him as 'demoniac'. But, however unsuited to that occupation he may have been, it must have been that which was used later on by chroniclers as a title by which to identify him. He escaped from that life, apparently leaving in 1190 when he heard that his father had been murdered, in order to pursue the murderer.

He is next heard of in the employment of the Count of Boulogne but he fell out with him and left, swearing vengeance. Outlawed from there, in 1205 he crossed the Channel to England and offered his services to King John. The king is said to have equipped Eustace with a number of galleys, who then established himself on the island of Sark, from where he could raid the coast of Normandy, encouraged by John, who was hoping for retribution, having so recently lost that duchy. During that time Eustace carried out at least one major and daring raid, in which he penetrated some distance inland up the Seine, and then escaped from his pursuers by retreating west to Barfleur. One account says that as a reward for that raid he was given a rich 'palais' in London, although another suggests that this 'palais' may in fact have been in Winchelsea, since that was his home port when in England. He was evidently receiving royal favours, and it seems that, one way or another, Eustace had also amassed a personal fortune, presumably on the proceeds of piracy.

Then, sometime between May 1212 and November 1214, he changed his allegiance for the second time. He crossed the Channel again, in order to support France. The reasons given for that move are contradictory. One source suggests that by 1212, having apparently overstepped the mark, he was expelled from the Channel Islands by the English keeper, Philip d'Aubigny, and escaped in disguise to France, taking five galleys with him. An alternative account of his defection says he went voluntarily. This seems not unlikely, as he would have been disenchanted with John's vacillation and weakness as a leader, and simultaneously attracted by the more positive approach of Philip Augustus.

From 1211 onwards both kings were jockeying for positions in Flanders. John still hoped to reconquer Normandy, while Philip Augustus had designs on England. Both of them needed a stepping-off base in Flanders, especially access to the harbour of the *Zwin*, and to Flemish mercenaries. Early in 1213 the Pope, after a long altercation with John, excused his English subjects from their allegiance to him and strongly encouraged all Christian leaders to unite in efforts to depose him. This, as described by the chroniclers, gave Philip Augustus the justification he was seeking for planning an invasion of England.

Events then led up to the episode known as the Battle of Damme, perhaps better described as an important raid. In the spring of 1213, Philip Augustus moved his land forces north and invaded Flanders. He devastated Bruges and attacked Ghent, at the same time ordering a 'large' fleet to move north up the coast. How large this force really was is not known, but it probably consisted mainly of sailors from Poitou, who were far from home and by no means entirely dependable.

John, having decided the best form of defence was attack, sent his half-brother William Longsword, Earl of Salisbury, over at the head of a considerably smaller fleet to reconnoitre and, if possible, to intercept the French. They probably sailed in mid-April, and would have reached the mouth of the Meuse (the *Zwin*) in a couple of days, where Longsword was surprised to find the port full of vessels.[49] Having established that the ships were indeed French, he took the opportunity to capture or burn the larger ones anchored out in the middle of the channel leading up to Damme while the sailors had apparently gone ashore to plunder what remained of the wealth of Bruges.

Hearing the news of this disaster and concerned particularly about the fate of his pay-chests which were on board one of the ships, Philip Augustus broke his siege of Ghent and hurried to Damme, where he found the remainder of his fleet, the smaller ships, still pulled up on the mud. However, confronted with the difficulty of getting those ships away from Damme in the face of the English fleet lying in wait outside, and mistrusting the mercenaries from Poitou, who might turn traitor and change sides at any moment, he burnt the rest of his own boats rather than let them fall into English hands. As a result, he was without a fleet and had to abandon any thoughts he may have had of invading England that year. .

Although Philip Augustus could not prevent John landing in Flanders the following year, he defeated him and the armies of his allies, the Holy Roman Emperor and the Counts of Flanders and Boulogne, in a decisive battle (on land) at Bouvines, between Lille and Tournai. This was the first great encounter between alliances of medieval European powers, and has been described as one of the most important in the history of medieval Europe. From the point of view of operations in the Channel, not only was John repulsed and thrown back on the defensive, but the way was laid open for the French (who were now led, for diplomatic reasons to satisfy the Pope, not by Philip Augustus, but by Louis, his son) to pursue their plans to invade England. They were further encouraged by the political situation in England, where John's tyranny was so intensely unpopular that a large faction of the English barons invited Louis to cross the Channel and claim the crown of England.

This was where Eustace, whose experience of dealing with ships and shipping, tides and currents in the Channel was evidently second to none, was indispensable. He was employed by Louis to assemble another substantial fleet, suitable for carrying a large force over to England. That was the official side of his activities. On the other side of the coin he played on his well-known personal reputation for inspiring uncontrolled terror, which was well illustrated by the caveat Philip Augustus gave to the papal legate, as reported by Matthew Paris, one of the more reliable of chroniclers: 'Through our land I will willingly furnish you with a safe conduct, but if by chance you should fall into the hands of Eustace the Monk or of the other men of Louis who guard the sea-routes, do not impute it to me if any harm comes to you.'[50]

In 1215, the year better known for the signing of Magna Carta, the international balance of power in the Channel was becoming critical and Eustace had begun preparations for their campaign. He took certain 'machines of war', possibly trébuchets, counter-weighted catapults to be mounted either on land or on the ships for throwing heavy stones at castles or onto the decks of enemy vessels, over to Folkestone to support the English barons. His fleet was then used to ferry Louis and his army over to Sandwich, of which they secured control in the summer of 1216. On 10 July Louis began to lay siege to Dover Castle but as that was skilfully defended by Hubert de Burgh, he failed to take it, and had to concede a truce on 14 October. Meanwhile, his forces went on to join up with the rebellious barons and together they gained control of a large area of north-east England.[51]

At the same time, John's fleet of galleys (incidentally one of the largest maintained by any of the medieval English kings) was feinting in the Channel with the French fleet. Considerable raiding and counter-raiding took place, but neither side seized an opportunity to confront the opposing fleet when they saw it emerging from port. It was easier to inflict damage on enemy shipping by raiding them while in port, with less likelihood of damage being sustained by the attacker.

In January 1217, in response to the critical situation, Philip d'Aubigny, described by then as a veteran seaman, was appointed to defend the coast of south-east England. According to one account, it seems that with the help of an irregular band commanded by one Willikin of the Weald, some of the Cinque Ports men managed to shut Louis up in Winchelsea. But at the end of February Eustace and the French broke out through that blockade. The town was apparently burnt, and one chronicler describes a dramatic rescue of Louis by Eustace.[52]

Whatever the truth of those stories, Louis then spent some two months in France, during which time he lost some support in England. He returned to Sandwich at the end of April, and by 12 May he was besieging Dover once more, control of which was highly important to him. But while there, on 25 May, news came through that his land forces had been disastrously defeated in a battle at Lincoln. To compound his difficulties, most of his ships were driven back to Calais by a storm. Louis could do little without reinforcements. He proceeded to London while Eustace retired to Calais and gathered together a new fleet which had been rapidly reinforced with more ships by the energetic wife of Louis, Blanche of Castile. On 24 August, St Bartholomew's Day, 1217, Eustace was sailing north up the coast of Kent at the head of this fleet, apparently bound for London in order to join up with Louis and the remaining land forces.

Having realised the very serious implications if the French reinforcements were to reach London, once the French had passed, Hubert de Burgh put to sea from Dover with a small fleet consisting mainly of royal galleys, reinforced by ships of the Cinque Ports. They started out on an eastern course, which gave the impression that they were making for Calais. But Hubert had a different object in mind. He made sure he had given himself the critical tactical advantage of having the wind and the sun behind him, and then turned north. The story goes that Eustace's ship was the largest and was weighed down by a trébuchet, with the result that it was lagging behind the rest of the French fleet. Be that as it may, somewhere in the narrow space between Sandwich and the Goodwin Sands the English caught up with the French fleet and English crossbowmen began the action. They

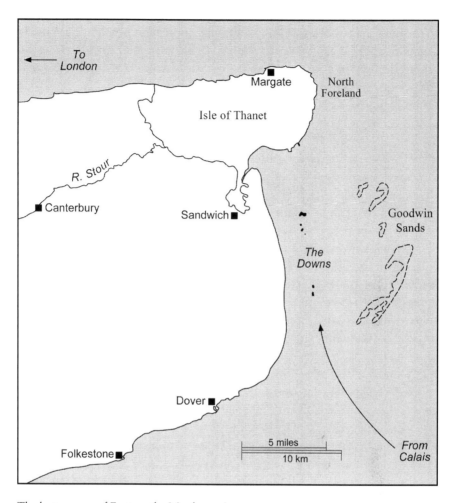

The last voyage of Eustace the Monk, 24 August 1217.

followed this by hurling pots of finely pulverised lime which blinded and paralysed the French, enabling the English sailors to board the French ships and slash down their rigging. As described by one of the chroniclers, this trapped everyone on deck 'like a net [falling] upon ensnared small birds'. Eustace was found hiding in the ship's bilges. Described by Mathew Paris as a 'master-pirate', he was a confidence trickster who in changing sides had inevitably made many enemies. He could expect no reasoned justice. He was brought out and summarily beheaded on his own ship, possibly by Richard, a bastard son of King John, possibly by Stephen Crabbe, a one-time friend whom Eustace himself had trained, who was now a rival pirate based at Sandwich.[53]

To sum up, Eustace made the most of the opportunities offered by rapidly changing political circumstances. Very little is known of his life before 1204 but, in the light of what followed, he must have made very good use of that early period, becoming exceptionally proficient in everything concerned with sailing ships and with navigation in the eastern half of the Channel. This can only have been the result of extensive experience at sea. Courageous and fearless, he established a fearsome reputation among other mariners and also, it seems, respect among the national leaders. He was flexible and adaptable and, unhampered by any sense of long-term allegiance, he offered his services wherever and whenever adventure and commercial opportunity arose.

Was it a coincidence that he appeared in England almost as soon as John had lost Normandy? Probably not. He lacked one thing, and that was ships of his own. It is probable that he saw England as a good source of ships with which to follow his piratical inclinations. Then, when Philip Augustus began to plan to invade first Flanders and then England, and John was on the defensive, Eustace went over to the French side in search of an alternative source of ships, more profitable adventure, and probably greater rewards. In both instances his maritime experience proved indispensable, so much so that he seems to have had a hand in planning, and certainly in executing, the French invasion plans.

It was perhaps unfortunate for Eustace that he was eventually defeated by a chance combination of circumstances, by the determination and the political and strategic acumen of Hubert de Burgh, and by a direction of wind which, although it favoured his final voyage, also proved conclusively helpful to Hubert. If the French plan had succeeded, and had Eustace arrived in London to be greeted by rebellious English barons as well as Louis with the remnants of the French troops who had survived the Battle of Lincoln, France would have had a strong foothold in the contemporary turmoil of English politics, and the succession to the English throne might well have been different. As it was, John died in 1216, and his 9-year-old son, Henry III, succeeded to a throne which was independent of France, with William the Marshall as his first regent. After this period of acute uncertainty, the Channel was firmly established as a political frontier – and a good hunting ground for pirates.

# 5

# The Cinque Ports

n 1200, a group of small English ports at the eastern end of the Channel was poised to achieve a degree of political influence far greater than their size or the economic value of their hinterland would suggest likely. By that date the original five Cinque Ports – Sandwich, Dover, Hythe, Romney and Hastings – had already been joined in their association by two so-called 'ancient towns', Winchelsea and Rye. So in this case the name *cinque* implied, in fact, seven. It is important to note that initially their association was informal. Not until 1260 was a charter directed to them as a group, rather than as individual ports. Before that date, they were bonded simply by strong mutual interests.

In an age characterised by violence, the men of these ports carried things to extremes, and showed no discrimination about whom they attacked. Their reputation as violent, independent, marauding pirates extended internationally, and they were also notorious for their long-lasting feuds with other ports, both at home and abroad. The Cinque Ports showed repeatedly that they were beyond the reach of authority, answerable to nobody, and over the course of the thirteenth century they secured for themselves a succession of unique concessions and privileges, which they valued highly.[54]

They operated from a position of potential strength, for which there were three underlying reasons. The first was the gift of geography. These portsmen, as much as any other, looked to the sea for their livelihood because, with the exception of Sandwich, which served as an outport for

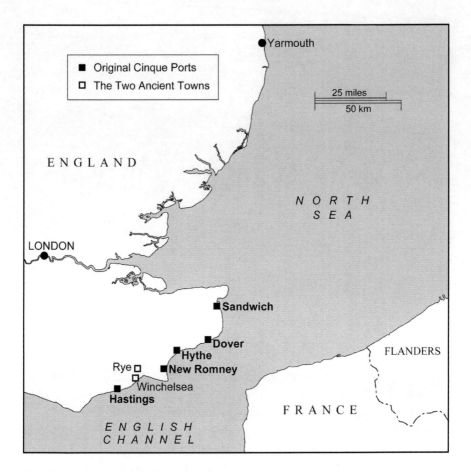

The Cinque Ports, and their constant opponent Yarmouth.

London, their Wealden hinterland was notably poor, the chief product being wood, an important but not valuable commodity. They were in a position of great strategic importance. They overlooked the narrowest part of the Channel so that on clear days from at least Sandwich, Dover and Hythe they could see the continental coast. The view from the hills behind their harbours was even better. They thus commanded, at least in fine weather, a view of all shipping using this part of the Channel, whether it was crossing between England and France, or heading up or down Channel in connection with the commercial centre of Flanders. In addition, they had control of their own ships and crews, and unequalled practical experience of sailing in what are daunting waters with a threatening combination of complex tides, shifting shoals and difficult tidal harbours. As a result of all this they were able, whenever they chose, to terrorise the shipping in what in the medieval period became known as the *Narrow Seas*, and is now known as the Straits of Dover. The other side of the coin was that, especially after the loss of Normandy in 1204, the Cinque Ports themselves lived constantly in fear, under threat of attack from the sea.

The second source of their strength was their involvement with the annual Yarmouth Herring Fair. Herrings are exceptionally nutritious, and since the Catholic Church at that time prohibited meat-eating on at least 135 (and probably a lot more) days in the year, they played a highly important part in supplying protein for the medieval diet. Indeed, it has been said that in times of famine the herring served to keep considerable numbers of people alive. Each year vast shoals of this fish migrated south down the North Sea to spawn off Yarmouth, and since before records began the Cinque Ports must have taken part in the great autumn fishing bonanza which took place there. Being highly perishable, as soon as they were landed the fish were smoked (to produce red herrings), or salted (producing white ones), then and there on the beach. They were caught in such vast quantities that subsequently they were shipped off to most parts of the known world, which meant taking them west as far as Ireland, south to Gascony (both destinations for Cinque Port vessels), and east to Poland.[55]

The third source of strength, an important bargaining lever for these ports, was the need of the Crown for vessels which could be used to fight, for both offensive and defensive purposes. By a strange paradox, William I, whose successful invasion of England had depended on his vast fleet, had let his fleet go, and showed no inclination to retain a fighting maritime force: his successors followed suit. Therefore, up to 1200, as far as England was concerned, shipping was almost entirely a matter of transport. Fortunately no foreign power had the motivation or the equipment to mount another invasion during that period of over 130 years.[56] However, by 1200, change was on the way and the ports of Kent and Sussex were obviously, with their active ships in sea-going order, poised to be recruited for either aggressive operations or for defending the coast.

Looking back, the individual ports had begun their accumulation of privileges at a very early date, for which evidence is very shadowy. But it seems that when Edward the Confessor (1042–66) needed ships in the 1050s, possibly to keep watch on potential invaders leaving the Flanders shore, he had to gain, or buy, the loyalty of these ports in the crucial geographical position. Hence some of the individual ports were offered privileges in return for guaranteed service. This was, apparently, the beginning of a sequence of negotiations between the Crown and the Cinque Ports, which became increasingly weighted in favour of the ports.[57]

Thus, by the end of the twelfth century, just before our period, certain 'ancient customs' had become well established. In return for providing the Crown with the (unpaid) service of fifty-seven ships, each manned by twenty-one men, for fifteen days a year, the Cinque Ports had gained certain rights. The most important of these concerned their interest in the annual Yarmouth Herring Fair, including the right of 'den and strand', to camp and dry their nets on the beach there between Michaelmas (29 September) and St Andrew's Day (30 November), the duration of the fair.[58] Other rights were held by the individual ports, but there was as yet no general charter, and no official organisation linking the ports. They were simply becoming gradually united informally by their two common interests, the Yarmouth Fair and piracy.

Disputes were a fact of fishermen's lives, and were much less easily controlled than those between men of communities on land. A record survives from as early as the time of Henry I (1100–35), to show that the Cinque Ports were causing trouble at Yarmouth. The portsmen 'tore down by force of arms' a church standing on the beach at Yarmouth, and that led to a riot. This was the forerunner of frequent disturbances and built up into the longest-lasting and deepest-seated of all the feuds in which the Cinque Ports involved themselves. It is not difficult to imagine the background of these fracas. A party of visiting fishermen, tough, energetic and mostly young, were based away from home for two months, living on a long narrow sandbank, part of which was already occupied by the settlement of Yarmouth. This was a recipe for dissension. Men of both communities must have frequently had time on their hands – waiting for the tide to turn, for a storm to abate, or simply hanging around until they could set out at dusk, since night was the prime time when the fish came near the surface. Quarrels broke out quickly and spread fast: they concerned space for drying nets, tangled nets, the control of fires, maintenance of harbour lights, removal of wrecks, petty thieving, prostitution.

The chaotic conditions during the English barons' civil war of 1215–17, coinciding as they did with the temporarily successful French invasion of England, provided the ports with a good opportunity to demonstrate their potential strength. Initially, Louis was able to establish his forces in England, which suggests that the ports had acquiesced, or more probably cooperated, in his crossing. They evidently did not support the defence of England at that point, in 1216. But William the Marshall soon realised it would be catastrophic for England if Eustace succeeded in reinforcing the French troops already in London, and he set about preventing that at all costs. An exceptionally able administrator, he rapidly assembled a small number of royal vessels and then did eventually succeed in persuading the reluctant Cinque Ports to put their ships at his disposal. This timing was crucial, because it allowed Hubert de Burgh (younger and more active than the Marshall, and equally effective) to lead that fleet out in time to finish off Eustace and put a conclusive end to those French aspirations to expand into England. It seems that the forces of the Cinque Ports, and their navigational advice, may well have tipped the scales in favour of England in the sequence of events which led up to the battle off Sandwich. At any rate, it was reported that they were well rewarded, and therefore would have emerged all the more confident in their own bargaining power. This short campaign served to emphasise their strength, not least in their own eyes.[59]

In 1216, at the age of 9, Henry III succeeded his father, and began a long reign which lasted until 1272. Even after the inevitable regency had come to an end in 1234, this period was distinguished from end to end by power struggles between various groups of barons. Henry, a remarkably literate but cautious man, was seldom capable of taking full control. During the first half of the thirteenth century, the complementary trade with Gascony became increasingly important to the English Crown, on account of the large revenue derived from taxing the wine as well as from the need for the drink itself. Besides the natural hazards encountered on the voyage, especially the rugged coastline of Brittany with its dangerous tidal races, there was always the threat of piracy, in which the Cinque Ports played a considerable part. That piracy increased after July 1224 when Louis VIII of France (1223–26), son of Philip Augustus, took advantage of a spell of internal disorganisation in England to overrun Poitou and capture the port of La Rochelle. In that way the French gained access for the first time to the Bay of Biscay, which afforded them the excellent possibility of interrupting English trade with Gascony, Castile and, later on, with the Mediterranean.

The Cinque Ports feature frequently in the national records throughout the century, but in a somewhat impersonal way. It is therefore fortunate that more personal details are supplied by the records of the extended family of Alard of Winchelsea, in many ways the most important place in Sussex. They are by far the best documented local family and their individual names are known although, unfortunately, relationships between the earliest members remain obscure. Together, these records serve to emphasise the dichotomy of the family's position, fulfilling two different, opposing roles simultaneously. On one hand they were fishermen and, to an increasing extent, merchants, who regarded piracy as a natural means of enhancing their personal incomes. Given a little extra encouragement, they extended that to terrorism. On the other hand, they were called upon to serve as maritime advisors to the Crown. To modern eyes these two roles may seem contradictory and conflicting, but their example is typical of the medieval relationship of the men of all the ports with the Crown. All along the coast, mariners added the proceeds of piracy to their incomes, while the Crown could not do without their ships and their navigational skills.

The Alards first appear in documents around the beginning of the century, as holders of land (an important indication of wealth) in the fertile marshes near Winchelsea. Since they are soon heard of as part-owners and masters of ships, they presumably also had fishing and probably trading interests. Castilian merchants had begun to travel inland to the great annual fairs in Winchester and Boston, where they may have been welcomed peacefully. It was, it seems, only on the coast that they had problems with hostility, which came from the Cinque Ports, and dated from at least as early as 1221. In 1227 a Castilian ship was ransacked in Sandwich harbour. Her cargo of wine, grain (the valuable scarlet dye-stuff), goatskins and skins of wildcat, hare, fox and lamb, cordwain, basan (tanned sheepskin) and thread was pillaged. Some, at least, of her crew were killed. This particular case clearly caused political embarrassment, because subsequently an unfortunate sailor named Dennis was sent to Newgate Gaol as a scapegoat. But much more

The Winchelsea Seal, *c.* 1300. A cog with furled sail. The rudder is on the starboard side. Two fighting castles are in place. Two men are pulling up the anchor.

frequently the pirates must have gone unpunished, although in some cases the government thought it politic to make compensation to those whose ships had been plundered by the Cinque Ports. A case in point occurred in 1225, when compensation was paid to a goldsmith, his seven companions and a woman called Margaret, from Norway.[60]

On the other hand, in the period 1225 to 1242 the portsmen were assisting in the building, maintenance and housing of the king's galleys and other ships, at Rye and Winchelsea as well as Portsmouth. William Alard was paid to accompany Richard, brother of the king, to Gascony and on his return was given royal compensation for the anchors and ropes he had lost there. In 1239 he personally was called upon to supervise the repairs of certain royal galleys and to mount guard on another in Winchelsea harbour. In 1242 the ships and sailors of the Cinque Ports were conscripted by the king along with those of other ports to take forces and supplies to Gascony: they were to provide ships capable of carrying sixteen or more horses. That same spring they were called upon to make provision for defence of the English coast.[61]

Meanwhile, they continued to pursue their activities as pirates and, given the opportunity, as terrorists. In 1236, for instance, merchants from San Sebastian in Castile were so intimidated by the Cinque Ports, who were

The Strand Gate, Winchelsea, *c.* 1300, looking out down the hill to the harbour.

said to be threatening every ship in the Channel, that they refused to bring their wares to England until they had been provided with safe conducts by the Crown. This, however, was by no means always a guarantee of a safe passage. In April 1235 three Alard brothers, Stephen, Henry and John, were prominent among a group of Winchelsea pirates who lurked among the rocky islets near Morlaix on the north coast of Brittany, waiting for the wine ships as they sailed past up the French coast. They boarded a small flotilla which was returning to Barfleur in Normandy, seized the merchants' documents and the king's letters of safe conduct, threw the documents and the crews overboard and made off with the ships, complete with their cargoes of wine and other merchandise. In the same year Stephen Alard attacked another similar ship: he not only robbed Reynard Bernard, a merchant of Perigord, of his wine but abducted Reynard's brother Stephen whom, we are told, he took to Guernsey, put him ashore there and abandoned him. It may be that his life was at least preserved until he could be ransomed, while the ordinary sailors, whose lives were worth nothing, would have been rapidly tipped overboard. After these episodes, the king ordered an officer named Drew Barentyne to search for and arrest Stephen Alard, 'if he can lay hands on him', a conditional clause which the historian L.F. Salzman suggested might be a hint not to be too zealous in the hunt. In any case, later that year the same three brothers were back at the Yarmouth Fair, accused of burglary. In 1240 William and John Alard – apparently the same John who was operating as a pirate off Morlaix five years earlier – were among nine commissioners appointed to keep the peace at the Yarmouth Herring Fair, a difficult and exacting task for anyone.[62] Thieves were thus similar to the proverbial poachers: they were serving simultaneously as gamekeepers.

When expedient, the Crown used piracy as an instrument of foreign policy. In 1242, the king was preparing to take an army to Poitou. In order for it to be safe for this force to set sail, he needed the Channel cleared of French pirates and so ordered the Cinque Ports to do as much harm to his enemies as possible, reminding them carefully that the Crown was due a share of all property seized from the enemy, 'Saving also to us our fifth, which you know belongs to us, of the profits which ye acquire in war'. Given this licence, they obediently set out on an orgy of plunder and slaughter. Their victims included returning English pilgrims as well as foreign vessels.[63]

The feud between the Cinque Ports and Yarmouth simmered on, and escalated in 1253 and 1254, when the king was already in Gascony dealing with unrest and the threat of invasion by the king of Castile. The high level of robberies and general disturbances continued throughout that decade. The king's appointment of his European relations and in-laws as well-paid

The Alard Tomb in Winchelsea church.

advisors, coupled with the failure of his expensive military expeditions, had for a long time made him unpopular with the barons. This dissatisfaction was compounded when he squandered further large sums, both in accepting the crown of Sicily for his younger son in 1254, and over the election of his brother as Holy Roman Emperor. Their frustration reached a peak after the king lost Wales to Llewellyn in 1256. In 1258 he was forced to sign the Provisions of Oxford and in the following year the Provisions of Westminster, both of which reinforced Magna Carta and reduced his independence.

In a highly charged atmosphere which seemed to be heading towards civil war, he turned abroad, looking for help. In an attempt to reduce the threat of French support for the barons, he signed the Treaty of Paris with Louis IX in 1259. Thereby, Louis undertook to withdraw his support for the English barons, while in exchange Henry renounced the English claim to all the French provinces originally lost by his father John, thus acknowledging for the first time a situation which England had never effectively challenged since 1204.

Another provision in the Treaty of Paris had much more damaging and long-lasting consequences. Henry was allowed to keep Aquitaine, including Gascony, but only on the condition that henceforth he and all his successors were to hold it as vassals of the king of France, so that at the beginning of every new reign, the king of England was to be required to pay homage to the king of France. Aquitaine, broadly north of the Garonne, had been part of the comité of Poitou, but Gascony, which stretched south from the Garonne to the Pyrenees, had hitherto never been part of France. The concept of one sovereign king paying homage to another was not only ridiculous; it was unacceptable to the medieval mind. But in 1259 Henry, already in a very weak position at home, was goaded by the French into making an under-taking which was to prove critically damaging to future relations between the two countries, and was to be one of the most important irritants which in due course led up to and perpetuated the Hundred Years' War.[64]

The unstable situation in 1260 played into the hands of the Cinque Ports. In an attempt to obtain their support, as a matter of political expe-diency Henry III gave them the first charter to be directed to all the ports combined. Having first thanked them for their loyal service, this confirmed their immunity from all external courts of justice, which was bound to be a matter of great aggravation to other ports, especially to Yarmouth because at the Herring Fair the visitors were to be subject only to their own bailiff.[65]

Simon de Montfort, ironically by blood and upbringing more French than English, emerged as leader of the barons. Against a background of momen-tous constitutional developments, in 1262 civil war broke out between a party representing many of the barons on one side and the supporters of the king on the other. As in 1215–17, control of cross-Channel traffic and therefore the support of the Cinque Ports was vital to both sides. The king and his elder son Edward (later Edward I) needed military reinforcements from France, while the object of Simon de Montfort and the baronial party was to prevent the arrival of these foreign troops. As on the former occasion, the portsmen followed their own agenda and preferred to sit on the fence. The king tried various means of attracting them. He took Dover Castle and the port of Sandwich into his own hands, dismissing the current warden and replacing him with his own man, Robert Walerand. He sent Prince Edward down to receive their homage in person. He also showered them with bribes and gifts. According to the chronicler Gervase of Canterbury, he tried to flatter them by inviting them to join him for a Christmas feast in Canterbury.[66] But all this was to no avail: the portsmen were not to be so easily bought off.

By 1263 Simon de Montfort already had control of most of south-east England, and his bribes to bring the portsmen within his influence were rather more practical than those of the king. He equipped them with ships, described as '*numeras naves piraticas*'. Early in 1264 the king came south and found that, prompted by Simon, the portsmen were already out at sea, beyond reach. On 14 May 1264 the two land forces met at the Battle of Lewes, during which both the king and Prince Edward were taken prisoner. As a result, Simon became the effective ruler of the country. On 28 May, only two weeks after the battle, he appointed his own eldest son Henry to be Keeper of the Cinque Ports.

On the continent on the other hand, where the queen and her younger son Prince Edmund were still at liberty, there was considerable support for the king. She raised an army of mercenaries together with a fleet of transports ready to take them to England from the *Zwin*. But their passage was held up, not by Simon de Montfort, but by persistent onshore winds, which therefore gave Simon time to fortify the coast – as far as practicable – against the possibility of her landing. For a few weeks, or possibly even a few months, the Cinque Ports evidently cooperated with him, for in July they were publicly thanked for their faithful service. In the middle of August Simon ordered as many ships as possible, properly equipped and manned with men-at-arms, to assemble off Sandwich. On 1 September he sent 300 of the best Genoese archers to defend Winchelsea. However, the queen's fleet was delayed so long by the contrary winds that her borrowed funds ran out, and so the threat of invasion from that direction evaporated.

Unfortunately for Simon, he ultimately proved no better than the king in controlling the Cinque Ports. In early October, at the beginning of the annual

Herring Fair, the portsmen resumed their old habits. Flattering praise for their 'labouring manfully about the defence of the sea and maritime parts' had to be sweetened with a bribe, a promise of compensation for the damages they were said to have recently suffered at the hands of Yarmouth, subject to the ruling of the king's court. It soon became obvious that the old feud with Yarmouth was escalating seriously, which implied that numerous ships and their crews were likely to be occupied about their own business at Yarmouth rather than helping to defend the Channel coast. On 5 October Simon, still operating in the name of the king, uttered a stark warning. It was essential, he said, that peace should be maintained at the current fair by every means possible. His order ended with an empty threat: if the two antagonistic parties did inflict grievances on each other, the king would 'betake himself so grievously to them that they and their heirs shall thence forward feel themselves aggrieved in no small measure'.

By December 1264 the Cinque Ports were evidently in control of the Channel, instituting a war of terror, plundering every ship they could find, English as well as foreign. Once more, returning pilgrims met the same treatment as commercial crews. The men of the Cinque Ports were described as 'the king's enemies and rebels'. A cardinal legate sent by the pope to arbitrate between the two warring sides was prevented from landing in England, as a result of which the ports found themselves excommunicated, of which apparently they took little or no notice. The continuator of the chronicle of Matthew Paris wrote that, 'More cruel than Scylla or Charybdis, they slaughtered the merchants who were accustomed to bring commodities to England ...' As a result of their activities the passage of trade was seriously reduced and the population was deprived of basic necessities. Salt, a vital commodity, became extremely scarce, and iron, steel, cloths and other imported materials were in very short supply. The price of wine tripled, that of wax (essential for lighting) rose fivefold and that of pepper sixfold.[67] The Cinque Ports had caused an unnecessary economic crisis and public opinion may well have been turning against them.

The tide of national politics was also now beginning to turn, albeit slowly. Prince Edward escaped from captivity, and Simon de Montfort himself was killed at the Battle of Evesham on 4 August 1265. It fell to Prince Edward, who had begun to assume royal authority in the name of his father, to find some way of regaining control of the Cinque Ports, who were still at large, in control in the Channel. The merchants of Flanders accused them of stealing 1,000*l* sterling over a very widespread area, on the coast of the North Sea, in the Gironde estuary and off Normandy. In another case, Pelerin, the merchant of Bayonne, complained that certain persons had captured his wines at sea, and they were now in the hands of the Cinque Ports, who would not release them. In both cases it was emphasised that these acts of piracy had been committed 'during the recent disturbances', in other words, during the civil war of Simon de Montfort.[68]

In November, Prince Edward imposed fines on them and hanged some of the malefactors at Dover and Winchelsea. That was no doubt meant as an example, a warning to others, but it proved a serious mistake. The Cinque Ports retaliated by sailing down the Channel and sacking Portsmouth. Why Portsmouth? Probably because it was the port from which royalty and their armies often set sail for Gascony, and the possibility of looting royal supplies stored in warehouses there was very attractive. Having failed to control the Cinque Ports by punishment, the only other possible recourse available to the prince was to order men from the ports of Norfolk and Suffolk, between (King's) Lynn and Orford, including those of Yarmouth, to come south to pursue the malefactors, whom he described as the 'king's enemies, the men in galleys (*galliots*) of the Cinque Ports'. Yarmouth and their associates failed to turn up on the first deadline, 1 January 1266, so the summons was repeated, with the promise that they should keep whatever goods and 'movables' which they obtained by land or sea. Various noblemen were appointed to supervise them. The prince sought help not only from other English portsmen, but also, in desperation, asked for help from steersmen and mariners of Flanders, Spain, Normandy 'and elsewhere'. It was during that time that Pelerin de Chapelyn, a merchant of Bayonne, complained to the Crown that it was impossible to trace wine which the Cinque Ports had captured from his ships at sea, because it had been distributed so widely. It was in the hands of many people who refused to give it up. This illustrates one of the perpetual problems involved in recovering pirate booty: it had usually been distributed widely and disappeared irrevocably.[69]

Eventually, having secured some of the ringleaders, on 30 March Edward was able to make peace with the Cinque Ports – but emphatically on their terms. They were admitted to 'the king's grace and peace' without 'peril of life and limb and imprisonment'. They were to keep their lands and chattels which they then had, which presumably included an impressive quantity of loot. They were allowed to keep all the liberties previously granted to them by the king and his predecessors. They were pardoned of all trespasses, exactions and damages they had committed during the recent war. The king also undertook to do his best to ensure that the same held good in Gascony and Ireland. All this was granted as long as they remained faithful to him and his heirs: if not, the grant said, they were to forfeit all their possessions and liberties to the king, which was yet another unenforceable threat.

Some form of normality had been resumed by 1267, because in that year the king handed back control of the port of Sandwich to Christ Church Priory, Canterbury. By June, too, the barons of the Cinque Ports, including Reynold (or Reginald) Alard, were themselves being used by the king to defend the coast and to pursue Henry Pethun, by then said to be a notorious pirate. Pethun and his accomplices were holding out on the Isles of Wight and Portland and 'elsewhere along the coast' and were evidently causing much havoc among trading vessels, so much so that, with the agreement of the merchants, it was decreed that the Cinque Ports should be rewarded for maintaining order with a tax of 40s on every laden ship and 20s on every empty ship arriving or leaving the country. Paradoxically, in the topsy-turvy world of the time, only in the previous year the ports had been insisting that Pethun, then held in custody by the king, should be kept safely and honour-ably 'until the peace in the realm is better assured'. Perhaps, in other words, they had wanted Pethun's rival parties of pirates out of their way?[70]

Events in the Channel during the reigns of John and Henry III made it obvious that an officer was needed to mediate between the king and the Cinque Ports. The king needed a means by which to communicate with, and if possible control, their activities while the portsmen needed someone who, on oath, would uphold their liberties. After various short-lived experiments, Stephen de Pencestre was appointed as the first Warden of the Cinque Ports, a position he held for thirty years, 1268–98. The position was held in conjunction with that of the Constable of Dover Castle, and as such was a political appointment.

After 1267 the level of piracy subsided, and it seems that the Cinque Ports were living a quieter life. They may have been respecting, for the time being, the authority of the new king, Edward I (1272–1307), or it may have been that, although still potential pirates, they were occupied with domestic problems, in particular the effects of the great storms of the second half of the thirteenth century. Winchelsea, to take an example, suffered worst. The inhabitants there had to deal with the later stages of erosion of its original town site and the transfer to an entirely new site. The original site is totally lost, but it must have stood on a shingle bank near the sea, some-where in the present area of Rye Bay. Documentary evidence shows that erosion threatened the town at least as early as 1244, after which it would have fallen progressively into the sea. Part of the church fell in 1271. In the same period of geographical transformation, the sea had flooded the marsh-land behind the shingle barrier and opened up several large tidal channels which became potential anchorages (Col. Plate 9).

Winchelsea was one of the leading Cinque Ports and, as relations with France deteriorated, Edward I particularly needed anchorages for both military and commercial vessels. The military potential of the new inlet, later known as the Camber, together with the evident organisation and maritime strength of Winchelsea, were essential to the Crown. So in 1280, when the old site was 'for the most part under the sea', he authorised the purchase of land and the rebuilding of the town on the present hill-top site.[71] Yarmouth too was occupied with internal disputes, and probably also with storm damage.

By 1277 Edward I was proposing to reconquer Wales. In order to get the support of the Cinque Ports, he took the necessary precaution of placating them with a new *dite*, or agreement. Encouraged by this favourable treatment, they not only provided seventeen ships (which on this occasion comprised his entire fleet, bar one which came from Southampton) to transport troops and supplies for his campaign in Anglesey and Snowdonia but they also, for the first and last time, formed part of a royal fighting force on land. After their cooperation in what proved a very successful expedition, in June 1278 Edward rewarded them with a second group charter. In addition to confirming all their former grants, he gave them new concessions. They received the ancient right of *utfangthelff*, which allowed them to punish a man who committed theft out of his own liberty, in other words, to punish sailors who visited the Cinque Ports. They were not to be put on an assize or jury against their will. And they were relieved of paying the duty on the wine which they imported: they had previously been paying for one tun of the wine carried before the mast and one behind it.[72]

This, however, made no difference to their usual behaviour at Yarmouth, and by 1289 a fresh spate of disputes had broken out, concerned particularly with removal of wrecks from the harbour and the access channel, and failure to maintain the harbour lights – which was all likely to result in further shipwrecks. Both sides seem to have been guilty of failing to take the necessary action. The Cinque Ports also complained that Yarmouth was building houses and too many windmills on the part of the beach which they expected to occupy. This complaint probably illustrated the needs of a population which, in line with that of the rest of England and Europe, was reaching saturation point, and the space available on the Yarmouth sandbank was limited. Indeed, the situation may have been further exacerbated by coastal change: space on the beach may well have been reduced by erosion during the tempestuous storms of the later thirteenth century. In order to settle these disputes, a new legal step was taken. For the first time representatives of all the parties, including the bailiffs of the Cinque Ports who attended that fair, Stephen de Pencestre, the Lord Warden of the Cinque Ports, and men from both sides, including some who happened to be overseas at the time, were summoned to appear at the next parliament.

In the early 1290s the level of hostility between the Cinque Ports and
Norman sailors was mounting. In the summer of 1292 two Cinque Port sailors
made a trip ashore to fetch water from a Norman port. A fracas ensued, which
led on to an obscure and bizarre set-piece fight at sea between the two. Then,
on 15 May 1293, an encounter with much more serious repercussions took
place. A Norman fleet returning from the River Charente, south of La Rochelle,
was intercepted off the Pointe de St Mathieu by a combined fleet of ships from
the Cinque Ports, Bayonne and Ireland. The Normans were defeated in the
fierce sea fight which followed. When, in around 1299, an inquiry was held
into this battle, the Cinque Ports claimed that they had been assailed by the
Normans who had 290 armed ships flying *bausans,* very long slender banners
of red *cendal,* a silken fabric, 'which among mariners means death without
quarter and war to the knife'. They claimed that it was the law and custom of
England that, when the *bausan* was flown, whether in peace or war, if a man
killed another in self-defence, he was not to be held responsible. Nor was he
required to make restitution for anything that was captured. They concluded
their evidence saying that if they were now treated unjustly (in their eyes),
they would 'forthwith forsake their wives and children and all they possess,
and go to make their profit upon the sea wheresoever they think they will be
able to acquire it'.[73] In other words, they had no intention of coming to heel.

The results of this unofficial battle, which was neither supported nor
sanctioned by either king, were welcome to neither of them, and were disastrous. Elated by victory, the Gascons went on to attack their long-term rival
La Rochelle, which since 1224 had belonged to France. Thus the Gascons,
subjects of the king of England, were attacking his own liege lord, which
was unacceptable. After diplomatic efforts to maintain peace failed dismally,
a war between the two ensued in Aquitaine, lasting from 1294 to 1298.
It ended with military stalemate and enormous debts on both sides, and it
marked a significant downturn in Anglo-French relations.

In the meantime, our focus moves to the eastern end of the Channel.
The Cinque Ports had evidently been involved in profitable piracy nearer
home, for in June 1293 small groups of merchants from Amiens, Abbeville
and Le Crotoy, and some representatives of the Knights Templars in France,
were given permission, with safe conducts, to search certain English ports,
including Sandwich, Winchelsea, Romney, Hastings, Dover and Faversham,
for wine which they asserted had been stolen from their ships at sea.[74]

Possibly as a result of aggravation, in the summer of 1295 a large fleet
of ships from Genoa and Marseilles sailed up the Channel. One of the
prime French galleys landed at Hythe where, as the chronicler's story goes,
the English apparently pretended to retreat but then returned and set upon

the French, killing some and burning the galley. (The real explanation is more likely to have been that the English initially took flight in disarray.) Then, on 1 August the French raided Dover and burnt a 'great part' of the town. Eventually, we are told, when English reinforcements arrived, thirty Frenchmen who had spent part of the night hiding in an abbey tried to escape in two boats under cover of darkness. But they were caught and their boats were sunk. About the same time, the Cinque Ports reportedly captured fifteen laden Spanish vessels bound for Damme.[75]

By 1297 Edward I was intent on attacking France from the north, but by then he had lost his former popularity. He was overstretched and seriously short of funds, and had great difficulty recruiting an army. Eventually, with contingents from both the Cinque Ports and Yarmouth, and also pardoned criminals let out of gaol for this purpose, he sailed from Winchelsea on 24 August and reached Sluys on 27 August. But, disastrously, even before they had disembarked, fighting broke out between the groups from the Cinque Ports and Yarmouth, and a bloodbath ensued. It is not at all clear what happened, but it seems that the Cinque Ports may have set upon their rivals. Certainly they came off best. According to an enquiry held in 1303, they burnt or destroyed seventeen Yarmouth ships and looted another twelve. The human toll amounted to 165 dead and material damage was estimated at 5,000*l* (one-third of the exaggerated claim made by a later historian). It was said by one source that finally two Yarmouth ships escaped and on their way home took the opportunity to pillage every Cinque Ports ship they could find.[76] This was far from the united display of strength which Edward wished to show.

After 1300, the Cinque Ports continued their feuds and their prominent piracy, especially during political crises during and after the Great Famine of 1315–17, but they had lost their bargaining power. Although they continued to have a high nuisance value, they were no longer exceptional, and from this point their activities seldom stand out from those of other pirates. Later on, in the second half of the fourteenth century, military, demographic and commercial factors combined with coastal changes to further diminish their importance.

The ports, however, have clung closely to their privileges, right up to the present day. But the suggestions repeated by romantic Victorian historians and still perpetuated in local tradition, that those privileges were acquired as a result of loyal service to the Crown in defence of the nation, or that their ships formed the original core of the Royal Navy, are very far off the mark. In the words of their biographer K.M.E. Murray, 'It is impossible to clear the reputation of the barons from the charge ... that [those privileges] bore witness to the terror inspired by the audacity of a group of pirates'.[77]

# 6

# Insolvency and Famine

or the first twenty years of his reign the overall management of Edward I (1272–1307) was remarkably successful, and acceptable to the English people. He conquered, or at least temporarily subdued, the Welsh. The Scottish border was relatively peaceful, and there was no insuperable political or financial crisis in England. In Europe, where he was closely related by kinship or marriage to most heads of state, the king had a well-earned reputation as a peace-maker, and a statesman. Relations with France remained peaceful. With Spain, relations had been good ever since 1254, when Edward's father, Henry III, had signed a treaty with Alphonso, king of Castile, and Edward himself had married Eleanor, the sister of Alphonso. Spanish merchants responded to English encouragement of remission of taxes, and small colonies of Spaniards grew up in Southampton and in London. As part of this friendly policy, Edward permitted his Gascon subjects to build galleys to assist Alphonso in his struggles against the Moors, which may have helped to give the sailors of Gascony a common purpose with their near neighbours in the ports of northern Castile, and damp down their potential antagonism. Overall, in 1292 Edward stood high in the estimation of his subjects. During a period of financial stability, maritime trade in the Channel prospered in tranquil conditions, not interrupted by piracy.[78] But this was not to last.

In the background, since at least the 1280s both France and England had been making preparations for possible hostilities across the Channel.

In France, Philip IV (le Bel) succeeded his father in 1285. He must have perceived the potential of the oared Mediterranean galley for raiding in the Channel, because he immediately began work to establish the *Clos de Galées*, a large-scale naval shipbuilding centre and arsenal on the left bank of the Seine at Rouen. His expenditure there over twelve years, 1292–1304, was equal to his highest annual budget. He also invested in defence along the Channel coast. For instance, in the winter of 1293–94 his expenditure on the garrison at Calais was unusually high.[79] In Castile, too, circumstances began to turn against Edward. In 1285 Alphonso was succeeded by his second son, Sancho, who was inclined to favour the French rather than the English, and by 1290 had a firm alliance with Philip le Bel.

On the English side of the Channel, the port town of Winchelsea had suffered progressive erosion since 1244, and by 1280 was 'for the most part under the sea'. Edward, needing a strong military base in that area as well as a new base for the wine trade, rebuilt the large town on a splendid hilltop site where it was not only secure from the sea, but also overlooked a capacious protected anchorage and had extensive views out to sea. In 1294, in anticipation of hostilities, he also organised English shipping into three large squadrons under three separate commanders – one dealing with the east coast ports centred on Yarmouth, one with the south coast based on Portsmouth, and one for the western ports and Ireland.[80]

When the attack did come, however, it was not by ships based on the Seine or in Calais, but from mercenaries hired by France from the Mediterranean. In the summer of 1295 a large fleet of ships from Genoa and Marseilles sailed up the Channel apparently reconnoitring. They took the opportunity to attack two of the Cinque Ports, Hythe and, more effectively, Dover. This drew attention to the weakness of English coastal defence, although if this was intended as an invasion of England, it was uncoordinated and ineffectual.

By 1293 Edward's resources had already dwindled seriously, on account of overspending on his wars. He had taxed the economy to the limit. Then, within the space of four years, he found he had to commit troops and supplies in four different directions. Recruitment of ever-increasing numbers of men, and raising taxation to meet the expenses of procuring and transporting the necessary support for his armies, made him ever more unpopular, which was not helped by the domineering, heavy-handed attitude of both him and a new generation of officials and tax collectors.

The fracas involving the Cinque Ports and others off St Mathieu in 1293 built up to further hostilities. The Gascons went on to attack La Rochelle. Following complex and abstruse legal arguments, Philip le Bel used the opportunity to declare war in the summer of 1294. Edward could hardly spare troops and military supplies but, very reluctantly, he had to send some south. When, as an example, *The Plenty of Winchelsea* left the Thames bound for the Gironde in October 1294, she was laden not only with a routine cargo of food consisting of 385 quarters of corn and 200 tuns of wheat and other cereals, but she also carried armaments amounting to three springals (the largest form of mechanical bow), forty-eight crossbows, of which twelve were 'great crossbows' with winding mechanisms, one coffer containing sixty bows and bowstrings, and other buckets and coffers containing large quantities of bolts for both springals and crossbows.[81]

At the same time, the king needed men and supplies for a campaign in Wales, where a serious revolt had broken out in September 1294 against English taxation and roughshod administration: it was not quelled until June 1295. Almost simultaneously, relations with Scotland were deteriorating fast and needed his attention. Edward's protégé king, John Balliol, proved too weak to stand up against the Scottish barons, and the Scots were particularly infuriated by Edward's demand for their support for his war against France. That demand had two highly important, unintended, consequences: it soured his own relations with the Scots further, and it drove them towards an alliance with the French.[82] In answer to the threat posed by a Franco-Scottish alliance against him, Edward resolved to remove John Balliol and to invade Scotland. On 30 March 1296 he laid siege to Berwick-upon-Tweed, the frontier town on the east coast which was strategically invaluable to both sides, and went on to sack it ruthlessly (Col. Plate 10).

Already committed in Wales, Gascony and Scotland, facing a Franco-Scottish alliance, and in the teeth of very considerable opposition at home to any further military expenditure, Edward determined nonetheless to invade France via Flanders. At great and fruitless expense he tried to form alliances with some of the small states bordering France to the north. Not surprisingly, he experienced considerable delay in his efforts to assemble an army, and the force he eventually collected was far from the cream of England. Recruits had been very reluctant to come forward and he was forced to include criminals whom he had let out of prison and pardoned rapidly. He finally set sail with them from Winchelsea on 24 August 1297, but by then it was too late. The French had already invaded Flanders themselves. As a military exercise Edward's attempted invasion was a fiasco due in the last resort, as we have already seen, to the riotous activity of the rival sailors from the Cinque Ports and Yarmouth.

With deep unrest over Edward's attempt to raise money from all sections of the community, the country was on the verge of civil war. Under these conditions of political disorder and uncertainty, piracy inevitably flourished. It took many forms.

A few examples show that the task of the commissioners appointed to find out what had happened, and where the stolen goods had fetched up, was complex and tortuous. Two very different versions of one case came before the king in January 1303. They dealt with the plunder of a cargo of ginger, cinnamon and other spices which was being imported from Provence for the royal household by Peter Andrew, the servant of a London merchant, in the ship *la Ludewyk de la Hoke of Dieppe*. According to the first enrolled complaint, the merchant alleged that the spices were stolen 'by certain Flemings' who broke into the ship while it was in the port of Winchelsea. That story sounds simple, but was quickly overtaken by the second version enrolled two weeks later, according to which the robbery had taken place at sea. The master, a Fleming named Lambert Labote, had tied up Peter Andrew and had himself stolen the goods, which were valued at 445*l* 2*s* 10*d*. However, Labote's luck ran out when, instead of making a safe passage back to Flanders, the ship was driven back by contrary winds to seek shelter in Winchelsea harbour, where he and some of his crew were arrested and summoned to appear before the Warden of the Cinque Ports. But then some of them broke bail and escaped in their ship, taking the 12-year-old son of Peter Andrew with them. The end of that story was unusual. Remarkably quickly, by 1 August those pirates had recompensed the merchant in full for the theft and damages by paying a fine of 2,400*l*.[83]

Around this time Genoese merchants were becoming regular summer visitors to Southampton, with the purpose of buying English wool and selling Mediterranean products, encouraged by very favourable taxation terms. Their experiences throw light on one focus of piracy. In 1303 two of them, Guidetus and Janotus Spinelli, shipped 400 sacks of wool overseas free of all customs. Two years later, another ship, the *Sanctus Nicholaus* of which Janotus Spinelli was part owner, arrived in Southampton with a safe conduct which covered both its crew and cargo.[84] Both of those ships seem to have sailed in and out of Southampton untroubled by piracy.

Further up the Channel, however, in the Straits of Dover it was a different matter. In the spring of 1303 the Spinelli were commissioned by the king to import from Wissant a cargo consisting of horses, armour, cloths of gold, silk and velvet and other goods valued in total at 522 marks, destined for Dover. Their ship was blown off course and anchored in the Downs off Sandwich where, while waiting for a favourable wind to enter the harbour (if the impression given by the scribe is to be believed, this was evidently a relatively small ship, or if larger, it would have been unloaded in the sheltered roadstead), it was boarded by armed pirates who removed the cargo and abducted seven servants of the Genoese, whom they imprisoned at Ypres. The negotiations which followed were complicated and protracted. The king wrote to the counts of both Namur and Flanders, requesting speedy release of the men and restoration of the goods or their value to the Spinelli. Simultaneously, he also ordered that goods of the same value belonging to Flemings should be impounded in London.

However, there were good reasons to doubt important aspects of this story. It became apparent that the miscreants included not only Flemings but also men from the Cinque Ports. In addition, the pirate ship, unnamed and described simply as 'of Dover', appeared to have returned later a large proportion of the stolen goods to Dover. So the Warden of the Cinque Ports, Robert Burghersh, was ordered to find out who was really involved and who benefited from the stolen goods. He was also ordered to identify the master of the ship, so that he could give a full explanation to the Spinelli. In the meantime, however, in order not to alienate the Genoese and risk losing their trade, in July 1304 an initial payment of 70*l* was made to them.[85]

Coastal traffic was affected by piracy just as much as international trade. English merchants were by no means safe simply because they were anchored within an English port. In the spring of 1303 Gerard de Vilars, a merchant of Lostwithiel, loaded *St Edmund's Cog of Fowey* with wine and salt valued at 300*l*, in order to ship it along the coast to Sandwich. On the way she put into Portsmouth harbour where she was commandeered by Flemish pirates who sailed her off to Flanders complete with her cargo, together with some unfortunate pilots, presumably local men, who happened to be caught on board.[86]

The next incident illustrates the wide range and coordination of the pirate world, with a suggestion of strong support in their home ports. In late summer 1304 the masters of seven ships from six widespread English ports, Yarmouth and Dunwich on the east coast, Shoreham and the Isle of Wight in the south, and Haverfordwest and Bristol in the west, teamed up to capture a large ship of Seville off St Mathieu, Brittany, where she was presumably waiting for a suitable wind to enable her to cross to England. She was laden with goods and merchandise valued at 4,200*l* which belonged to merchants of Majorca and Seville. The pirates took the goods, plus the ropes, anchors and other moveable gear from the ship, thus effectively disabling her. They then transferred both the goods and the ship to England, possibly to a depot on the Isle of Wight, where they divided or sold the goods, because the commission sent out in late September shows that those were widely dispersed round eastern and southern counties, from Norfolk to Gloucestershire (though not, it is interesting to note, including

Devon and Cornwall). Only two days after the complaint of the robbery was put on record William Pierre, the merchant of Majorca whose goods were concerned, was already seeking justice in England, presumably to trace his wares. He was given a safe conduct for one year. However, the fact that they had been distributed so widely must have made it particularly difficult for anyone to trace the stolen goods.[87]

What could be done to protect these cargoes against pirates? In October 1301 the masters of all wine-ships taking goods to Gascony or coming north with wine were directed to travel in a fleet, a convoy. But there were always good reasons why some masters would flout this. They preferred to sail in their own time, and when the weather favoured them. Others became separated from the convoys by adverse conditions. Local arrangements were sometimes made, but one instance showed that they proved far from reliable. In this particular case, the king had ordered the barons of Sandwich to choose a ship to be sent to sea 'for the security of merchants and others [making the] Channel crossing'. But in this context, in April 1305 four London merchants complained that they had recently freighted a ship at Calais and crossed towards England, but when they reached *St Margaret's Stairs* (now St Margaret's Bay, between Dover and Sandwich), the so-called security vessel, the *Snak*, appeared, and itself attacked them, stealing 250*l* and a minor quantity of other merchandise.[88]

A temporary amelioration in Anglo-French relations was brought about by the betrothal of Edward I's son and heir to Isabella, daughter of Philip le Bel of France. This seems to have resulted in some respite from piracy, and to have given a window of opportunity to investigate the 'excesses, violences, wrongs and robberies' which were being inflicted on each other by the Cinque Ports and the men of Calais. This had mounted to the scale of a private war and was one important reason for serious disruption of trade. The two kings agreed on a very high-level meeting in an attempt to sort matters out. Robert Burghersh, Constable of Dover Castle and Warden of the Cinque Ports, and Master Philip Martel, doctor of civil law, were to establish as many details as possible and two weeks after Easter 1304 were to go to negotiate with two similarly high-ranking Frenchmen. It was, however, one thing to arrange a meeting, and quite another for all the delegates to appear. If this meeting did indeed take place, which is doubtful, it was evidently unproductive, because in June the king issued far more peremptory instructions. Robert and Philip were to go and see Philip le Bel in person and demand satisfaction for the depredations caused by the men of Calais. There was no mention this time in the English documents of the undoubted parallel activities of the Cinque Ports.[89]

Edward I died in July 1307, near Carlisle while on his way to Scotland. At his death he left a disaffected country on the verge of rebellion. England faced huge debts to Italian bankers, a war in Scotland which was already going badly and to which there was no foreseeable end, and a high level of piracy which threatened both trade and military operations at sea.[90] Only an exceptionally strong successor could have hoped to restore confidence and stability. His only surviving son Edward II (1307–27) was far from that. A degenerate individual, he failed to command respect and his government was, inevitably, exceptionally weak. His own attention was largely focused on his favourites, who wielded great influence and, together with the king himself, were objects of intense baronial jealousy and mistrust. The first favourite, Piers Gaveston, was murdered in 1312. The second was Hugh Despenser the younger, who also met a violent end.

At the beginning of the new reign piracy was flourishing, reflecting a similar degree of violence and lawlessness on land. Fishermen of north Norfolk complained of wrecking and physical violence. Ships bringing cargoes from Wissant or Calais fell victim to Cinque Port pirates, either in the Channel or in the Thames off Sheppey. In February 1311 merchants of Calais complained that the Cinque Ports had stolen woollen cloths and money which they were importing, and those goods had been distributed round Kent and Sussex. Other named men from Sandwich and Hythe were active further north, in Yarmouth, and men from Orford wrecked a vessel from Bruges, having previously stolen the goods on board.[91]

Men of the Cinque Ports were also busy further down the Channel that spring, collaborating with others from Somerset and Dorset to capture goods coming up from Aquitaine. In April that year the master of a ship, the *St. Mary* from Fuenterrabia, complained with merchants of Pamplona, over the mountains in Navarre, that their ship had been wrecked in a storm near Shoreham in Sussex. They had escaped alive from the wreck, which entitled them to part of the value of their goods and possessions, but men including some from the Cinque Ports had stripped the ship of its gear and carried off the wine, cloth, linen, wheat, bran, spices and other wares she was carrying, plus their armour, robes, couches, chests, gold and silver money, precious stone, gold rings and other things they had found on board. The names of the commissioners appointed to enquire into this incident implied that the Cinque Ports were at least among those involved.[92]

The mariners of Dorset had evidently earned themselves a reputation for attacks on foreign merchantmen, because the three commissioners appointed to investigate a case of piracy had handled similar matters before. Stephen de la Fonteyne, a merchant of Périgueux in Gascony, complained that summer that one of his wine ships, the *Seint Goymelote of Gerunde*, had been attacked between Weymouth and the Isle of Portland (now the area of Portland harbour) by pirates who removed most of the wine. As a parting shot, they cut her anchor cables, so that the ship was blown help-lessly onto the isle, where shore-based robbers finished the task of removing the cargo.[93]

Since 1265 the wool trade with the Flemings had been interrupted by embargoes and confiscations, the result of the policy of Countess Margaret. English relations with the Scots had also deteriorated, and so by May 1313 piracy had taken a new political slant: the Flemings were supporting the Scots in their struggle against the English. *La Welifare*, a ship belonging to Richard Randolf, a burgess of Yarmouth, was attacked near Dover by thirty-two men from Flanders in *La Cruxesbergh*, a ship of Sluys. They slaughtered the Yarmouth master and fifteen of his men, and then split their party in two. Half of them sailed the ship on to offer it to 'the king's enemies' in Scotland: the other half took the cargo, principally wine, back to Sluys in their own ship. Requests for repayment to that value met with no response. [94]

In 1314, the year of the military catastrophe at Bannockburn, Winchelsea was allowed to fit out two ships on the pretext of defending the east coast against Scottish pirates, on the one condition that the crew did not attack friendly merchants. Ralph Ambrois and John Styward, both of Rye, then set off in the *St John of Rye* in direct contravention of that understanding, on a piratical spree which apparently had nothing to do with the Scots. They crossed to Sluys, where they stole iron, steel, copper, furs and wax from some Hanseatic ships, killing some of the merchants, wounding others, and finally scuttling those ships. Back in the Orwell in Suffolk they stole cloth from newly arrived Flemish merchants and various goods from the Dutch, and at Harwich they plundered cloth from Flemish ships. In August 1316 the king was informed that the pirates of Kent, Sussex and Hampshire were gener-ating, through robbery and homicide, such an atmosphere of terror that both foreign merchants and local fishermen were reluctant to bring their cargoes of food and other goods into English ports.[95]

The problems of uncertainty posed for the merchants by piracy resulting from weak government were compounded by the greatest environmental crisis in medieval memory. The Great Famine of 1315–17 generated a uni-versal atmosphere of insecurity, lawlessness and violence which permeated all levels of society across the whole of northern Europe. This promoted both an increase in shipping and encouraged a further very strong political incentive for piracy. The population had been increasing and the economy expanding rapidly since the eleventh century, but expansion could not continue indefinitely. Inevitably, a point was going to be reached when demand for food exceeded the supply. Signs of food shortages had been seen as early as the 1280s. The scales were disastrously tipped for the whole population by continuous torrential summer rains which may have begun in 1314, and certainly took place in the summers of 1315 and 1316, affecting northern Europe at least as far south as the Garonne. Grain had to be left to rot in the fields. Harvests were decimated and prices rose sharply. Murrain, a mysterious deathly disease, struck sheep in January 1316. Terrible floods destroyed the land-based fish 'stews', another important source of nourishment. Flooded roads and broken bridges interrupted communications across the country. The wet and cold also destroyed the wine harvest in Poitou and prevented salt production in southern Brittany, both of the greatest importance to the people further north. An epidemic which affected cattle and the oxen, essential for ploughing, continued until 1321. Misery was compounded by several bitingly cold winters, especially that of 1317–18, when the Baltic and part of the North Sea froze over. People fought over food and resorted to cannibalism. The proportion of the population who died from starvation and disease in these years of famine and terrible weather is impossible to estimate, but it must have been very high.[96]

The famine demanded swift reaction from the northern rulers, which they did in different ways. The English Crown gave especially favourable terms to merchants of Spain, Sicily and Genoa, encouraging them to send urgently needed grain and other foodstuffs. Not only was it imperative to feed the population of England, especially in the towns, but the isolated garrison town of Berwick was, if possible, in even greater need.

In May 1316 several 'great ships of Genoa', in fact the very large cumbersome vessels known as dromonds which would have seldom ventured out of the Mediterranean in other circumstances, carried supplies as far as Sandwich, the outport for London. Three arrived, more or less in convoy. Anchored in the Downs, however, these large craft were conspicuous targets for French pirates. With the full support of his king, the French admiral Berenger Blank set out with a fleet of armed ships to capture some of them and sail them back to Calais. He secured his first prize sometime before 18 May. It was carrying a cargo of at least 500qtrs of wheat and wheat flour, oil and honey destined for the beleaguered army in Berwick. The French explanation for attacking this ship was that she was suspected of visiting a 'Saracen shore' on a previous voyage. They subsequently agreed that English representatives could go to Wissant to discuss her return with her cargo to the Downs, however improbable that seems with hindsight. Anyway, the English delegation waited there for six days and the French party failed to turn up.

A second dromond was captured by Blank and went the same way on Ascension Day, 20 May. She was carrying 2,100 quarters of wheat valued at 2,362*l* 2*s*, plus almonds, 20 casks of oil, flour and leather goods. A full list of the value of this ship, her equipment, stores and armament, plus the cost of putting up forty-five mariners marooned for three months in Sandwich, and subsequently travelling home overland, is given in the Appendix (page 173). A third dromond, captured before 23 May, was carrying wheat and 'other corn' which was partially unloaded at Sandwich before unidentified pirates arrived and carried her and the remainder of her cargo off towards an unknown destination. However, their luck ran out: adverse winds blew them back to Sandwich where they were imprisoned and the cargo immediately disappeared – in that case into English hands. Two other dromonds survived their visit in that stressful summer of 1316 without trouble, but they belonged to Venice and their destination was Southampton, and thus they never risked entering the terror-dominated Straits of Dover.[97]

It is probable that, because of the large urban population there, the Great Famine hit Flanders even harder than most places, and certainly their count assembled a fleet with the express aim of capturing ships carrying food. An early victim of this state-sponsored piracy was *La Coga of Valencia*, hired by the Earl of Pembroke, a cousin of Edward II, to import wine and wheat to England. Her cargo also included armaments such as helmets, together with sailcloth from Brittany. On 1 August 1316 three armed Flemish vessels captured and escorted her across to the *Zwin*, where the food and wine was immediately sold off. Arguments about possible compensation for this were still going on seven years later.[98] A chorus of complaints that Christmas signalled losses from the new season's wine ships arriving from Bordeaux. There were at least three victims: the *Coga of Valencia* (confusingly, the second ship of that name), *La Mariot of Goseford*, and the *Bona Navis of Strood,* which was seized by the notorious Flemish pirate John Crabbe, an event described in the next chapter.[99]

In April 1317 Flemish pirates captured the *Coga Sancte Marie*, due to deliver a cargo of wine to Antwerp. They also struck, between Beachy Head and Winchelsea, at *La Johanette*, which was bringing home a cargo of corn from Cornwall for Stephen Alard. The following year it was the turn of *La Nicholas of London*, carrying wine, wheat flour and whale meat, together with nut oil, vinegar, saffron, pepper and armour. Sometime before February 1318, *La Swallow of London* was captured while anchored off Margate, her master and crew were slaughtered, and the ship was taken to Sluys, complete with her cargo of wine, canvas and linen cloth, and money in sterling. These were understood to have been taken for the count's use, though he later denied all knowledge of them. A boy who hid on board had to stay in Flanders for nearly a year, being cared for by one of the pirates and the Bailiff of Sluys, and that ship was repaired in such a way as to be unrecognisable when she next went to sea.[100]

Vessels carrying food and wine were not the only victims of piracy. The French had an eye on the wool ships leaving London for Antwerp, in Brabant. After spending several days negotiating the shoals of the Thames these ships called at Margate, probably to take on water and victuals. They anchored offshore, and at low tide came to rest more or less upright on the exposed chalk platform, over which it was possible to walk ashore. *La Petite Bayard of London*, whose capture in May 1316 involved a spectacular chase, was the third victim of the French in two years. Her crew, who saw the French admiral coming with an armed company, fled up the hill into the town taking with them the ship's sail and rudder, thereby disabling her. The French pursued them into the town, retrieved the essential tackle and made off back to Calais with the ship and her cargo of wool worth, it was claimed, 2,000*l*.[101]

The Cinque Ports' habitual feuds continued unabated, ranging from one end of the Channel to the other. In the summer of 1316 an armed party from Yarmouth attacked the Cinque Ports and then proceeded along the south coast as far as the Isle of Wight and Southampton, plundering cargoes, killing crews and burning ships. In June 1318 the Cinque Ports were in conflict with both Flanders and Wissant and in December 1320 they were again preying on the men of Flanders.[102]

Meanwhile, as the chief creditors of the English king, Italians in general were not popular. Especially in lean times, it was not difficult to whip up jealousy against them. Until 1319, the undemonstrative Genoese had been accepted as traders visiting Southampton for several decades. They brought goods which were needed locally. But that year, five Venetian galleys anchored in Southampton Water for the first time, and they were a different matter. Flamboyant in style, their vessels were long, graceful and highly coloured, with a high-peaked prow, lateen rigging and triangular sails. They appeared more extravagant than anything the local people had seen before. What was more, their cargo of luxuries, spices and jewels was not especially welcome, either. It is not therefore entirely surprising that when some of the crew came ashore, an affray broke out, resulting in an international incident. For many years after that the Venetians neglected Southampton and took their trade elsewhere.

In January 1321 the Cinque Ports were sent by the Sheriff of Kent to preserve peace at sea, which predictably had the opposite effect. They encountered some ships from Yarmouth which they pursued into the Fowey estuary, where they killed one sailor and, within that small space, committed general plunder. Some of them were put in prison by the Cornish justices,

1 Lostwithiel Bridge. The river channel is partially filled with rubble from medieval tin-working upstream on Bodmin Moor.

2 A wine cellar in Winchelsea, dating from *c.* 1300. The staircase at the end admitted traders direct from the street. Thirty-three cellars are accessible today, and eighteen others are known to exist beneath the town. Subterranean, they have consistent year-round temperatures, ideal for storage of wine.

3 Salt-working in southern Brittany. Small sluices admit a controlled quantity of sea water at high spring tides in the summer.

4 Salt-working in southern Brittany. After evaporation in sun and wind, the final product, pure salt, is raked in.

5   Pointe St Mathieu, rocky and remote, on the western tip of Brittany.

6   Le Conquet, a small, secretive harbour, the only one near Pointe St Mathieu. This
    dries out at low water, but the number of ships using this in the fifteenth century
    suggests that it may have been larger, less silted, then.

7   The town wall of Montreuil-sur-Mer, which dates from the early thirteenth century.

8   Castle Gorey, Jersey. (© Dr Janet Stuart)

9 The new site of Winchelsea, built on a rectangular plan, similar to many bastides in Gascony. The door at the side of the house on the right leads directly to the cellar.

10 Berwick and the tidal River Tweed. Berwick was a vital frontier town and port whose garrison depended on seaborne supplies.

11 Dartmouth,
rising steeply
above
the harbour.

12 Dartmouth.
A deep, enclosed,
harbour,
looking towards
the entrance.

13 The brass of John Hawley in St Saviour's Church, Dartmouth. (© Rebecca Wright Photography)

14  Fowey harbour, another deep, enclosed harbour, with Pont Pill, a creek on the east
    shore. Mixtow Pill (sharing the name with privateers) is the adjacent creek upstream.

15  Harfleur. Houses of merchants built beside the once-tidal waterfront, now the River Lézarde.

while others were killed resisting arrest. Yet others then stayed around, in protest at the imprisonment of their fellows, threatening the trade of the Cornishmen.[103] This was hardly a peaceful start to the year.

That summer the Cinque Ports were continuing to cruise around the south-west, threatening Poole, Weymouth, Melcombe and Lyme (Regis), with a record of 'homicides, depredation and burning of ships'. The mounting catalogue of violence culminated on 30 September, when they appeared at Southampton. They came in force, armed under the guise of coast protection. Having rejected that port's offer to contribute two fully armed ships to help in policing the Channel, they proceeded to burn fifteen ships there. The next day they returned and burnt two more.[104]

The Alard family were still very much to the fore. In May 1322 a group which included Gervase Alard the younger and Henry Alard of Winchelsea overcame a merchant of Bremen in Harwich harbour and went off with his ship and cargo. In the winter of 1323 a merchant of Bayonne who was carrying a variety of wares from Sluys to Spain ran into the port of Sandwich to escape pirates but then, while he was anchored there, a formidable group from Dover, Battle and Winchelsea, among whom were Stephen, Gervase and Reginald Alard, took over his ship and divided up its cargo between themselves.[105]

The Straits of Dover and the north coast of Thanet were evidently especially dangerous, but piracy was universal – off Sussex, off the Isle of Wight and Dorset, off Cornwall, off the Somme, off Guernsey and down the coast to Gascony. A salt ship was captured off Brittany, and near La Rochelle one English vessel intentionally rammed another as part of a feud between a merchant of (King's) Lynn and another from *Goseford* (on the Deben estuary, north of the Orwell). Life and death continued in this vein.

When England emerged from the trauma of the Great Famine, it had entered a period dominated by the Hugh Despensers, father and son, whose influence led to increasing anarchy. Intensely ambitious for wealth and power, they were already unpopular with the other magnates. The son, already very rich by virtue of his marriage to the heiress of the Clare family and as a result of his own personal acquisitions, became an inseparable favourite of the king. With his position and influence at court, nobody could expect reasoned justice. Extortion, corruption, rape, pillage and murder were the order everywhere. Acute tension among the magnates led to a number of political executions. When parliament exiled both Despensers in August 1321, the father went off to Bordeaux but the son indulged in piracy in the Channel, capturing a Genoese ship and drowning the crew, possibly in the company of the Cinque Ports. Their exile was short-lived, and after only a few months the son was back at the king's side.[106]

There was little hope that this climate of anarchy on land and sea would cease while Edward II remained king, and his degree of unpopularity was such that he only survived a few more years. At the end of another short war in Gascony, Queen Isabella, the king's French wife, was sent to negotiate terms of a truce with her brother, Charles IV of France. Her son, the future Edward III, aged 12, was permitted to leave the country with her, to pay homage to his uncle. The queen and her lover Roger Mortimer, another English exile, then plotted to overthrow the Despensers, and when they landed with a small force at Orwell on 24 September 1326 they met very little opposition. In the face of growing opposition to them, the Despensers and the king retreated west, and by the end of November both the Despensers had been hanged by the barons. The king was imprisoned in Kenilworth Castle and later removed to Berkeley Castle, where it seems he also met his end. The young prince Edward officially succeeded as king on 25 January 1327, but as he was only just 15, the queen and Mortimer ruled as regents – and their regime gave the country no more security than the previous one. Their peace treaties in Gascony and Scotland were deeply resented in England because they both conceded territory to the opposition. Grasping power and possessions, Mortimer quickly fell out with the barons. It was only a matter of time until he too was overthrown. On 19 October 1330, the young Edward and a small band of followers, with considerable support from elsewhere, overcame Mortimer and Isabella.

Edward III's personal rule began then, and although that does not seem to have made any noticeable difference to the level of piracy, there was a subtle difference as to its cause. It no longer reflected the weakness and chaotic state of the central English administration, but rather the increasing animosity between England and France, which led on to the outbreak of war in 1337.

# 7

# Portrait of a Pirate: John Crabbe (c. 1290–1352)

ohn Crabbe was one of a very few medieval pirates who stood out as extraordinary, independent opportunists. Unlike the majority of these men, he operated without a lifelong base. On the contrary, he sought adventure by serving several different leaders, one after another. To each of them in turn, he could be relied on for very efficient and effective service, while it lasted, but not for consistent allegiance. There was nothing which tied him down.

During the period of thirty-five years when he was active at sea, he served the heads of three states, Flanders, Scotland and England, changing sides twice, as well as living through a period when he fluctuated between Flanders and Scotland. As a result he became one of the most celebrated, the most feared and, in several quarters, one of the most hated seamen of his day. However, in contrast to Eustace the Monk, a similarly independent character, Crabbe managed to live to an advanced age and die of natural causes.[107]

Crabbe was probably born around 1290. His family circumstances went unrecorded, but he came from Muiden (alternatively known as Mude, now Sint Anna ter Muiden), near the mouth of the *Zwin*, on the left bank of the channel leading from the North Sea towards Damme and Bruges. He therefore grew up surrounded by the busy commercial life of the sea. As a small boy he is most likely to have witnessed with excitement the chaos which attended the arrival of Edward I's fleet in 1297: if not actually present, he would have heard about that soon enough.

His name first appears in 1305 or '06 in connection with the violent seizure off La Rochelle of the *Waardebourc*, a ship belonging to John de le Waarde, a merchant of Dordrecht. This was just one event which reflected a long-running dispute between the counts of Holland and Zeeland on the one hand and the counts of Flanders on the other. The bone of contention was ownership of Walcheren, Noord Beveland and Zuid Beveland, then three separate islands (now united as one) lying between the two mouths of the Scheldt. On this occasion Crabbe and his companions seized 160 tuns of wine and all the other goods on board with a total value of 2,000*lt*, and kidnapped the crew. Despite determined requests for justice and compensation, de le Waarde received no satisfaction until seven years later, when a treaty was signed between the two opposing sides.

Shortly before 28 May 1310 Crabbe struck again, this time far up the Channel, much nearer his home base. By then he was master of the ship *de la Mue* (Muiden) and accompanied by a second Flemish ship, he seized

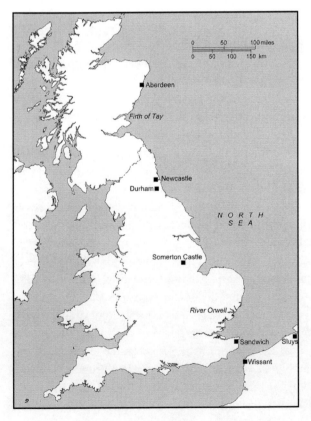

The world of John Crabbe, 1310–40.

a vessel carrying the possessions of Alice, Countess Marshall, the widow of Roger Bigod, hereditary Earl of Norfolk. She was planning to leave London shortly to go 'overseas' – which may have meant she was going to Hainault to her father, John de Avennes, one-time count of that province. She had sent her clothes, jewels, gold and silver valued at 2,000*l* on ahead (into a pirate-infested sea!), only to lose them to Crabbe as her ship approached Wissant. Repeated calls to Robert, Count of Flanders, for return of the goods met with no response for five years, that was until 1315, when the count replied that a number of culprits had been punished. Whether that was true or not, Crabbe himself had evidently escaped some time previously, for by then he was living in a Flemish colony in Aberdeen.

Crabbe's first phase of living at least part-time in Scotland had begun around 1311, when the Flemings were uniting with the Scots to exploit the continuing enmity between England and Scotland. On 3 September 1311 Crabbe and a collection of men from both Aberdeen and Flanders stole eighty-nine sacks of English wool from two ships sailing together from Newcastle to Flanders. Crabbe then sent the Scots on to sell the wool in Flanders, which may imply that he himself was already outlawed from Flanders. Then, in May 1313, Edward II asked Robert, Count of Flanders, to do justice to English merchants for the robberies committed by John Crabbe and other Flemings, on the understanding that the king would reciprocate by compensating Flemings who had suffered at the hands of English pirates at *Crasden* and elsewhere since the time of the king's accession.[108]

The Great Famine of 1315–17 hit all the northern countries, but Flanders probably suffered especially badly on account of its large, concentrated, urban population. The count reacted to the situation by assembling a fleet to send to sea at public expense 'to acquire victuals for the sustenance of the men ... where there is great need and famine'.[109] In other words, this was state-sponsored piracy, and such was Crabbe's reputation as a fearless and successful pirate that in this state of emergency he was recalled and, having been swiftly pardoned of all his previous wrongdoings, he was made leader of this Flemish fleet. He set sail on Ash Wednesday, 24 February 1316. Five days later they captured two Yarmouth ships on their way home from Rouen laden with provisions. It seems highly probable that other victims followed.

Crabbe was still in the southern area just before Christmas 1316, because then he captured a wine ship in the Downs off Sandwich. The *Bona Navis de la Strode* (Strood, on the Medway in Kent), with John Springer as master, had probably reached the end of her voyage when Crabbe and his associates attacked and made off with both the ship and the cargo – 86 tuns, 25 pipes of wine belonging equally to two merchants, Aymer de Insula, a merchant of Bordeaux and Arnold Dosyngham, described as a citizen of Bazas, 50km south-east of Bordeaux. The value of the wine was quickly established by the Sheriff of Kent at 788*l* sterling. Other goods and merchandise belonging to various merchants together with the ship's tackle and beds and chests and other small belongings of the master were valued at 210 marks. The king immediately ordered the sheriffs of London, Lincoln, Norfolk and Suffolk to arrest various proportions of goods belonging to the Flemings up to this value, allowing 8*l* per tun and 4*l* per pipe of wine, and to keep them safely.[110] Three demands met with no response from Robert, Count of Flanders before he eventually replied in April 1318. He was, he said, ignorant of the whole affair. This was greeted with astonishment in England, since it was well known that at that time Crabbe stayed in Flanders whenever he chose, that the count had appropriated the wine for his own use and had already passed the ship on to someone else. It was not until July 1332, sixteen years after the seizure of the ship, that Edward III finally instructed the sheriffs of Kent, Suffolk and Norfolk to produce the sums from Flemish cargoes which they had impounded, so that he could indemnify the merchants and owner in full.

Soon after his capture of the *Bona Navis*, and apparently banished from Flanders for murder, Crabbe began his second Scottish phase. Ever since the Battle of Bannockburn in 1314, bitter fighting had been taking place on the Border, and on 1 April 1318 Berwick-upon-Tweed was captured from the English and became a vital Scottish outpost. Crabbe was certainly living there by August 1319 when the English tried to recapture it. His help in strengthening the town fortifications was invaluable, and he carried on serving the Scots, harrying the English on land and at sea.[111]

A change in his fortunes, however, happened in 1332, coinciding interestingly enough, with the effective beginning of the reign of Edward III. The English destroyed all the ten Flemish ships Crabbe had taken north to the Firth of Tay in response to a request for support by the Scots, and later that autumn he himself fell into their hands during a skirmish near Kelso. Being extremely unpopular with the English, his life was in jeopardy. The parliament which was convened at York in January 1333 was in angry mood, demanding recompense and retribution from this man who had robbed their merchants and hanged their seamen from their own masts for many years past. They demanded that he pay the full penalty, and meanwhile he was to be kept in chains. It was an ignominious beginning to the final, English, phase of his life.

The English were then besieging Berwick, and Crabbe played the only card available to him. Against strong odds, he persuaded Edward III that his knowledge of the defences of that town would be useful. In the event, his inside knowledge and practical help proved so valuable that the king saw fit to pardon him of 'all homicides, felonies and other offences of which he might possibly be accused, whether on land or sea'.[112] He was also created constable, for life, of Somerton Castle, Lincolnshire. Seen in retrospect, his survival and recovery was remarkable. But his former friends, the Scots in Berwick, were furious at his treachery and apparently vented their wrath by killing his son.

Crabbe continued to provide advice and materials for the English war against Scotland. In March 1335 he assembled a fleet of ten ships, complete with 1,000 mariners and archers, to go to sea to try to prevent French support reaching the Scots. In December 1337 he was to be paid 100s for his expenses incurred while staying in Berwick, and all the engines there were to be repaired according to his specification.

In February 1339 he was to be paid a further 24*l* for surveying the construction of certain engines and 'hurdis', which were either siege towers or wooden galleries to attach to the castle, at Dunbar. This payment seems to have been for clearing up matters prior to his departure, since he was about to set out on the king's service overseas. That June he was paid for going north with another hundred archers 'for the defence of the realm' and, described as the king's yeoman, he was also allowed 100*l* to repair his houses at Somerton.[113]

In the meantime, in 1337 war with France had begun. As Edward III was hoping to use the Low Countries as a base for invading France, it was highly important to keep the sea lanes in the North Sea open and free of French marauders. To that intent Crabbe, the former pirate who probably understood more than anybody else about the geography of the *Zwin* and about navigation in the North Sea, was brought south in the summer of 1339 to work with Robert Morley, a Norfolk knight who had recently been recruited as admiral of the fleet north of the Thames and was to become one of the most able and energetic of naval commanders. It was this somewhat improbable combination of two men who, that year, took a convoy of ships carrying supplies of money, wool and military reinforcements over to Sluys. There they did raid an enemy merchant convoy and took numerous prizes, but they also attacked without discrimination neutral Flemish and Spanish escort vessels which they had been expressly told not to tamper with. To make matters worse, when they returned to the Orwell, they quarrelled over the division of the spoils of their plunder, and the fleet which had only been assembled with difficulty scattered and some of the vessels sailed off, beyond recall.[114]

Edward III was still hoping to take an army across from the Orwell to Flanders, but he suffered repeated frustrations when his hoped-for force of men, supplies and ships failed to materialise. While he was delayed, Philip VI of France was also frustrated, because the Genoese who had added their important support to the French for nearly two years had mutinied and taken their ships back to the Mediterranean. Thus weakened, Philip fell back on the only policy open to him – using those ships which remained at his disposal to block the mouths of the Scheldt. At least the English would not be able to enter and anchor there.

Edward too had only a limited force, and in view of the great risks to the king himself, the Archbishop of Canterbury intervened and strongly advised him to be cautious about going. The king turned to Morley and Crabbe looking for more encouraging support, but he found that their advice confirmed that of the archbishop. In spite of this unanimous advice to the contrary, Edward pressed ahead and on 22 June 1340 sailed out of the Orwell estuary accompanied eventually, but possibly still reluctantly, by Morley and Crabbe. On the afternoon of the next day he reached the coast of Flanders, off Blankenberg. They were within 10 miles of the *Zwin*, probably within sight of the French galleys, which had been chained together across that estuary.

The most experienced of the French seamen, Barbavera, had pointed out the dangers of a large fleet being shut inside that inlet without room to manoeuvre, but this was a piece of good advice which the French admirals Quiéret and Béhuchet chose to ignore. Having held back until conditions were right, on the afternoon of 24 June, Edward seized the combined advantages of having wind, tide and sun all strategically behind him and went into the attack. The French were indeed trapped inside the estuary, unable to manoeuvre, and by nightfall they had been nearly annihilated by the hail of arrows from English longbows. Both French admirals lost their lives and 190 of the 213 French vessels were captured.[115] Towards the end of the engagement, Crabbe was given forty ships with which to chase a few French ships which had escaped led by a notorious pirate called Spoudevisch.

This victory, which came to be named after the port of Sluys, seems to have marked the end of Crabbe's maritime career, although subsequently he continued to work on land for the king. He collected taxes, a highly important duty since the Crown was once again bankrupt, and he took into custody at Somerton Castle one of the many important Scottish prisoners taken at the Battle of Neville's Cross near Durham. His last years seem to have been spent peacefully at his castle, and he died in 1352.

Crabbe was a remarkably gifted man, who combined a high level of skill in seamanship and navigation with equal qualifications as a military engineer. In other words, he was particularly unusual and useful, being an expert in warfare both at sea and on land. He was also an adventurous, independent spirit and a political strategist. In him we see an excellent example of a symbiotic relationship, in which a medieval pirate was able to exploit various rulers to achieve his own ends, while simultaneously those same rulers were using his expertise to further their own objectives.

# 8

# Raids, Devastation and Fear 1337–89

n 1337 England and France began a conflict which was to last spasmodically until 1453 and became known, only some centuries later, as the 'Hundred Years' War'. The fundamental reason for the outbreak of war was, once again, the argument over the status of Gascony. French support for the Scots against England was a further aggravation, and the final and most pressing reason was Edward III's recent claim to the crown of France. This chapter charts the progress and implications of raids and counter-raids across the English Channel until the truce of 1389.

The economic and military strength of England depended on the continuity of prosperous maritime trade, and in that respect the ports were an essential, vital link. Without their operation and facilities – the import, export and storage of raw materials and manufactured goods, the collection of large sums from customs, and above all the continuing supply of ships and crews – the nation would be critically weakened. It was also essential to keep up the confidence of the foreign merchants who carried the trade, and that could evaporate all too quickly, those merchants preferring to visit foreign ports.

However, and working against the likelihood of prosperity, the French wars greatly increased the demands by the Crown upon the ports and their shipping. The king expected to commandeer at will and at short notice unlimited numbers of merchantmen and fishing vessels to fulfil his needs for troopships and supply vessels, thus prejudicing not only the sources of trade which provided the national wealth but also local supplies of food. On top of all that, he looked to the same source to provide men of war whenever needed to defend the coast against the depredations of foreign fleets and pirates. This procedure was inherently unsatisfactory from the points of view of both the merchants and the king. Without their ships, the merchants went without their annual income, while for the king this procurement of shipping was uncertain and always delayed. The French, on the other hand, supplemented their shipping by hiring galleys from the Mediterranean. Those were more suitable for raiding than the short, tubby, northern sailing cogs, although the cost of hiring them was high and the galleys were not necessarily in the place and at the time when they were most needed.

All the ports on the south coast were in the front line. Southampton and Sandwich were especially important since both served as outports for London. Winchelsea (which dealt especially in wine) and Portsmouth were also in the top rank since both commanded extensive sheltered inlets of the sea where fleets could be assembled and Edward's armies could embark. In addition, every smaller port involved in trade or fishing was expected to subscribe ships and crews on demand. All of them were thus likely targets for the French.

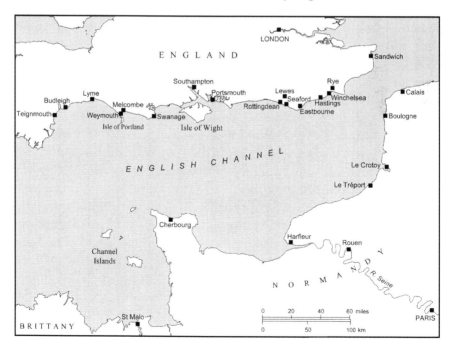

Targets for attack 1337–89: the ports of southern England.

Defence was always much more difficult than attack. It was also less attractive for funding or any other form of support. The galleys struck without warning, suddenly and effectively, on a coastline which was then deeply indented by tidal rivers which could only be crossed some considerable distance upstream by ferries or bridges, so even if there had been a national defence force, it would have been impossible to move it along the coast. Therefore for defence of the realm Edward III relied first on the coastal communities themselves, each in their own locality. The tenants, under the direction of their feudal overlords, were expected to line up along the shore, which meant abandoning their normal way of life. In theory, they were to be reinforced by large numbers of men drawn from other parts of the country, according to a system of array laid down by Edward I in the Statute of Winchester in 1285. This specified that all non-military men between the ages of 15 and 60 should equip themselves with weapons according to their means, which in fact were very limited. Commanded by the local gentry in units defined by their hundreds, they were to be prepared to leave home and set off for the coastline of the appointed county. For example, the men of Berkshire and Wiltshire were expected to go to defend Hampshire, those of Essex to go to Kent (travelling across London and round the Thames estuary!). Those of Gloucestershire were to defend Devon and Cornwall. As a result, the southern ports and their surroundings sometimes suffered acutely from having to support large numbers of visitors who arrived officially to defend them. In addition, Southampton, Portsmouth, Winchelsea and Sandwich periodically endured the presence of large armies who were waiting for the order to embark on overseas campaigns. Those armies might wait bivouacked for several months, and their needs for food, shelter and other support were enormous. Arrangements to feed them were always inadequate. Moreover, all these men had been uprooted from home and from their place within the normal system of law and order. Lawlessness, stealing and personal violence were rife. As an example, as early as February 1338 the people of the Isle of Wight registered a 'loud complaint' that many 'vagabonds and others infested their boroughs, market towns and other places'.[116] The demands of the king and his armies quickly proved to be well beyond the resources that the ports could provide. In addition, they had to face the French.

In February 1338 the French king appointed as Admiral of France one of his financial officials, Nicholas Béhuchet. A low-born Norman of unimpressive appearance, this man did not by any means command respect in all quarters. However, he seems to have been very shrewd. A memorandum he wrote to the royal council shows that, decidedly in advance of most of his peers, he appreciated the economic importance of command of the sea. At a time when soldiers regarded naval warfare as an awkward extension of that on land, he pointed out that a powerful fleet could destroy the English trade in wine, fish and salt. Nothing was specifically said about the strategy of raiding the English ports, but this must surely have been implied in view of what followed so swiftly.

On 24 March, only six weeks after his appointment, Béhuchet led a party of Frenchmen to raid Portsmouth. They hoisted English banners to disguise their identity. They met with no opposition, so they were free to pillage and plunder at will and then set fire to part of the town before departing on the next tide. That raid was sufficiently severe for the town's taxes to be remitted the following year, although its political fallout was minimal compared to what was soon to happen to Southampton.

The Channel Islands were another obvious target. Two days after attacking Portsmouth, the French descended on Jersey where, although they narrowly failed to take the stronghold of Gorey Castle, they did a great deal of damage to crops and buildings. The same combined French and Monegasque force then made its way north, until off the island of Walcheren (near the mouth of the *Zwin*) they captured five large English vessels including the *Cog Edward* and the *Christopher*, the pride of the English king's own ships, laden with wool and victuals, and killed the sailors they found on board while the masters and merchants were safely ashore.[117]

Frequent threats of invasion made the people living along the English coast increasingly insecure and unsettled, and repeated royal demands requiring the coastal authorities to reinforce their defences met with very mixed response. One of the few large local landowners who actually lived in the area (as opposed to being a distant absentee) and was attentive to both the needs of his tenants and the defence of the realm was the Abbot of Battle. In June 1338 he was reported to be fortifying his abbey, and by October his men were arrayed along the coast near Winchelsea 'for the safety of those parts against invasion'.[118] It may well have been that display of strength which caused the French to head further west – to Southampton.

On Sunday, 4 October 1338, a fleet of some fifty French, Scottish and Genoese armed galleys was seen advancing up Southampton Water. They had with them an experimental military 'machine', a *pot au feu* equipped with gunpowder and forty-eight iron bolts, which was almost certainly more frightening than dangerous. Whatever effect this invention may have had, however, when the leaders in Southampton saw what was coming, they panicked, abandoned the town defences, turned tail and fled with all their men. The French then landed undeterred and plundered hundreds of bales of wool piled up on the shore awaiting exportation by the Genoese on behalf of Florentine merchants. The invaders found the wine stored in the cellars, and no doubt made free with that. They rampaged through the houses, hanging the elderly and infirm who had been unable to flee. Before leaving on the tide next morning they set fire to large parts of the south of the town, causing a conflagration for which there is good archaeological evidence. Portsmouth was burnt again on this occasion, and either then or soon afterwards Swanage and its neighbour Studland shared the same fate.[119]

As a result of this raid, Southampton was wrecked. The instruments of its government, the charters and their seals, the equipment for weighing the wool, the customs seals, and the book recording debts to be collected had all disappeared. The French had caused havoc to the leading port on the south coast, and the English had apparently offered no opposition. The king was furious and desperate. He took this raid as a severe blow to his personal prestige, and he had little choice but to take Southampton temporarily into his own hands and establish, in effect, a form of local martial law. He ordered an immediate enquiry into what had happened. Why had the defence failed? Where had the local defenders been? And where were the men of Berkshire and Wiltshire who should have been there in support? This was followed very quickly by other enquiries into the whereabouts of his personal supplies of wool and wine which had gone missing. It became apparent from complaints by some Catalonian merchants anchored out in Southampton Water that their cargo of rice (*rys*) and other goods had been lost to *English* looters after – and possibly even before – the French raid. Although these enquiries did nothing to establish the identity, or even the nationality, of the culprits, it was established that of over 1,100 sacks of wool awaiting exportation, less than 100 had survived being stolen or burnt. The king's wines had suffered equally badly: of a special purchase of 194 tuns of red wine only two survived the raid. It was also clear that the arrayers from Berkshire and Wiltshire had simply failed to provide the men intended to help defend this part of the coast, and had pocketed the money intended for paying those men. The merchants had disgraced themselves and the king may have been looking for a scapegoat. At any rate Nicholas de Moundenard, four-times bailiff and once mayor of the town, spent a short spell in the Tower the following summer, for good reasons. His activities, by no means exceptional among his peers, had included helping himself to a considerable quantity of the king's wool and turning a blind eye to evasion of customs. He had also sold some ships to the king's enemies in Spain.[120]

Any possible improvement in conditions in Southampton was prevented by an exceptionally inclement winter, very wet up to Christmas and extraordinarily cold after that. The site was hardly attractive, and people who had lost their homes and others who were very frightened by the possibility of further raids had migrated inland. Although in March 1339 all earlier inhabitants were ordered to return to the town, to rebuild their houses and live there 'for the safe-keeping of the town', it is very doubtful how many returned. Similarly, Bartholomew de Lisle, one of the major landowners on the Isle of Wight who had retreated with his men to the mainland, was ordered to return and reprimanded for behaviour 'not becoming of belted knights'. But again, how many people actually obeyed these orders is not known.[121]

The climate of fear generated by the devastating success of the French at Southampton also permeated the government, whose members became seriously concerned about their own position in London. Somewhat irrationally, considering that the success of raids depended on surprise attack and it would have taken three or more days for a raiding fleet to negotiate the constantly shifting sandbanks in the Thames estuary, the mayor and his officers were ordered to fortify the waterside of the city with stone or timber and install a line of piles across the river (which would, if they ever had been erected, have seriously hampered the capital's trade).[122]

The following spring men and materials were indeed sent to the south coast to improve the weaker defences of Southampton. The king himself stayed at Winchester in March. He visited Southampton and gave detailed directions for strengthening and maintaining the defences on the seaward side of the port. But even then there is considerable doubt about how much was actually carried out. However, the presence of workmen on the shore may have acted as a deterrent to the French. Another, probably more important, factor was the presence of a Cinque Ports fleet in the eastern Channel. They had obligingly provided at their own expense sixty armed vessels which in 1339 were not required as troop-carriers, and so were available to cruise around in aid of coastal defence.

Anyway, probably for a combination of reasons, there was no French raid on a major English port in the summer season of 1339. In May and June they only feinted at Southampton. They then sailed west to plunder merchant vessels off Devon and Cornwall, but suffered heavy casualties in a skirmish at Plymouth. Returning east, they made for the smaller ports. They razed some fishermen's huts, and possibly more, at Hastings. The castle there had been allowed to decay since 1264 when it was given to the Duke of Brittany, and that port was already well past its prime on account of erosion of the cliffs and silting of the harbour. At Eastbourne, however, the French were less successful. Andrew

Peverel, who was in charge of men at arms, light horse and archers based nearby at Pevensey, repulsed the crews of fifteen French galleys. In July the French appeared off Rye, but the Cinque Ports fleet was on hand and chased them back across the Channel, cornering them in the harbour at Boulogne, where they captured several vessels, hanged twelve of the ships' masters from their own yards, and set fire to the lower part of that town.[123]

That summer the French had their own problems. It seems that Ayton Doria, the Genoese admiral, had not passed on the funds given him by the French for his sailors. Unpaid, the sailors mutinied at Boulogne. They deserted and took their galleys back to the Mediterranean. This left the French naval force depleted by nearly two-thirds, and put the English in a relatively strong position. Hence in January 1340 the Cinque Ports, acting on intelligence obtained from merchants captured in the Channel, were able to carry out another raid on Boulogne in which, although they suffered considerable losses themselves, they destroyed eighteen French galleys and twenty-four merchantmen. The portsmen were then able to go further confidently, and raided Le Tréport and Mers.

Both kings – of England and of France – were aiming to invade one another's countries, but neither of them had yet managed to build up the very complex organisation required to mount such an operation. However, after repeated postponements and in the face of considerable opposition at home to his proposed expedition, Edward III left his anchorage in the Orwell and sailed out past Harwich on 22 June 1340, aiming for the *Zwin*. As we have already seen, at the ensuing Battle of Sluys he captured most of the French ships there, which were unable to manoeuvre and escape. He also recovered the *Cog Edward* and the *Christopher*.[124]

This battle at Sluys has long been celebrated as the first in a long line of great English naval victories, and as a disaster for the French. So it must have seemed at the time, and it provided a great boost for English morale. But close beneath the surface England was already badly weakened. The adverse effects of the French raids, and almost continuous threats of raids, cannot be overemphasised. Both economically and socially, the damage they inflicted was long-lasting. On the south coast this was all too evident. One parish in Hampshire reported that much of their land lay uncultivated because the peasants had been diverted to cut down trees and transport the wood to bolster the defences of Southampton. In another, the tithes in wool were much reduced 'because sailors and others coming to guard the shore stole both ewes and lambs'. Elsewhere, the men were occupied guarding the shore rather than sowing or harvesting the grain. Thus in various ways the supply of food was seriously reduced, and social structures were severely disrupted.[125]

After Sluys too, although he remained in Flanders and intended to fight on, Edward was bankrupt for the second time in three years. The government promised him funds but was then unable to deliver them. The English, who had been taxed repeatedly to support his wars against Scotland and on two fronts in France, would not, and possibly could not, provide any more. Tax collectors met with organised, armed resistance. The government warned the king: 'We dare not do more than we have, for we shall have a civil war on our hands; the population will fight us rather than give us their wool.'[126]

For the French, in contrast, the supposedly disastrous effects of the loss of a fleet proved remarkably short-lived. By the beginning of August, only five weeks after Sluys, Robert Houdetot, an energetic Norman knight who had replaced the two admirals killed at Sluys, had assembled a new, if small, fleet. He landed on the Isle of Wight. He was eventually beaten back, but not before the commander of the local militia, Sir Theobald Russell, had been killed. He then moved on with characteristic French speed. Within a week he had burnt Portland, raided and burnt Teignmouth, and tried, without success, to do the same at Plymouth before returning to Normandy to deposit the booty. He planned to return. This rapid resurgence took the English by surprise, but stirred them into action. The English admiral Robert Morley was transferred from the North Sea and was able to ensure that Houdetot's second visit was much less successful. Morley also regained control of the vital Channel Islands, went on to raid Brest and take possession of some Genoese galleys. [127]

In 1346 Edward III assembled a large army at Southampton and Portsmouth. Such was the secrecy, it was not known whether his destination would be Gascony or Normandy. After being held up for a fortnight by changing, unfavourable winds which took him from one end of the Solent to the other and back again, he sailed the army over the Channel and landed on the wide open beach south of St Vaast La Hogue, on the Cotentin peninsula of Normandy (a site near that of the right flank of the equally secret Normandy landings in 1944, 600 years later). His eastward march across Normandy took him through some of the most fertile land in France. The army was large, but there was no centralised command, and it was best described as a disorganised rabble. In spite of Edward's personal if unrealistic instructions to the contrary, they left a wide trail of destruction, looting and burning as they went. The towns they passed through, including Caen, suffered that treatment. They met little effective opposition until, having come within sight of Paris, he was held up for a few days before crossing the Seine. Eventually his army met and annihilated the French army at Crécy, north of the Somme, on 25 August.

This victory made the way clear for him to move further north to besiege Calais, at that time only a relatively minor fishing port but nonetheless a source of great aggravation to the English because its sailors also specialised in the profitable activity of piracy. Thanks to its position, it held a key to controlling shipping in the Channel. Any ships heading to Flanders from the south had to pass nearby, and it was also not far from the passage from London or Sandwich to Flanders which was essential to English commerce. As long as Calais remained in French hands it posed a serious threat to the English ships, and therefore the possibility of capturing it attracted much more willing support from the English merchants and burgesses than any of the king's other military ventures. Besides, for Edward himself that harbour was potentially a very useful place to land his armies in future.

The town had grown up on a coastal sandbank. With the sea on the north-west side, it was otherwise surrounded by marshes which were flat, below sea-level, mainly stagnant and very unhealthy. They were crossed by an intricate network of watercourses, only occasionally bridged, so communications were limited, difficult and, often in wet weather, impossible. Since Calais was very close to the frontier with Flanders, the town had long had a fortress and was enclosed by strong walls and a moat (which is still there). With no chance of breaking through the defences, Edward began his siege on 4 September 1346, preparing to starve the inhabitants out, using a combination of land forces and a blockading fleet. To sustain his own army, which probably numbered over 10,000 men, large quantities of provisions were supplied from England and more were imported from Artois.

To begin with, things did not go his way. The Genoese captured twenty-five of the ships in his blockade, and one French convoy got through with relief supplies before winter set in. Then, during a very grim wet winter, both sides were weakened by disease and his own forces were reduced by desertion. In March and April 1347 two more convoys broke through the blockade, bringing some relief to the beleaguered town. But a third was apprehended by an English fleet while it was being assembled at Boulogne and Le Crotoy, and after early April no more supplies got through. As a result the townsfolk suffered terrible privations and ultimately, on 3 August, after eleven months under siege, during which cannon were used for the first time, followed by several days of negotiations, Calais capitulated.

As had been widely predicted, it was found that the people of the port had amassed great riches from their piracy. The chronicler Thomas Walsingham described the 'coats, furs, quilts and household goods of every kind, table cloths, necklaces, wooden bowls and silver goblets, linen and cloth' which were found, goods which had been derived from south and north, from Spain to Scandinavia, from England and especially from Flanders.[128]

Determined to eliminate this base of French pirates and trouble-makers once and for all and to establish firm control there himself, Edward expelled all the French inhabitants and sent a group of prominent English merchants over for up to six weeks to set up an appropriate English administration in Calais. These included John de Pulteney, a four-times mayor of London, William de la Pole, a leading merchant from Hull, and Roger Norman, the rich and successful burgess from Southampton who held estates spread out across four southern counties. In early October the captain and the marshall of the town were appointed. Free grants of properties in the town were advertised by proclamation throughout England. The response was remarkable and very rapid. On 8 October nearly 200 names were entered in a roll allocating the vacated buildings and a few empty plots. They came from every area of England, and included merchants, mercers, leather-workers (cordwainers and saddlers), a taverner and the king's sergeant at arms. Each of them was granted the property on condition that they and their heirs would remain loyal to the Crown and do all that was neces-sary to safeguard and maintain the town's defences. Queen Philippa also received a large block.[129]

As the result of the victory at Crécy and the capture of Calais, English morale was high, although it is important to note that the new conquest marked the beginning of a huge financial commitment for England. A perma-nent garrison of some 1,500 soldiers was needed to defend the town, and they had to be continuously provisioned and supplied, a burden which fell mainly on Essex and Kent. This arrangement lasted (at times with a much reduced commitment) until Calais was finally lost to the French in January 1558, when invaders gained access over frozen marshes.

After the defeat at Crécy and the loss of Calais, the French were in desperate straits, and turned once more to the South for additional shipping. They had already, in January 1347, concluded an agreement with Castile, which secured the use of some of the renowned Castilian galleys, although the first payment did not reach the Castilian commander, Don Carlos de la Cerda, until early in 1350 when he was in Flanders on a commercial trip. The danger to English shipping was immediately apparent and near-panic set in along the south-east coast. Men were arrayed to guard the coast and a fleet consisting mostly of commercial vessels, equipped with wooden castles and manned by men at arms, was hurriedly assembled at Sandwich. The king himself, the Prince of Wales, and the king's cousin Henry 'Grosmont', Earl of Derby (soon to be created Duke of Lancaster), were on board. The Castilian galleys began their voyage home, laden with merchandise bought in Flanders. Sailing close to the English coast, they were intercepted by the English fleet as they passed Dungeness on their way down the Channel and somewhere off Winchelsea a battle, later known as *Les Espagnols sur Mer*, took place. The Castilian galleys had the great advantage of superior height, from which they rained missiles down on to the English decks but, once the English had overcome the difficulty of establishing grappling irons and had boarded the Spanish vessels, they cut down the Castilians and Flemings with swords and axes. Although the English won the day, it was at great cost. Many ships were lost, and the king's own ship nearly sank and could only limp back into Winchelsea. And this battle did little to curb the Castilians, who threatened the English wine fleet when it sailed from Portsmouth that autumn.[130]

Meanwhile, piracy and small-scale raids had continued in the Channel and some of the smaller ports were paying a heavy price, as is demonstrated by a petition in 1348 to the king from the people of Budleigh (now Budleigh Salterton), some 5 miles east of the River Exe in Devon. The townsfolk said that they were no longer able to defend the local coastline as they were supposed to do, because they had been ruined by the enemy, to whom since the previous Easter they had lost not only three ships and twelve boats but also 140 merchants and mariners, including some of the richest men of the town. Some of those men had been killed, some had been ransomed and the rest were still imprisoned in France because the town was unable to afford their ransoms.

The ports were already suffering from a long-term recession. The damage wrought by the enemy was made worse by the depopulation caused by the Black Death (1348–49) followed by further outbreaks of the plague in 1361 and 1366. In 1356 Seaford complained that whereas it used to provide several warships for the king, had defended itself and its neighbourhood against attack, and used to pay the taxes expected of it, none of that was now possible. It had recently been burnt, devastated by the plague and the 'chances of war' and by then, in addition, men were demolishing the remaining buildings and selling the timber, lime and stone, presumably for it to be used in rebuilding further inland.[131]

Overall, in France, the defeat at Crécy, the loss of Calais and further failures in Aquitaine led to acute dissatisfaction with leaders and to prolonged civil disruption, which in turn gave the English armies an advantage over the French throughout the 1350s. The French king, John II, was captured at the Battle of Poitiers in 1356. After a year imprisoned in Bordeaux, he was brought to England where he was maintained in some state, and at great expense, first in the Tower of London and then at Windsor. In July 1359 he was transferred to a safer site well removed from the coast, Somerton Castle in Lincolnshire (see map on p. 100). The French government was virtually powerless, recovering from a recent revolution in Paris.

For England, in contrast, 1360 should have been an exceptionally high point. Yet, when a French splinter group made a bid to invade England and rescue King John, Edward and his government failed to react. Edward III may have been exhausted, having reached an age when the fight had gone out of him, and he had, once again, run into serious debt. But, following several months of rumours of invasion, by the end of February 1360 Jean de Neuville, a nobleman of Picardy, had gathered a fleet at Le Crotoy in the Somme estuary and was preparing to strike at Sandwich, apparently in the mistaken impression that this would lead to King John. It was not, however, a good time of year to stage such an invasion. At the outset de Neuville was frustrated by the weather. After a week pinned by onshore winds against his own coast, he finally crossed the Channel. He failed to reach Sandwich, but he landed easily on the sheltered and relatively remote marshy shores of the extensive tidal inlet below Winchelsea on Sunday, 8 March. His forces went forward and met no opposition, we are told because it was a Sunday. The 'great host of armed men with their horses took the town, barbarously slew the men therein found, and [rode] over the county, slaying, burning, destroying and doing other mischief'. In other words, they were a frightening rabble. However, having – hardly surprisingly – not found their king, this invading party soon lost its impetus. Disputes broke out among them over dividing the booty. They made tracks for their ships, where local levies caught up and slaughtered some of them before they could re-embark and sail away. Although on this occasion the French were disorganised and did not achieve their principal objective, this raid was yet another bodyblow towards the depopulation and decline of Winchelsea. A schedule of the mid-1360s indicates widespread desertion across the entire town, with a high number of tenements (not far off half of the original town) being 'waste, burnt and uninhabited'.[132]

The occasion also showed how slow, inadequate and uninterested the government's response to protection of the south coast had become. Not until the news that the French had actually put to sea reached London were the arrayers of southern and midland counties told to assemble their men and march them to their allocated places on the coast. In theory this should have formed a defence all the way from Lincolnshire to Cornwall. The men of Essex were brought to London, but only when the French were already on English soil were arrangements made to ship them round to Winchelsea. At best, they could only have arrived some days after the French had retreated.

On the other hand, the government managed to make some capital out of the widespread fear induced by this raid. It was able to raise some money, officially in order to finance a fleet for coastal defence – but then promptly diverted that to a potentially more spectacular activity, a raid at the end of April on Leure at the mouth of the Seine and on nearby Harfleur, an adventure which proved as ill-conceived and fruitless as the recent French raid on Winchelsea had been.

Almost immediately, on 8 May, the Treaty of Bretigny was agreed and sealed, signalling a truce, the principal provisions of which were that England would gain all the extensive land in the south-west of France which in the twelfth century had belonged to the Angevins. A huge ransom of 3 million gold crowns would also be paid for King John. In return, Edward III agreed to give up his claim to be King of France. Although at the time this must have appeared a very low point in the fortunes of the French, that was not to last long. The truce only lasted nine years.[133]

For the south coast of England this truce proved to be no more than a welcome period of respite. No attempt seems to have been made to restore or strengthen defences. Edward III, now elderly, issued what seems today an amazingly irrelevant instruction to men who were hungry and frightened: when at leisure the men of Kent should practice with bows and arrows, pellets and bolts, rather than indulging in football, quoits, cock-fighting or other *useless* games (the italics are mine). France, in contrast, soon had a dynamic young king, Charles V (1364–80), famous for his administrative ability as well as his military prowess. He, perhaps better than any of his predecessors, realised the importance of control of the English Channel if the English were to be defeated, and his practical approach contrasted sharply with the empty claim of Edward III to be 'Sovereign of the *Narrow Seas*'. Charles V revived the shipyard at Rouen, the *Clos de Galées*. He also arranged a new alliance with Castile, which meant that when hostilities were renewed the formidable maritime strength of the Spanish galleys was combined with that of France.

When war was resumed in 1369, it was the signal for twenty more years of raids and scares for the southern ports while, during the first few of those years at least, Edward III or those who governed in his name chose to concentrate their resources on campaigns in France and to neglect the defences of the coast of England. To make matters worse, in June 1372 an English fleet of seventeen vessels taking an expeditionary force and £12,000 in cash to pay troops in Gascony, defended by a mere three fighting ships, was wiped out by twelve Castilian galleys off La Rochelle.[134] And in 1375 the French destroyed another English convoy, of thirty-nine merchantmen which were loading salt in the Baie de Bourgneuf. The losses on that occasion were valued at £18,000. Together, these were catastrophic for England's already much-depleted stock of ships. After that, England could only rely on arrayed defenders standing on the coast which, particularly when it involved bringing in men from other counties was always unpopular, was subject to widespread evasion, and became increasingly ineffectual. A few galleys were hired from Holland and Zeeland but that, of course, involved more expense.

The next major round of French raids began in June 1377 (coinciding almost to the day when Edward III died), and their effects were worse than ever before, partly because of the strength and organisation of the French, and partly because they were descending on ports which were already so seriously weakened. These raids were neither the work of an independent splinter group, nor forays by enthusiastic adventurers: they were the result of the deliberate policy of a now-strong French monarchy, and followed three years' naval preparations conducted by a new admiral, Jean de Vienne. He masterminded the work at the *Clos de Galées*, implementing a programme of building both galleys and clinker-based oared barges. The Castilians provided reinforcements and they, in their turn, looked to the Portuguese for support. The fleet he led out from Harfleur towards the end of June 1377 therefore included eight galleys from Castile and five from Portugal, together with a number of armed Castilian merchantmen.

On 29 June, Jean de Vienne anchored in marshland channels between Winchelsea and Rye and quickly took possession of the latter, where the inhabitants had made themselves scarce. He advanced on Winchelsea but made no headway against stout resistance put up by Abbot Hamo of Battle. So he went on to sack Hastings, which was long past its prime owing to movement of shingle and silting of the harbour, and he then returned to set fire to Rye on the evening of 30 June. At much the same time (the order of events is by no means clear) the French also attacked further west in Sussex. They landed on the beach at Rottingdean, a small settlement some 7 miles west of Seaford and 4 miles east of the even smaller village of Brighton. They advanced inland. The Earl of Arundel, who owned the castle at Lewes and was responsible for arraying the local defence, was absent, so not only the town but also the castle were undefended. Before reaching the town, however, the French met a party of local peasants, led by the prior of Lewes, John of Charlieu, and two experienced local knights. A sharp skirmish followed, in which a hundred of the local men were killed and the three leaders taken prisoner. The prior remained a prisoner in France for a year before being released in return for a large ransom, and the Poll Tax record of 1379 shows that two years later some men from Sussex ports were still being held captive in France. Meanwhile, the French went on to burn Lewes.

In July the French returned to their base in Harfleur, to land their plunder and their prisoners, and to refit. Jean de Vienne intended to return to England in mid-August to strike at Southampton. However, the weather took a hand and his ships were driven onto the Isle of Wight, where the opposing forces were better balanced, as the Isle was by then well defended. In 1378 it was the turn of some of the Cornish ports, including Fowey, to be attacked and have their ships burnt.[135]

In 1380 the French returned to Sussex with a vengeance and even the redoubtable Abbot Hamo was driven back, one of his monks was captured and Winchelsea was burnt. In March 1384 it was reported that the town which 'was once well inhabited but by being burned by the king's enemies, and much more by the withdrawal by its burgesses, is now so desolate and almost destroyed, so that the ownership of vacant plots and tenements can scarcely be known'.[136] The contemporary records of Battle (some 6 miles inland) show that some of the more enterprising burgesses of Winchelsea and Hastings had settled there permanently, and had abandoned their way of life based on shipping for more secure, inland, pursuits like cattle farming and trading in timber.

Acute insecurity pervaded the south of England amid very real threats of permanent French invasion. A number of decayed fortifications in Kent and Sussex were revived and strengthened, and new ones were built, inland as well as on the coast. In 1385, for example, Bodiam Castle was built some 10 miles up the Rother above Rye. But what was achieved was much too little, much too late. In the face of renewed scares, masons, carpenters and other labourers were sent to work on the defences of Rye and ordered not to leave until the work was completed: defaulters were threatened with imprisonment. Everyone living within 6 miles was then told to move with their possessions into the town. A tax was levied on all fish sold in the ports of Kent and Sussex, an unwise move at a time of simmering unrest since it both struck at the livelihoods of fishermen and reduced the food available to the poor. In 1384 and again in 1385 it was only unrest in Flanders which prevented the French from arriving with a large fleet from Sluys. By 1386 they were so confident that they constructed an elaborate wooden fortress with watch-towers, to be floated across the Channel on seventy-two ships, to act as their base for a bridgehead at Rye. But this was captured by Sir William Beauchamp, Captain of Calais, and was said to have been used to augment the defences of Winchelsea.[137]

By the time a truce was called in 1389 between the two war-weary countries, the ports of the south-east were shadows of what they had been when the war began, two generations earlier. The ports had suffered depopulation as a result of the Black Death and further epidemics, an effect which was further increased when, in response to French attacks and as a result of general xenophobia, the portsmen had migrated inland. Harbour channels became irrevocably silted or blocked by shingle. For a combination of these reasons, houses and warehouses were abandoned, in ruins. Some of the smaller ports like Melcombe, near Weymouth, and Lyme (Regis) never recovered their commercial significance. In 1405 Lyme, for example, was 'so wasted and burned by the attacks of the sea and assaults of the king's enemies, and frequent pestilences, that scarcely a twentieth part is now inhabited' (compared, that was, to the time of Edward I, a century earlier). Others like Southampton did recover, but did so only gradually. More importantly for the immediate future of the country, it had lost a large proportion of its ships and their crews, particularly from the ports east of Exeter.

# 9

# Privateers of the West Country

he first few years of the fifteenth century were a time of danger for the new king, Henry IV. They also witnessed an outburst of violence in the English Channel as intense as anything which had gone before. This part of the story focuses immediately on the ports of south-west England, about which very little has hitherto been said. They had begun life as little fishing ports, whose men gained challenging experience venturing out into the rough waters of the Western Approaches but were too far away, too far west, to benefit from the twelfth- and thirteenth-century trade with Normandy. The local wool, too, was of poor quality so they were not involved with the wool trade with Flanders. Instead of that, they developed a modest general trade, mainly in foodstuffs, with Brittany, to which they were almost as close, after all, as they were to Southampton. The only local product of exceptional international importance was tin, which at that date was mainly shipped abroad by foreigners.[138]

In the fourteenth century, however, these ports became increasingly important as sources of ships for the carrying trade and as ports of call for ships sailing from Flanders and eastern England which, having followed the south coast of England, were about to strike out across the Channel to Brittany and on to the Bay of Biscay, Iberia and the Mediterranean. They also served as harbours of refuge from storms, although some of the ships which had sought shelter paid a hefty price to wreckers who exploited the special conditions provided by those sheltered harbours.

Moreover, in that century their remoteness proved a great advantage: those ports were scarcely touched by the French raids which progressively crippled their counterparts in the south-east. The supply of ships based in the south-east dwindled away, lost in French wars and raids and so, to protect the convoys on their way to and from the Bay of Biscay, and to defend the south coast against raiding parties, the Crown was forced to call upon the mariners of the West Country. Those men willingly and easily answered his call, using their own fleets – although to a great extent they served on their own terms, following their own agenda. In this way they became privateers, and a serious power to be reckoned with.

It is worth stepping back and investigating the source of that power. To do that there is no better way than taking a look at the family history of John Hawley of Dartmouth (*c.* 1340–1408), the most prominent and by far the best documented of all those privateers. It has been claimed, very plausibly, that he was the model for Chaucer's shipman.[139]

About the time of Hawley's birth his father, also named John, abandoned his existence as an agricultural tenant on the upland and, presumably attracted by potential advancement in the world of shipping, migrated down to a site beside the River Dart. He established himself with 'a quay' (which probably implied simply a 'hard' on which to draw up his boats) beside a tide-mill

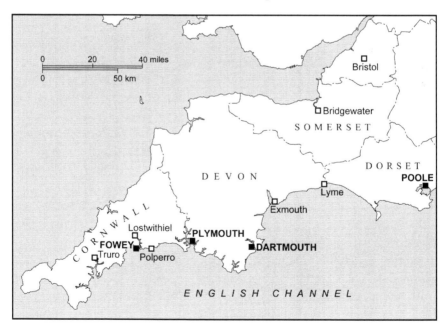

Ports of the south-west, thriving as centres of privateering especially from around 1400.

on the Fosse. This was the causeway which dammed a side stream and also linked the two original settlements, Hardness to the north and Clifton to the south, which eventually merged to form Dartmouth.[140] The family prospered, and in 1372 the young John Hawley already owned one ship and was part-owner of another which was requisitioned for royal service. In 1379 he was licensed with two other Dartmouth merchants, Thomas Asshenden and Benedict Bottesano, to go at their own expense to attack 'the king's enemies' for a year, an early example of the privateering which was to come. On that occasion he contributed one ship to a fleet of seven.

In the mid-1380s, by which time Hawley was already an important figure in his community, having been mayor of the town four times, he was sending his ships to join others from Dartmouth, Plymouth and Fowey playing a prominent part in organised piracy off Brittany. They were lying in wait in the roadstead off the Pointe St Mathieu where there were, as ever, prizes to be taken in the form of ships coming up from the south. Most of the losses to Hawley and his friends at that time were sustained by merchants of Genoa or Flanders, both neutral states, but the losers were by no means all foreigners. In one case a ship of Southampton fetched up at Topsham on the Exe.[141]

The evidence indicates that by the later 1380s Hawley had been able to accumulate a considerable personal fortune. For example, in 1387 he was able to pay for some of the captured goods landed at Dartmouth, over and beyond his own share. He was also able, in November 1389, to pay two sums totalling over 1,000 marks for several manors and some potentially very remunerative tin-works in Cornwall, all of which had recently been forfeited to the Crown by the chief justice Robert Tresilian who, having been condemned to death, was then killed by the mob in London. In 1388, when tension with France was at a peak, the king had the confidence to instruct Hawley to use his own funds to summon carpenters and other labourers from ports all round Cornwall and Devon and build a barge at his own expense – and gave him the power to imprison defaulters. He is also credited with building a fort on the southern promontory commanding the entrance to the Dart, to defend the town and the port against attack from the sea, although whether this was built then is open to question. The Dartmouth Castle seen today stands on the same site but was built a hundred years later and must have almost obliterated the work of Hawley's generation, though it is sometimes confusingly known as Hawley's Fortalice.

In November 1388 Hawley obtained royal exemption, for life, from undertaking any official duties against his will, which included sitting on assizes or inquisitions, being mayor or the collector of subsides and taxes, or the leader of military contingents.[142] This was very unusual. Why did he seek

The fruits of privateering. Hawley's Hall, Higher Street, Dartmouth, is the second house on the left. Painted in August 1839 by Miss C.B. Hunt before demolition in 1864.

this? It has been suggested that he may have been seeking release from the mounting burden of civic business. But that suggestion is contradicted by his continuing in various public offices for more than another ten years. It seems rather more probable that, in the wake of the purges of the Appellants in London, he wisely sought a guarantee that he would be able to stay clear of any possible involvement in the turbulent politics of central government and could then concentrate on his more profitable life in the south-west.

Altogether, he was Mayor of Dartmouth fourteen times between 1375 and 1401, eight of those years after 1388. As mayor, he was responsible for the distribution of the goods entering the port, whether they came by means of regular trade or more irregular piracy. He was elected to represent the town in the parliaments of 1393, 1394 and 1402. He served as escheator for the ports of Devon and Cornwall, managing the reversion of property to the feudal lord (often the Crown) in the absence of a legal heir, or after outlawry of the tenant. He was appointed to a commission concerned with setting up new metal mines in Devon and Cornwall, though in fact he was relieved of that office before taking an active part. In December 1390 the town received a grant for three years of the exclusive right to ship tin abroad, because 'above other places in the realm [it] has long been, and still is, strong in shipping, and therewith has wrought great havoc on the king's enemies in time of war'. It is not difficult to detect that the town owed this reputation in considerable part to Hawley.[143]

By one means and another, John Hawley amassed a very considerable fortune. During the 1390s the truce with France held good, and this was probably the period in which he had the time to build for himself what was surely the largest house in town, later described as Hawley's Hall. This stood on Upper Street, only a few hundred yards along the hillside from the church and probably with a second frontage on the street below. This was a prime position with an excellent view of the harbour entrance from the sea, as well as of the anchorage upstream. That house continued to provide a centre for civic meetings until it was demolished in 1860 to make way for road-widening on the very steep slope at the junction of Newcomen Road and Higher Street.[144]

Hawley also built the chancel of Trinity (now St Saviour's) church, in which in due course he was buried in 1408. For his impressive memorial brass he chose, very significantly, to be shown dressed in the armour of a knight, a fighter, rather than associated with a wool-pack and other symbols of a

Plaque of Hawley's House on wall today.

Hawley brass from
St Saviour's Church,
Dartmouth.

merchant. His first wife, Joan (d. 1394) is shown on his right, and his second, Alice (d. 1403) on his left.

But that is to anticipate Hawley's final decade, which included an unprecedented peak of piracy. His authority, his influence in maritime affairs and his benevolence undoubtedly served Dartmouth well, and the pattern of his rising wealth and that of the port in the fourteenth century must be echoed on various scales by the other, less well documented, mariners and ports of the south-west in the same period. The same rising tide of prosperity must have affected other

men about whom much less is known. How otherwise could Robert Bolt and
Edmund Arnold, also of Dartmouth, Mark Mixtow of Fowey and William
Meer of Truro suddenly spring to life in the records as well-off shipowners and
men of substance at the beginning of the new century? In addition to those and
many more from the West Country, there were just a few who managed to
rise to prominence further east, like William Prince of the Isle of Wight, and
the Spicer brothers, Richard and John, of Portsmouth, who did so in spite
of the adversities in their area.[145]

We can now put them into their national and political context. Richard II
(1377–99) had proved a volatile and inconsistent ruler, immoderately
extravagant and, for the final two years, tyrannical. In a climate of fear,
something had to happen before a very large number of the nobility and
officers of the Crown were eliminated. In the summer of 1399, while Richard
was away in Ireland, his cousin Henry Bolingbroke landed at Ravenspur on
the Humber estuary with a small force and moved west, rapidly gathering
more support. Richard was captured and held secure. With no serious
opposition, on 30 September Henry was pronounced king by Parliament,
and so became Henry IV (1399–1413). As soon as he took up the reins of
power he was, predictably, immediately faced by a wide variety of problems.
On land, these included a short-term baronial uprising in support of Richard
(who eventually met his end in Pontefract Castle, probably in February 1400);
repeated rebellions led by Owen Glendower in Wales; and almost continuous
disturbances in the north, which forced Henry to declare war against the
Scots in August 1400.

However, the greatest, and continuous, challenge which Henry faced
was on his southern flank, where renewed and increasing violence was
seriously threatening the trade which was vital to his interests. As ever,
a large proportion of the English national income came from taxes on
imports and exports, especially on wine and wool, which were essential to
maintain both economic and social stability at home. This was threatened
by political repercussions of the activities of English pirates interfering
with the ships of neutral nations, principally Castile and Flanders but
including others in the Mediterranean and the Baltic. If diplomatic relations with those countries became soured by the depredations of those
English pirates, the southern galleys could easily bypass Southampton
and other English ports and make straight for Flanders; and Philip the
Bold, Count of Flanders (also Duke of Burgundy and uncle of Charles VI
of France), could place embargoes on the import of English wool. It is
easy to see that any of those moves would plainly be against the interests of those foreigners as well as of England: they all needed the English

wool and cloth, and the Iberians needed access to the northern markets. But, once more, politics threatened to overrule economic need.

Because neither France nor England had the will, or the resources, to resume full-scale war, unofficial hostilities increased. The French especially lost no opportunity to go on the offensive. They were quick to support both the Scots in their struggle against the English and also, in due time and on a lesser scale, the Welsh rebels. On 20 January 1401, they made a political move which gave a clear indication of their intention to reconquer English Gascony: their government awarded the duchy of Guyenne to the king's brother Louis. Nearer at hand, they were very ready to support their own pirates who, thus equipped and supported by government officials, they described as corsairs.

On the English side, the merchant-privateers were, in effect, both Henry's merchant navy and the forerunner of men who would eventually become the royal navy. He was dependent on them to serve and guard England's commerce in general, and especially to bring the Gascon wine north twice a year, while at the same time he needed them to protect the English coast-line against French incursions. For their part, these men were also freelance pirates, whose activities Henry needed to control if they were not to offend the neutral nations upon whom his economy depended. The problems he faced were thus complex and interrelated, and the situation was to prove extremely difficult.

In theory, the famous 'Twenty-Eight-Year Truce' signed by Richard II and Charles VI in 1396, the terms of which Henry anxiously renewed in the summer of 1400, still held good and should have prevented English mariners from plundering shipping. He therefore made considerable efforts to protect foreign shipping including, initially, that of France. For instance, in April (even before he had declared war on Scotland) a commission was issued to William Prince, master of a barge called *Le Cristofre* of Arundel, to take her to sea with sufficient mariners on the king's service, 'provided that neither he nor any of liege of the king in his company on that barge take any ships, barges or other vessels, merchandise, goods or chattels of any of the realms of France, Spain, Portugal or other parts *except ...* of the realm of Scotland'. Similarly in June, relying on the merchant/pirates to respect the truce, his tone was one of firm encouragement. He ordered the sheriffs of London, the 'keepers of the passage of that port', and the bailiffs or mayors of ports all round the coast to make a proclamation that no merchant or any other Englishman was to 'take or send out of that port any ship, barge or balinger armed for war to damage the French or their allies, *the Scots excepted*'.[146]

If the king really had confidence that this policy of limited violence would succeed, he was soon disillusioned. However clear his instructions, the exception in the case of Scottish vessels and those of other countries which were carrying goods to Scotland was bound to run into trouble, not least because the majority of commercial vessels carried mixed cargoes which belonged to merchants of various countries who, of course, had varying political allegiances. For instance, to take an example from the summer of 1401, John Hawley himself ran into trouble when he captured a French vessel from Abbeville commanded by Jean de la Chapelle, which was taking a consignment of wheat, flour and canvas, which appeared to belong to Scottish merchants, from Sluys to Scotland. The capture itself was acceptable, since England and Scotland were technically at war, but then two Flemish merchants of Bruges claimed that a quarter of the flour and all the canvas belonged to them and demanded their return. A year later Hawley was still refusing to obey the order to hand them over, arguing that the merchants of Bruges were in fact partners of the Scottish merchant who owned the rest of the cargo! Maybe their claim was specious?[147]

From the start, in order to deal with French attacks on English shipping, Henry had been forced to invoke the help of privateers. In 1400 he had established a semi-official fleet under the joint command of John Hawley and Richard Spicer of Portsmouth. In spite of almost continuous scares to that effect, the French did not attempt an invasion at that time. But in the spring of 1402 the level of piracy escalated sharply as a result of a French agreement to support a specific request for help from the Scots. A fleet which they had assembled at Harfleur was sent to sea at the end of March. Instead of making straight for Scotland, which it did not reach until July, that fleet spent three months scouring the Channel for English shipping. Meanwhile, English spies based in Calais had given an early warning of those French naval preparations, and the admiral of the southern fleet, the authorities in Southampton, Poole, Dartmouth, Fowey and, notably, John Hawley in person, were all instructed to send their ships to sea. In command of their own fleets and unencumbered by the trappings of official bureaucratic organisation, they were able to react very quickly. Thus, while the French corsairs captured some thirty-three English merchantmen in those three months, their English counterparts took, in return, forty-eight foreigners.

This escalation of piracy had two important consequences, neither of which was welcome to Henry IV. Firstly, the cover afforded to the neutral powers by the Twenty-Eight-Year Truce had been blown. They became involved either because their ships were carrying some French goods, or their cargoes were being conveyed in French ships, or simply because the pirates did not or could not discriminate as to whose vessels they were attacking. Secondly, and most importantly, the English privateers became increasingly confident in their independence from the government. Eighteen of their forty-eight captures were taken by a Dartmouth fleet under Hawley, Robert Bolt, John Corp and Edmund Arnold, another ten by a Fowey fleet under Mark Mixtow and the Russell brothers, and six by a fleet from Southampton commanded by Henry Pay of Poole and Richard Spicer of Portsmouth.[148]

Robert Bolt, Mark Mixtow and Richard Spicer had been part of the scene since at least 1400 and Hawley for many years before that but Henry Pay was, apparently, a newcomer to this privateering and, even in that toughest of environments, was an exceptionally rough diamond. Unlike Hawley, nothing is known of his background and, in contrast to Hawley, Pay has left no record of trading activities, of public-spirited benevolence, or (before this date, at least) taking part in public administration. In addition, there is a strong probability that he was not a shipowner. On every occasion except one in his very active spell in 1403 he was reported to be using other people's vessels. Only once is there a suggestion that he sailed in his own ship, and that may be a clerical error in the record. On the other hand, he was evidently an expert and experienced seaman and navigator. He was a thorn in the side of Henry IV, and yet it was to him, as one of the toughest of the privateers, whom Henry turned for help in his greatest crisis.

At sea, the high level of violence continued, and the Channel was in ferment. By mid-winter 1402–03 representatives of both the Flemings and the Castilians had arrived in Westminster with long lists claiming damages incurred when English pirates had broken the truce and stolen their ships and goods. While the French obfuscated, Henry did everything in his power to defuse the situation

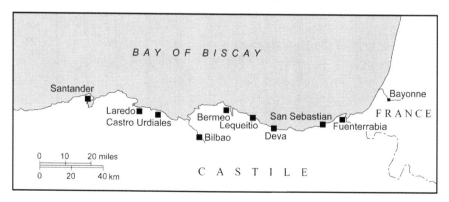

The ports of northern Castile, whose trade suffered at the hands of English privateers.

and, since the two lists consisted of almost identical names, dealt with both cases almost identically. The example of the Flemings can therefore serve for both here. On 19 December 1402, Henry wrote to the privateers individually in the strongest possible terms, leaving no doubt about his anger: his language is in marked contrast to that in 1400. His letters went to, among others, Richard and John Spicer of Portsmouth, John Hawley, Mark Mixtow, Henry Pay, John Trieman of Rye and Hugh Bodrugan of Cornwall. Each of them was ordered 'at his peril and under pain of the king's wrath to leave all else and ceasing every excuse to be in person before king and council at Westminster on the morrow of the Purification next (i.e. on 3 February) to answer ...'.

The response of the pirates to this summons was simple: none of them turned up to the appointed meeting. So the order was repeated: they were to appear on 7 March. That date came and went with no response and, with the continued absence of John Hawley and the others, the council had no option but to postpone the matter until July, when a meeting with delegates from Flanders was scheduled to take place in Calais. On several other similar occasions over the next six months, the reaction was the same.[149]

Faced with this total lack of cooperation on the part of the merchant-privateers, the king turned to the only possible alternative solution, diplomacy. On 7 March 1403 a provisional agreement was reached with the great towns of Flanders. The Flemings were, in principle, to be allowed to travel freely on the seas and to enter English harbours unmolested, subject to certain conditions. All their ships were to be marked so that they could be easily identified. All their goods, whether being carried on Flemish or on foreign ships, were to be accompanied by sealed letters certifying to whom the ship and the goods belonged. No enemy goods were to be hidden on board, and no Fleming was to disguise as his own any goods which in fact belonged to the French, the Scots or any other rebels or enemies of the king of England. In May a similar treaty of friendship was pending with Castile, and in the summer the Portuguese ambassador informed Henry that England had been included in a new truce between Castile and Portugal. The diplomatic net was spreading wider. But, while theoretical diplomacy continued to stagger on throughout the year it made as yet little, if any, difference to what happened at sea.

Around the end of March seven vessels sailing in convoy, some of whose principal cargo was the reek wines while others were carrying iron, were captured by pirates who included Mixtow, Edmond Arnold, William Meer of Truro, others from Lostwithiel and Polperro together with, perhaps more surprisingly, two from London. About the same time the Flemings recorded another twenty-six attacks on their ships by the English, and by

15 April 1403 the patience of Philip the Bold, Count of Flanders, had run out. A year earlier, he had been persuaded not to take punitive action against English shipping, but not this time. Now he instructed the maritime bailiff of Sluys to confiscate goods worth £10,000 from English ships anchored in that harbour, which was exactly what Henry IV had been trying to avoid.[150]

That, however, made no difference to the behaviour of the privateers and for the next three months Henry Pay seems to have dominated shipping in the western Channel, operating out of Dartmouth. In April, accompanied by others from the south-west including some from Cardiff, he captured a French ship, *St Anne of Guérande,* carrying a cargo of wine from La Rochelle to London. In May, in the company of Robert Bolt he captured the *St Marie of Prussia* laden with wax, hides of oxen and cow, suet, iron and olive oil, goods which belonged to Domingo Dyas, a merchant from Logroño (over the Pyrenees in the Ebro valley). In June, using ships belonging to John Hawley and Robert Bolt, his victim was the *St Marie of Lequeitio*, carrying wine from the south of Spain. This included bastard wine, and *Lepes* which came from the area west of Huelva and was a wine well-regarded in England. Three years later, in 1406, Richard Garner, a merchant originally of Piedmont who was then living in London and was soon (in 1408) to be naturalised as an Englishman, was still demanding restitution of some of this wine, and the magnates in the parliament of that year agreed that all who refused to accede to this were to be arrested personally, or if that proved impossible, their goods to the same value were to be impounded. Whether this was achieved is doubtful.[151]

Then, one night that August the long-anticipated and long-feared French attack on England occurred: a party of Bretons landed and burnt part of Plymouth. The subsequent commission described, probably with considerable exaggeration, that the Bretons had 'burnt divers towns and killed, wounded, robbed and captured [the king's] subjects'. Arguing that the Bretons were allies of the French, the king reacted by ordering the privateers to concentrate on protecting the autumn wine fleets and to make war on the Bretons or any others who broke the truce of Leulingham, the isolated church which stood on neutral ground outside Calais, where he had recently renewed the Twenty-Eight-Year Truce. This may have been a knee-jerk reaction, and it did nothing to calm a very tense situation.[152]

Whatever the king's instructions, the privateers had their own priorities and that autumn a northward-bound convoy proved overwhelmingly attractive. On 18 and 19 October the official English fleet carried out their most spec-tacular exploit yet. John Hawley, with Thomas Norton of Bristol and other ships from Plymouth, captured eight ships carrying a large and very valuable quantity of iron and other goods. One of these ships, the *St Julian of Plesancia*, was beached on the coast of Brittany, relieved of its cargo of 2,036 bars of iron and taken out to sea and sunk on 22 October. The implication is that this ship was in poor condition: otherwise they would have taken more trouble to keep her and take her to England.

The remaining seven victims were all landed at Plymouth, where a distinction was made which illustrates a noteworthy degree of organisation which probably, in turn, reflected a great deal of experience in handling prize goods as well as more regular trade. The cargo which belonged to merchants of Castile, consisting principally of iron, wheat and cloth, was kept intact, initially at least. In contrast, goods which belonged to merchants of Florence and Piedmont, or to those of *Plesancia*, Spain and Navarre, which included a significant amount of olive oil and white soap which came from Seville, was 'divided'. Their containers were opened up and the contents sold off: they were later reported to be widely scattered – in the ports of south Devon, in Bridgwater and in Bristol. Some of the ships themselves were moved on quickly. Two were taken to Dartmouth, and two to Bristol. The *St John of Laredo*, for example, was in Bristol by 12 January 1404, although minus 1,382 bars of iron and 30 quintals of resin which had already been extracted in Plymouth. The *Sta Maria of Deva* was also taken to Bristol, from where Thomas Norton returned her to the master, Sancho Martens, also promising him one-third of the freight she had carried. But that generosity was apparently an exception. Indeed, in November 1403 John Hawley and Thomas Norton were instructed to bring four of the ships, those laden at Seville with oil and white soap belonging to Italian merchants, to the Pool of London, but showed no inclination to do so. And then, at a subsequent inquiry John Hawley's son asserted defiantly that all these ships and barges and all the goods on board had belonged to the king's enemies, therefore implying that they were fair game for pirates and there was no reason for returning them. Hawley had evidently chosen to believe that a state of war existed. It is interesting to note that, unusually, in the wake of this piratical extravaganza several of the ships' masters intervened, anxiously demanding the return of not only their ships and crews, but also the armour which belonged personally to them and their crews. This proves, in case there was any doubt, that those crews were well armed, which must have considerably increased the cost of transport for the merchants.[153]

The following spring, the offensive by French irregulars began again. A Breton fleet arrived off the River Dart and then hesitated. Although Dartmouth, as the headquarters of their principal opponents, was an attractive target, they were cautious about risking being surrounded in that enclosed estuary. Hesitation was their undoing. Eventually, having given due warning to the defenders of their presence, on 15 April they tried to land at Blackpool, a small shingle beach exposed to the sea some 2 miles south of the Dart. But that was hardly ideal since it was surrounded by high hills which gave the defenders an excellent view. The Bretons were picked up individually as they came ashore. Their commander Castellis, who had led the incendiary raid on Plymouth the previous year, was slain and three lords and twenty knights were taken prisoner, providing useful hostages whom the king was very keen to interview on the subject of French plans.[154]

That August, what seems to have been a larger French and Breton fleet arrived in Milford Haven in support of a Welsh insurrection led by Owen Glendower. Some of their forces landed, took Carmarthen and advanced nearly as far as Worcester, while their fleet moved towards the Bristol Channel. But that was intercepted by Henry Pay, who had performed an abrupt *volte-face*. Whereas in the autumn of 1403 he had been active as a pirate near the Isle of Wight and had captured at least two freighters, now, nine months later, he had changed his allegiance and he was working for, rather than against, the interests of the king. Having been commissioned to 'make war on the king's enemies', he was jointly in command of an official fleet and was said to have inflicted significant losses on the French.[155]

The following year, the warlike conditions in the Channel attracted an adventurer from further away. Pero Nino was a young Castilian nobleman whose story was written down thirty years later by his companion and standard bearer, Gutierre Diaz de Gamez. Making allowances for Gamez's ridiculously exaggerated praise for his 'ever-conquering hero', the most significant event of Nino's foray with five galleys up the coast from Cornwall to Southampton was his ferocious attack on Poole. This was motivated by Castilian hatred of 'Arrypay' with whom they had many scores to settle, as he had reputedly terrorised their coasts, burnt Gijon and Finisterre, and carried off the exceptionally sacred crucifix of St Mary of Finisterre. The Castilians failed to find Pay himself, but killed one of his brothers. By the time the little party reached Southampton in September their oarsmen were exhausted and certainly not equipped to face the northern cold. So they retreated to spend the winter up the Seine. Meanwhile, Pay visited Rouen and Paris where he received some financial support, though not as much as he hoped. The following season he made purchases at the markets in Bruges and raided Jersey before, once more running out of funds, he made his way back south.

Nino's trip had little or no political significance, but for historians the account by Gamez is very valuable as the only contemporary eyewitness account of the management of the ships and their crews, and of the places they visited. His galley, for instance, had both main and mizzen sails, proving that she had at least two masts. He describes, individually as he came to them, how Calais, Le Crotoy and the Isle of Portland were only accessible from the land at low tide. He mentions the defensive bridge of boats at Plymouth, similar to that at Seville (and perhaps that across the Golden Horn at Istanbul). Militarily, we learn from him that Nino was advised that it was impossible to take control of Jersey without first securing all the four fortified castles on the island.[156]

In conclusion, the record of this short period of less than five years shows that privateering was firmly established. With the minimal evidence available, it is impossible to say what proportion of the stolen ships and their cargoes was ever returned to their original owners, but it appears likely that it was very small. Further to that, a commission granted with parliamentary support in April 1406 to Richard Garner, the expatriate Italian merchant from Piedmont then based in London, proves that could be fraught with difficulty. The commission shows that Garner had a substantial record of losses covering a wide range of commodities, going back over three years. Between March 1403 and July 1404 alone, he had lost goods to the total value of 2,109*l* from six ships, which were intended for either London or Flanders. Overall these amounted to 235 tuns of wine, 19 tuns of olive oil, 1,108 pieces of fruit, one bale of wax, 7,000 unspecified units of iron and 62 cases of white soap, the last of which had been stolen from two Venetian galleys captured on the orders of the king's admiral of the fleet in the Thames. On one occasion English soldiers from Calais were involved in stealing from him. It also shows that, presumably frustrated by failure to retrieve his goods through legal processes, he had taken matters into his own hands. Sometime around the beginning of 1406 he sent his attorney Peter King 'on certain business', to make his on-the-spot investigations in Dartmouth. That man was attacked, robbed of valuable goods and 44*l* of money, and imprisoned by one of the original pirates. It seems that a personal feud existed between John Hawley III and Garner.

Retrieval of stolen goods was by no means easy to achieve and even John Hawley spent a short sojourn as an old man in the Tower, from 15 December 1406 until 4 February 1407. Slightly later, it is clear that Richard Garner himself did not disdain from illegal practices: early in the next reign, he sought sanctuary in Westminster Abbey on account of certain offences he had committed. John Hawley, the outstanding English privateer, died, as we have seen, in 1408. His son, John III, entered royal service as a young man but continued with piracy when opportunity offered.[157]

Surprisingly little is known about Henry Pay's subsequent history, but what glimpses there are suggest that he settled into royal service. In November 1406, he was in charge of fifteen vessels, part of a larger fleet, waiting outside the Garonne estuary to pounce on ships attempting to bring supplies to the French forces besieging the town of Bourg, close to Bordeaux. Considerably later, in October 1413, he was water bailiff of Calais, an important member of the administration there, and on 19 July 1414 he was paid for ascertaining as quickly as possible the state and conditions of the soldiery in Calais, and reporting back to the Earl of Arundel. He died on 26 March 1419 and was buried in Faversham, Kent. His very battered gravestone now forms a rather strange step to the north aisle of the church, where it was probably placed in the major Victorian reordering of the building. Although this resting place might suggest that Pay had some connection with the Cinque Ports, a search has produced no reliable evidence to support the claim that he was at one time in charge of that fleet. On the contrary, the position and condition of the gravestone go further to indicate that he was never a valued member of either the town of Faversham or of the Cinque Ports.[158]

While piracy persisted after 1404, complaints with strong political overtones diminished, as did the incidence of the Breton/French raids.[159] One reason for this quietening down was increasing discord within France which reduced and weakened her hostility to England. Since 1392 Charles VI had suffered from recurrent bouts of madness, and competition for power between his uncle Philip the Bold and his brother Louis of Orleans increased. Relations deteriorated progressively, leading to civil strife. Following the assassination of Louis in November 1407, the country was on the verge of civil war. Back in England, Henry IV himself began to suffer from an unknown, spasmodic, debilitating illness, which was first manifest in 1405 and forced him to give up his intention of leading an army over to France. Under these less aggressive circumstances, the treaties guaranteeing safe passage for the merchandise of neutral countries probably became more meaningful. Thus, the privateering which came to the fore in the early years of Henry IV, diminished later in his reign. Although piracy in general was then suppressed under Henry V (1413–22), in the longer term it resurfaced, fiercer than ever.

# 10

# Henry V: Pirates Suppressed

enry V (1413–22) was the first, and indeed the only, medieval king who included among his top priorities the eradication of all piracy and other violent maritime activity in the English Channel. He understood that peaceful conditions at sea and security for cargoes were essential for national economic prosperity, for maintaining good relations with other maritime nations, and for the success of any overseas military expeditions he was likely to undertake in the future.

He achieved that objective as part of his overall policy of establishing law and order. In just a few years he virtually eliminated all the activities which led to insecurity. Maritime plundering and pillaging, privateering and cross-Channel raiding of ports became things of the past. He also quenched retaliation by the English in response to foreign piracy. By 1417, for the first time since 1200 (and indeed before that) he had reduced the Channel to a peaceful waterway, where all commercial shipping of whatever state could go about its rightful business with relatively little fear of interference – except, of course, by that natural hazard, the weather.

Therefore, whereas all the other chronological chapters have traced the progress of piracy in its various forms, the slant of this one is different. It describes the means by which that piracy was eliminated, at least for this short period. First, we need to look at the man who brought this about, for it rested to a large extent on Henry's own personality. By all accounts he was an exceptionally able, energetic and determined, but pleasant, individual. His early upbringing and experience built on his natural talent. Born in 1386 or '87, he was the eldest of the four sons of Henry (the eldest son of John of Gaunt) who was to become Henry IV, and the heiress Mary de Bohun. (Even the year of his own birth is uncertain: since he was only a 'minor royal', it went unrecorded.) After their mother had died giving birth to a second daughter in 1394, every year the boys were moved round several family estates where their education was well looked after. They were taught field sports, including riding, hunting, and using the falcon (all a suitable training for warfare), while on the cultural side they became 'wel-boked', able to read French and Latin and to write in English. All of them were clearly well above average intelligence. In addition, Henry benefited from the advice of his step-uncles, John, Henry and Thomas Beaufort, who were as talented as the royal brothers and, being older and more experienced, gave him consistent, valuable guidance in his earlier years and support throughout his reign. He was thus able to rely on the support of a large and exceptionally united family.

When only 12 or 13 he was made Prince of Wales, and from then on he took increasing responsibility for dealing with the rebellion headed by Owen Glendower. There, he gathered invaluable field experience of warfare. He learnt that it was essential to plan campaigns so as to ensure that armies were supplied with food, and were paid, as well as receiving the necessary

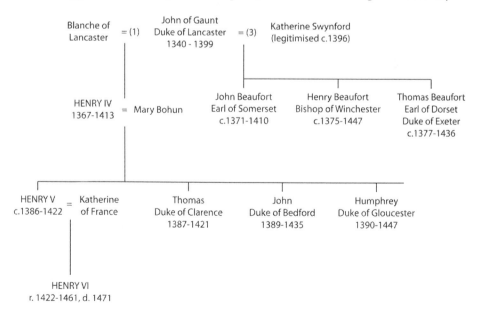

Family tree of Henry V.

military equipment if they were to succeed. By then, the equipment included cannon-balls, saltpetre and gunpowder, whose transport was both difficult and dangerous and were better carried by water. He learnt other advantages of water transport and the importance of sea power in general, in which the Welsh were deficient and the English used to their advantage. He was also learning the importance of having good, trustworthy friends.

By 1406 the Welsh problem was quietening down – it virtually ended in 1408 – and Henry was free to move forward elsewhere. In December 1406 he became a member of his father's ruling council (since parliament met only occasionally and for short periods, much of the direction of government rested with the council). There, the main, important, responsibilities included reordering the chaotic royal finances, and bringing the interests of Crown and parliament together. The near-fatal illness of Henry IV in the spring of 1409 helped to promote the prince. While a member of the council, Henry had an excellent opportunity to develop good relations with parliament and with many members of the nobility. Among the leaders, his prominent supporters included the Beauforts, and also Thomas Chaucer, their first cousin and son of the poet, who was speaker of the last three parliaments in the reign of Henry IV. Encouraged especially by Henry Beaufort, who was twice chancellor, he learnt to recognise the importance of order, efficiency and justice in government and of close personal supervision of all expenditure.

Since most of Henry's adult life was to be concerned with France, it is important to outline the complications of the political situation there, for from 1407 to 1435 that country was locked in civil war and throughout his reign Henry had to face two parties, each headed by men who were contenders for power in the vacuum created by the intermittent madness of Charles VI. On the one side was the party led initially by Louis of Orleans, the brother of Charles, known successively as the party of Orleans, of Armagnac and of the Dauphin, and often referred to as 'the French'. They usually dominated Upper and Lower Normandy, and the valley of the Seine up to Paris. On the other were the successive dukes of Burgundy, led from 1404 by the singularly ruthless John the Fearless who controlled a large area of the present-day eastern France and also, as Count of Flanders, the northern part of present-day France and the southern Low Countries. Simmering antagonism between those two flared up into almost continuous open warfare after Burgundy arranged the assassination of Louis of Orleans in Paris in November 1407. Thus, while Henry was to face principally the Orleanist (Armagnac) forces on the opposite side of the eastern Channel (his main sphere of activity), he also had to consider interference by the Duke of Burgundy, and the vacillating independence of the Duke of Brittany.

It was essential that England should hold on to Calais, at that time her only possession on the Channel coast, because that was critical for the protection of English trade and for the defence of the English coastline. Against that was set, however, the expense involved, which was a great burden on the English exchequer. During the reign of Henry IV, in spite of the fact that the town was threatened by the Burgundians, it still suffered from chronic underfunding by government, and in 1406 conditions of near-starvation were exacerbated by the failure of ships bringing vital supplies to break through the Burgundian blockade. Matters came to a head in February 1407, when the garrison mutinied because of lack of pay and seized the stores of wool belonging to the merchants of the staple.[160] After that John Beaufort, who had been captain of the port since 1401, was able to persuade the Council, of which he had also been a member in 1404 and 1406, to allocate revenue to Calais on a more continuing basis. When Beaufort died in March 1410, Prince Henry, who was already Constable of Dover Castle and Warden of the Cinque Ports, was made Captain of Calais in his place. This promoted him to the front line, with responsibility for defending the English coast against spasmodic threats by the French.

In August 1411 the French civil war reached a new peak. Both sides approached England for support, and although Henry IV and his son had the same ultimate aims in mind, which were to restore to England all the territory promised to Edward III under the Treaty of Bretigny, and to retrieve the large sum outstanding on the ransom due on John II, both of which dated back to 1360, father and son supported different sides. Henry IV chose to support the Armagnacs, still led by the Duke of Orleans, and sent his second son Thomas, now Duke of Clarence, with a force of some 6,000 to help them out in Aquitaine. This, however, came to nothing.

Prince Henry, in the meantime, supported the Duke of Burgundy, no doubt keeping an eye on the economic benefits such an alliance would bring, and probably foreseeing merit in having Burgundy as an ally if, or rather when, he went to war in France. There was also talk of his marriage to Anne, daughter of the duke. But none of these negotiations came to anything.

All this time, the prince had been accumulating not only experience but also very considerable influence and popularity. For reasons unknown, but perhaps because the king felt power was slipping away from him, in November 1411 the prince and his supporters were abruptly excluded from the king's council. There is no evidence of reconciliation before Henry IV died on 20 March 1413. It is important, in addition, to realise that there is no actual evidence for Henry having spent a madcap, adventurous youth: that was a powerful and long-lasting myth of imaginative propaganda put out by Shakespeare to influence his Tudor audience. Indeed, Henry's youth was so fully and positively occupied, there would have been little time for such intrigues and escapades.[161]

When the prince eventually became king, the nation generally was well united behind him (apart from a year's uncertainties over the Lollard revolt), and so, working carefully in a spirit of reconciliation with all possible adversaries, he was able to begin to put into effect plans which must have been gelling in his mind for several years. He kept himself closely informed of all royal and government finances, and surrounded himself with a hierarchy of trustworthy administrators, all of whom shared his ideals of social justice, stability and economic prosperity. Henry Beaufort was immediately reappointed chancellor. Their joint priorities were to establish law and order at home and, if possible, to reach settlements which to their eyes were satisfactory in France and with the Duke of Burgundy.

To achieve his aims in France, Henry moved forward diplomatically as well as on the practical, shipping, front. On the one hand, he continued to make truces with all the nations whose mariners were using the Channel. In January 1414 a ten-year truce was signed with Brittany (though he was to discover that the Bretons were not the most reliable of allies). In the same year, he was negotiating with the Count of Aragon, the Emperor Sigismund and, most important of all, with the Duke of Burgundy. He also concluded a truce with France at Leulingham (a deserted church whose significance lay in the fact that it stood on neutral ground outside Calais) on 23 September 1413, which was to be renewed in January 1414 and again in January 1415.[162]

On the other hand, Henry was going to depend heavily on ships, which served several different vital functions, both offensive and defensive. At irregular intervals he would need large numbers as troop ships to take thousands of men and the supplies for his armies across the Channel. Slightly later on, from 1417, smaller but still substantial numbers were needed to provide frequent ferries to service the English settlers in Normandy. And, if peace was to be maintained in the Channel, Henry's government also needed one or more flotillas on a seasonal, semi-permanent basis, to chase off foreigners intending to attack English ports and shipping.

Working towards this, Henry progressively accumulated a flotilla of his own ships, on whose finances, manning and deployment he then kept a very close eye. He is said to have started out owning two vessels as early as 1410, a number which had increased to six or seven when he became king in 1413. After that, he went on to acquire more by one means or another, by purchasing them, or as prizes taken through piracy by the merchants, in the course of war, or by building them. Looking forward, what was most remarkable was his programme of construction and innovation, especially of four 'great ships'. The first, the *Trinity Royal*, 540 tons, which was built at Greenwich in 1413–15, may have been a reconstruction of the *Trinity* which had previously belonged to Richard II and Henry IV. In Southampton William Soper, evidently an extraordinarily capable man and one of the wealthiest burgesses in town, began a long association with the king's ships, first as clerk and then as keeper, a post he held until 1442. In February 1414 he started rebuilding and converting a Castilian ship he had captured: that became the *Holy Ghost of the Tower* of 750 tons. Within months of completing her, in 1416 he laid down in the River Hamble the *Gracedieu*, which at 1,400 tons was the largest, most impressive, and as it turned out the most useless of all Henry's ships. Marine archaeology has shown that she was 125 feet long, and like many outsize, innovative vessels built at various times through the ages, she was built before her time, an expensive experiment which failed to live up to expectations. The fourth of the 'great ships', the *Jesus* (1,000 tons) was built between 1415 and 1417 in the Winchelsea estuary, mainly up the River Rother at Small Hythe, below Tenterden. Then there were various smaller ships, barges, balingers (including two built in 1416 by Soper at Southampton, the *Falcon* of 80 tons and *Valentine* of 100), a galley and a couple described as cogs. Seven southern carracks captured in the engagements of 1416 and 1417 were renamed and added to the royal fleet. The total number of Henry's own vessels was eventually over thirty, though they were never all in service, or even afloat, at the same time.[163]

At the beginning of his reign Henry had to deal with piracy by English merchants and others who were, as ever, enjoying and exploiting their freedom. Wool ships on the way to the staple at Calais and corn ships visiting the east coast from Dutch ports were in danger, while the wine ships were instructed to sail together for their protection. John Hawley III was carrying on his father's traditional way of life, in and out of Dartmouth. The case of the *Seint Croice*, a Spanish balinger which he had retained since November 1412 when she put into the port in bad weather, was only one of several in which he was involved simultaneously. Throughout the spring and early summer of 1413 he prevaricated, refusing to release either the ship or her cargo of 85 tuns of wine which had been destined for London, despite much legal wrangling which included his failure to honour a recognisance of 500 marks to be levied on his property in Devon. On 10 August the order was given for his arrest, and he was commanded to appear before the king and council at Westminster. Whether Hawley chose to appear there and what transpired from any meeting is not known, but clearly an overall policy, with stronger measures, was badly needed.[164]

To address the pressing problems of piracy, the Parliament which met in
May 1414 enacted an important measure, the Statute of the Truces. Under
this, truce breaking and contempt of safe conducts, together with hiding
and maintaining the offenders, became acts of high treason, for which the
penalty was death. To enforce it, conservators of the truce (officers who
already existed in the major ports) were established in every port, and now
everywhere they were to be backed up by two legal officers and the ultimate authority of the admiral – at that time Thomas Beaufort, Henry's
uncle. The master of every vessel, or the owner if he happened to be on
board, had to swear an oath each time he left port that he would not break
the truces which Henry had achieved with most of the seafaring nations.
On returning, the master had to account for every article he had captured
from 'the king's enemies' before it could be unloaded and sold. To a class of
men who for generations, for centuries, had been used to playing the game
their own way, these measures must have seemed draconian. (They may,
however, have been designed in part as a gesture to placate the merchants
and authorities of Brittany, Portugal, Castile and Flanders, matters which
were also of great importance to Henry.)[165]

Opinions differ as to how effective this measure was, whether it 'worked'.
If the statute suppressed the would-be English pirates, it did nothing to
touch the government-sponsored French vessels or the carracks of their allies,
the Genoese and Castilians. Certainly it was very unpopular: in 1416 the
English parliament heard that the king's enemies overseas and in Scotland were
breaking the truce with impunity, because the English mariners dared not retal-
iate. On the other hand, it did curb the pattern of reprisals and counter-reprisals
between English and foreign mariners. There is no doubt that complaints from
foreign merchants concerning English piracy were almost eliminated. And the
offences of foreigners still had to be dealt with by the long-established and
long-winded processes of letters of marque. For several years a Dutch widow,
Katherine Kalewartes, attempted to recover goods which had been captured in
the previous reign and were still held in Sandwich.[166]

Behind a thin veil of international negotiation and truces, in July 1414
Henry laid claim to the French throne, and throughout most of that year
and the first half of 1415 he was preparing to invade France. From the
winter of 1414–15 his maritime expenses showed a marked increase.
In anticipation of crossing the Channel himself, he could not risk
neglecting his back, leaving the English coast unprotected. So, while he
planned to take two of his brothers with him, he left behind John, Duke of
Bedford, the most reliable member of the family, to take charge of matters
in England and of defence of the English coast. The council arranged for

two large ships, five barges and five balingers, all filled with men at arms, archers and sailors, to cruíse and defend stated lengths of the coastline between Plymouth and Berwick.

Having rejected a last-ditch appeal from French ambassadors, who chased him across England from London and caught up with him at Winchester with elaborate offers of peace, he superintended the embarkation of his troops and then boarded his own ship, the new *Trinity Royal* at Southampton. On Sunday, 11 August 1415, he sailed out past the Isle of Wight at the head, it was said, of 1,400 vessels, some 700 of which had been hired for the purpose from Holland.[167]

His target was Harfleur, and although this was officially kept secret until the last moment, it is not at all difficult to see the reasoning behind this. Guarding the mouth of the great River Seine, and backed up by the

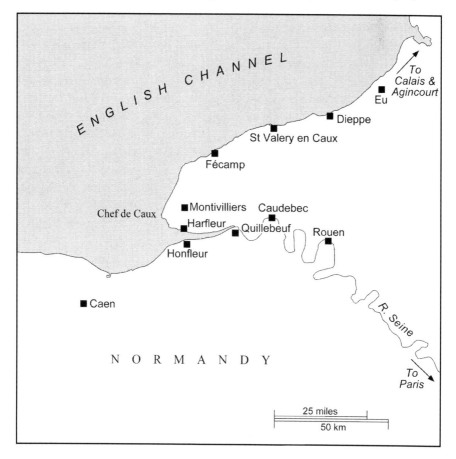

Harfleur, the Seine and the ports of Normandy.

shipbuilding centre and arsenal of the *Clos de Galées* at Rouen, that port had been the stepping-off point and servicing base for antagonistic French fleets since the days of Philip IV, le Bel, in the 1290s. As we have seen, the raiding fleets so dreaded in England in the late 1370s and the 1380s set off from there. So did the contingents sent to support Scotland and Wales during the reign of the new king's father. Besides that, ever since France had lost Calais to Edward III over sixty years earlier, Harfleur had been the principal nest of French irregulars, pirates who caused unpredictable but incessant trouble for shipping in the Channel and the North Sea. It is not too fanciful either to suggest that Henry must also have been looking forward to more offensive ventures, to future conquests, when he hoped the Seine would become an essential routeway, an artery for transporting his own supplies into the present French heartland – to Paris and beyond. Altogether, therefore, possession of Harfleur was of immediate importance to the English commercial community and to the king himself.

Conditions for Henry's passage were good, and on 13 August his fleet anchored off the Chef de Caux (now Cap de la Hève), the cliffs some 4 miles west of Harfleur, where it was safely outside the treacherous shallow and shifting sand banks in the estuary of the Seine. His target lay astride the little River Lézarde where that broke out through the chalk cliffs of the great river valley. In the fifteenth century the tides flowed up to the southern gates of the town so that, when Henry's siege began, while his army enclosed it on the landward side, he also had ships blockading it from the sea. The town held out for six weeks, but capitulated on 22 September, with its walls badly damaged by artillery and the men on both sides seriously weakened by dysentery. Henry sent numerous Englishmen, including his brother Thomas, Duke of Clarence, back to England to recuperate.

Henry may have taken possession of the town, but capture was only a first step. His position there was still very vulnerable because Harfleur was as important to the Armagnacs as it was to him and they held all the surrounding territory. Retaining it was going to be a serious, ongoing problem. Before he left, Henry did all he could to secure it by deporting all the French inhabitants who refused to swear allegiance to him and installing a garrison of some 1,200 (300 men-at-arms and 900 archers) under the command of Thomas Beaufort.[168]

By the time he was ready to leave, autumn was advancing and Henry could easily have sailed directly back to England, well satisfied with what he had accomplished for one year. But against all advice, he decided to march the remainder of his army to Calais, 120 miles away to the north. After a variety of difficulties and delays, including crossing the Somme, he was intercepted near Agincourt by the Armagnac army and, although pitted against vastly superior numbers, he annihilated them by a combination of outstanding leadership and strategy. His reputation and standing was greatly enhanced, at home and abroad, which made it easier to obtain funds for future campaigns, and encouraged wavering supporters like the Duke of Brittany. After being held up in Calais for two weeks by adverse winds, he was greeted with euphoria on his return to England that November by the people, as well as by the government and the city of London, both of which were important as potential sources of further finance. The French, in contrast, had suffered a grievous number of casualties, a very severe blow to morale, and serious loss of support from elsewhere.

Although Agincourt was a great triumph for Henry, it did not by any means imply that the Channel was yet under his control. Nor was the passage of the wine fleets secure. One contemporary example is of interest, not least because it shows how the convoys were organised. The master of the ship named the *Christopher* of Hull, which was carrying 240 tuns of wine, was elected admiral of a forthcoming convoy 'by all the merchants, masters and mariners of England'. According to established custom, those individuals also swore before the Constable of Bordeaux that they would stay together, not leaving the admiral, until they reached England. Contrary to that undertaking, when the convoy was intercepted by hostile carracks, the other vessels fled, leaving the *Christopher* to be captured and relieved of her cargo. Subsequently, the owner petitioned that the other ships should pay for his losses.[169]

During the following spring, too, maintaining Harfleur became increasingly difficult. The Armagnacs were tightening their blockade. It became too dangerous to replenish the town's supplies by means of raids out into the surrounding countryside, and so the town became dependent on supplies delivered by sea from England. Fish, beer, cannon and other military equipment were among the commodities delivered that way. Then, sometime after Easter (19 April) the French blockaded the seaward approaches as well, with vessels which included eight carracks, as many galleys and 600 crossbowmen, all hired from Genoa. Throughout May, however, the blockading force was temporarily weakened as troops had to be withdrawn to deal with a Burgundian uprising in Paris. A temporary truce was made, and one ship may have got through with supplies. But in June Thomas Beaufort sent an urgent appeal to Henry: his situation was becoming impossible. Without meat and grain, without horses and with his men afflicted by sickness, he said he would be forced to evacuate the town within two months.[170]

Owing to diplomatic distractions, including discussions with the Holy Roman Emperor who had arrived to try to make peace between England and

France, Henry was slow in assembling a fleet to relieve Harfleur. In the meantime, the French had established a naval headquarters at Honfleur and were
making trouble for English shipping in the Channel. Even ships going from
London to Southampton needed to be guarded against the enemy 'who were
assembling in large numbers at sea'. The French appeared in Southampton
Water, raided the Isle of Wight and made hostile demonstrations off Calais.
England began to fear an invasion and, as early as April, some ships and
sailors were impressed and told to gather in the Orwell estuary. When he
went down to inspect his fleet at Portsmouth in July, Henry found that the
French were forming a blockade and thus preventing the ships gathered there
from joining the others out in Southampton Water.[171]

In line with Henry's peaceful policies towards almost everyone except the
French, all the English ships going to sea that year were instructed to abstain
from attacking those of friendly countries, including Portugal, Denmark,
Sweden, Norway, Holland and Prussia, and told not in any way to break the
truces in force with Castile and Flanders. The only foreign exception was
Genoa, with whom (unusually) a trade war had broken out, and hence the
Genoese carracks were sailing with the French fleet.[172]

Eventually, in August 1416, Henry sent his brother John, Duke of Bedford,
across in command of a task force, a fleet of miscellaneous vessels, to
confront the Franco-Genoese blockade of Harfleur. On 15 August they met
the enemy fleet among the shoals of the Seine. Fortunately some details of
this engagement have survived. The opposing ships were shackled together,
enabling intense and prolonged hand-to-hand fighting which resulted in a
high number of casualties on both sides. But the French expectations of their
high-sided carracks, which were supposedly difficult to board and each of
which had two even higher castles and from which it was easy to project all
kinds of missiles, proved misplaced. Those large vessels were very difficult
to manoeuvre in the restricted space between the shallow sandbanks, and
the manoeuvrability of the smaller English vessels counted for more than the
height of the Genoese carracks. As a result, the English defeated the French,
capturing three of the carracks in the process, while a fourth was wrecked
trying to escape. Harfleur was relieved, at least for the time being.

In the meantime, Henry had been making diplomatic, financial and
practical preparations for what he envisaged as the permanent English
occupation of Lower Normandy. After Christmas 1416 he began piecing
together a large army, the necessary equipment and, once again, the ships
needed to transport it all. By mid-summer, the only remaining obstacle
was a small enemy flotilla consisting of twenty-six ships including nine
Genoese carracks with 700 or 800 crossbowmen on board, which was

lying off Honfleur on the opposite bank of the Seine to Harfleur. It had
been guarding the mouth of the river for some three months. The Earl of
Huntingdon was sent across with another task force and on 29 June 1417
he fought and defeated that flotilla, capturing another four large carracks
– which, like the earlier three, were transferred to Henry's fleet under new
names. The remaining five carracks found refuge in Brittany.[173]

The sea was now as clear as possible and at the end of July all was ready.
For the second time, Henry sailed down Southampton Water at the head of
his fleet, this time on board his brand new clinker-built, 1,000-ton flagship
the *Jesus*, only recently delivered from Winchelsea. On 1 August he landed
with his large army near Touques, 10 miles west of Honfleur. From that
bridgehead he went forward and within a year had taken all the fortified
towns in Lower Normandy.

First, he advanced on Caen, a river port with excellent communications by
water with both England and Harfleur, which was to become his headquarters. The town surrendered on 4 September after a siege of only two weeks,
but it involved great loss of life – which he had hoped to avoid. He had hoped
to win over the French population and keep some of them in their former
positions, but the French chroniclers speak of a mass exodus of refugees to
Brittany and other parts of France. It is impossible, however, to estimate the
real extent of that migration.

Leaving Caen on 1 October, he moved forward with remarkable speed.
The Duke of Brittany, eager to support the successful side, appeared at
Alençon on 22 October, and signed a further non-aggression treaty, which
seemed to secure Henry's western flank for him. Elsewhere there was likewise
little or no opposition. Possibly the carnage at Caen served to frighten some
into submission or maybe, as so many Norman lords had fallen at Agincourt,
there were very few strong adult Norman leaders left.

The port of Cherbourg was the last to be taken. It was somewhat remote,
new supplies could be brought in by sea, and also part of the besieging army
had to base itself and its heavy equipment on 'shifting sands', probably
dunes, to the west of the town. Humphrey, Duke of Gloucester, besieged
it for five months before the starving inhabitants eventually gave in at
Michaelmas in 1418.

Meanwhile, in February Henry himself had hurried back to Caen and,
having consolidated his administration there, turned his attention to Rouen
and the valley of the Seine, control of which was essential if shipping in
the Channel was to be rendered safe. The river itself was a considerable
obstacle, since it was wide, deep and swift-flowing, and an unknown
number of the French were defending the northern bank. Henry managed

brilliantly, organising a temporary pontoon bridge just downstream of Pont l'Arche, some 10 miles upstream of Rouen, and the army crossed without major incident.

By then, John the Fearless of Burgundy was in political ascendancy. He had taken Paris on 30 May 1418, and during bitter fighting John's opponent the Duke of Armagnac had been killed and the young Dauphin, the new leader of that party (which henceforth became known as the Dauphinists) only narrowly escaped with his life. Henry found that Rouen too was in the hands of the Burgundians and well prepared for a long siege. In addition, the *Clos de Galées*, the dockyard on the south side of the river which had served them so well since the 1290s, had been destroyed so that he could not make use of it.

Almost as soon as the siege began at the end of July, Henry's supplies of beer, wine, food, utensils and all kinds of munitions from England were interrupted by marauders stealing them from the flat-bottomed transports further down the river. However, a 400-strong band of gangsters operating near Quillebeuf was dealt with in August, and opposition from the castle which dominated the river at Caudebec was neutralised by agreement in September, thus clearing the passage up the river.[174] Famine and disease within the city became dire, and by Christmas the surviving merchants, whose interest lay in resuming their normal business as soon as possible, were in revolt, demanding that the political leaders should capitulate. The city officially surrendered on 19 January 1419. For the first time since 1204 Rouen, the centre of Norman administration, justice and finance, was in English hands. Once that had fallen, many smaller places followed quickly. According to a French source, which on this occasion was probably not exaggerating, thirty-five towns and castles surrendered rapidly, including Montivilliers (whose inhabitants had threatened Harfleur for the past two years) on 23 January, and the ports of Honfleur, Dieppe, Eu, and probably Fécamp, in February, all of which reduced the risk of attacks in the Channel.

The remarkable success of all his operations in France had depended on keeping control of shipping in the Channel, and for that, characteristically, he had made careful provision. Every year from 1417 to 1420 squadrons were specially organised for 'skimming', or safeguarding, the sea in the dangerous summer months with a force which consisted of one-third men at arms and two-thirds archers. From 1 March 1417 Sir Thomas Carew, based in Dartmouth, directed a group of eleven ships, with 950 men, during which time he seems to have captured five French ships and one Spanish vessel in the harbour of St Valéry. A similar group mustered at Winchelsea. In 1418, when there was fear of attack by a Castilian fleet, squadrons were kept at sea in the

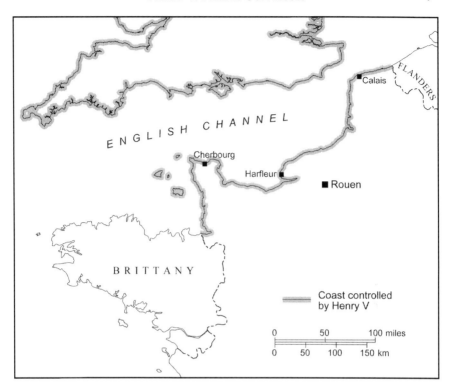

Coastlines controlled by Henry V in 1319–22, which enabled his control of piracy.

Channel and in the North Sea. Thomas Beaufort, Lord High Admiral, made arrangements to keep fifteen vessels and 1,000 men at sea that spring and summer, under Sir John Arundell. The following year Hugh Courtenay, Earl of Devon, took over, indenting 1,160 men in nine vessels for a shorter period, from 1 May to 1 August. In 1420 he maintained 1,500 men at sea with instructions to make war on all Genoese, Scots, Spaniards and Dauphinois. In the succeeding year, however, Courtenay was serving in France and there was apparently no need for special patrolling forces in the Channel. It is, incidentally, notable that the people employed in safe-guarding and manning these fleets included Richard Spicer and others, who were the very men who would have been tempted to turn once again to piracy or privateering if they had not been otherwise employed.[175]

Nonetheless, while Henry made careful precautions in the Channel, he could not control the activities of England's opponents elsewhere, notably the Scots in the North Sea, and the Castilians in the Bay of Biscay. In 1419 a Castilian fleet was still able to slip through undetected, to collect some 6,000 Scots from the east coast and carry them south, through the Channel and round the capes of Brittany, to deliver them to the Loire. By the end of October those mercenaries had joined the Dauphin's army near Tours.[176] Added to which, John of Brittany either could not, or would not, control the Breton privateers who began to make undeclared war on the English at sea, running between St Malo and Le Crotoy, the fortress at the mouth of the Somme which was still in Armagnac hands. Not much later, after Henry had died, they dared to raid the harbour up the river at Caen.[177]

With hindsight, the siege of Rouen can be seen as a watershed in Henry's fortunes. Until then, his progress had been relatively easy. After that, he pushed on east, towards Paris. But there he met with stronger resistance, while his hold on areas previously captured became weaker. Brigands made his supply line dangerous. Moreover, the longer his campaign continued, the government became increasingly reluctant to provide funds for his war.

In addition, both French parties were beginning to gain reinforcements from the Castilians and the Scots. By the spring of 1419 Scottish troops were already serving in the armies of the Dauphin. The English government interpreted the Castilian threat in its own way, and on 5 March 1419 the whole country was arrayed 'to be on the watch for …. a great armada of vessels of Spain [coming] shortly …. to burn and destroy the ships of [this] realm, and especially the king's ships, most of all the ships at Southampton and Portsmouth and invade the realm….'. In both 1418 and 1419, Richard Spicer, the potential pirate, was prominent among those involved in the preparations for defence in Southampton.[178]

In France, Henry's military resources were too thinly spread, and it was essential to negotiate peace, or at least a truce. Negotiations were difficult and tortuous, because they were essentially tripartite, and because Henry's demands were well in excess of what the French were prepared to concede. Deep mistrust existed on all sides. Then, on 10 September 1419, a catastrophic event played into Henry's hands. John the Fearless of Burgundy was assassinated as he walked across the bridge over the River Yonne at Montereau, 50 miles south-east of Paris, to a meeting with the Dauphinists. This seriously weakened the French bargaining position.

In those changed circumstances, terms for the peace were agreed with Duke Philip, the son of John the Fearless, on 2 December 1419. Henry was to marry Katharine, daughter of Charles VI (a union which had been discussed for some years) without any dowry at all, and their children were to succeed to the throne of France. On Charles' death which, since he was 53, infirm and had suffered bouts of insanity for over thirty years, could with good reason be anticipated before Henry's, the crown of France was to pass to Henry and his heirs, for ever. These provisions were ratified in the Treaty of Troyes on 21 May 1420 by Henry, the French queen (in the place of Charles VI) and Duke Philip of Burgundy.

The merchants of Paris and Rouen were particularly pleased that the Seine, their commercial life-line, was now safely open for the first time since Henry began his war. The terms were not, however, universally welcome, and ominously Charles, the young Dauphin, leader of the 'other' French party, was not included in the discussions or the treaty.[179]

Henry and Katharine were married at Troyes on 2 June 1420. He continued to campaign locally against the Dauphin's supporters and, having celebrated Christmas with their families in Paris, the royal pair crossed to England in January 1421. However, during their absence, Henry's impetuous brother Thomas, Duke of Clarence, was killed taking part in an ill-advised, ill-planned skirmish against a large Franco-Scottish force on 22 March, at Baugé, almost as far south as the Loire. The news of an English defeat and the death of a royal duke together with several other important leaders was a very damaging blow to English confidence and prestige.

By the time Henry returned to France in June 1421, he found things were going against him. The Duke of Brittany had changed sides and was now supporting the Dauphinists, and the terms of the Treaty of Troyes were not universally accepted by the people. Furthermore, supplies for his army were short and morale was low. But he was still determined to set siege to Meaux, a major fortified town some 30 miles east of Paris, which was occupied by the Dauphinists with the support of the Scots. Seven months of bad winter weather, from October to May, took a heavy toll in sickness and disease, and soon Henry personally had to admit to the first signs of sickness. He died on 31 August 1422.

He left a world shocked by the news of his death, a large English settlement in Lower Normandy and conditions in the Channel more peaceful than they had ever been in the last two centuries. The question was how long these would last without his outstanding leadership.

# II

# Henry VI: Resurgence of Piracy

he unusually peaceful conditions in the Channel left
by Henry V were the result of English control of both
shores, combined with the essential support of the Count
of Flanders (otherwise known as the Duke of Burgundy)
and a series of truces made with the other countries whose
merchants used the waterway. Englishmen continued to be restrained from
piracy and privateering by the 1414 Statute of Truces. In addition, any
potential offenders were busily occupied ferrying soldiers, officers of the
government, the new settlers and all their respective supporters and equipment across to Normandy, and were paid for doing so.

In the background, however, the premature and unexpected death of
Henry V brought to light other circumstances which were both complex
and threatening. The so-called 'dual kingdom' was ruled by one king, but
nonetheless consisted of two distinct countries. Behind the veil of Henry's
'permanent' settlement of Englishmen in Normandy, each of the two
countries, England and Normandy, still had its own government, its own
laws, its own customs, and its own language. Henry's failure to include the
Armagnacs in the Treaty of Troyes meant that he bequeathed an ongoing
war being fought against them on several different fronts, but mostly in the
general area round Paris. In England, there was mounting opposition to
this continuing war. Overall, the political portents for longer-term stability
were not good.

Henry's heir was the nine-month-old Henry VI (1422–61), born to Catherine at Windsor the previous December. A long regency was inevitable and the responsibility for continuity of government lay with the remaining members of the royal family, who were now reduced to four, Henry V's two youngest brothers and two Beaufort step-uncles (see below). Almost immediately it became clear that it had been Henry V's personal leadership and charisma which had provided the cement to give the family its former, remarkable, cohesion. Once that leadership had gone, cracks quickly appeared. The two remaining brothers were very different characters. John, Duke of Bedford was cast in the same mould as Henry himself, to whom he had already served as a trusted lieutenant. He was to prove wise, diplomatic, capable, energetic, and dedicated to the cause of England. Humphrey, Duke of Gloucester was, in contrast, much less reliable. His one military success had been conducting the conquest of the Cherbourg peninsula in 1418. Otherwise he lacked discretion and diplomacy, and was emphatically not a team player. He evidently had not been, and would not in future be, entrusted with important responsibility by other members of the family and nobility, which was a constant source of grievance to him. Apparently feeling cheated of opportunities to achieve military honour and glory, he was to prove himself irresponsible and self-seeking, an irritant and, increasingly, a danger to national and international stability.[180]

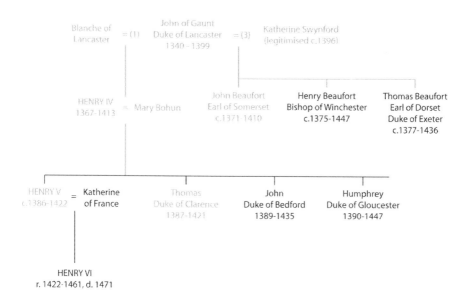

Family surviving into the reign of Henry VI.

Henry V's wills, codicils and the other verbal directions he gave when he knew he was dying did not cover all eventualities, and were open to different interpretations. They opened the door to controversy. Henry had stipulated that Duke Humphrey should have the wardship of the infant king, but when the duke chose to assume that included running the country he found, to his intense frustration, that he was opposed by the council led by Henry Beaufort and his brother Thomas, and that all his activities were to be scrutinised by parliament.[181] This initiated a series of fierce disputes between him and the restraining arm of his step-uncle, a bitter feud which continued to dominate English politics until they both died in 1447.

In France, Charles VI died fifty-one days after Henry V and, ignoring the Treaty of Troyes, his 19-year-old son, the Dauphin Charles, immediately claimed the throne. But that claim was supported by little substance: Charles had no financial resources, no body of loyal nobility and no centralised army. Much more important at that time, by mid-November John, Duke of Bedford, had emerged as the English regent of France.

Bedford was well aware that to maintain peaceful conditions in the Channel, which implied preventing a resurgence of piracy, it was essential to remain on good terms with Burgundy and, if possible, with Brittany. After some six months' negotiation he achieved a triple alliance which bore fruit on 17 April 1423 in the defensive and offensive Treaty of Amiens, signed by himself, by Duke Philip of Burgundy and by Arthur of Richemont, brother of the Duke of Brittany. It was cemented by the marriages of Bedford to Anne, a sister of Philip of Burgundy (on 14 June), and of Arthur de Richemont to another sister, Margaret. The treaty recognised the French, the Dauphin's party, as the common enemy.[182]

He continued fighting to mop up remaining pockets of opposition on the Channel coast. For instance, he captured Le Crotoy, now a sleepy silt-bound fishing village but then one of the more important of the Channel ports, with an impressive fortress guarding the mouth of the Somme. Until then, lying too far from Flanders for Burgundy to reach it from the north, and too far north for the English to reach it from the Seine, it had remained in Armagnac hands, and had proved a useful base for Breton pirates. On 17 August 1424, Bedford also inflicted a massive defeat on the Dauphin's much larger, but badly organised, force of French and Scots at Verneuil, some 60 miles west of Paris. As a result the Dauphin went into retreat, leaving the French temporarily leaderless, and the slaughtered Scots were never replaced, showing that Scottish support for France was dwindling.

However, two developments already threatened to destabilise Bedford's triple entente. In or about January 1423 Humphrey, Duke of Gloucester, had married Jacqueline of Hainault, and together they set out to recover Hainault from her estranged first husband, John of Brabant, and Holland and Zeeland from her uncle, John of Bavaria. Having landed with an army at Calais, their campaign was short and ended in fiasco. Nonetheless, both their objectives were bound to stir up antagonism on the part of the Duke of Burgundy. Secondly, the Bretons, as ever, were shifty allies, and despite the encouraging result at Verneuil, Arthur of Richemont reneged on the Treaty of Amiens and changed sides. He and his brother then proceeded to take control of the Dauphin's side of the war, which aimed to expel the English! In spite of these checks, and continuing piracy by the Bretons, for six years Bedford was able to maintain the areas conquered by Henry V, and even to extend his land down to the Loire.[183]

Then, on 3 November 1428 the military tide turned. The English forces suffered their first serious defeat. The Earl of Salisbury, their leader, was killed by a gunshot during the siege of Orleans and, following that, they failed to take the town. Soon afterwards, Jeanne d'Arc intervened. Her story is well known, but in short, she led the French troops to rapid victory over the English in a series of battles, and ensured that the Dauphin was crowned King of France at Reims on 17 July 1429. Although she herself was captured by the Burgundians in May 1430 and tried and burnt at the stake by the English in Rouen on 30 May 1431, she had restored French morale, and became a martyr. The loss of Salisbury, failure of their siege of Orleans, and the contributions of Jeanne d'Arc combined to seriously weaken the English position in France, and in December 1431 the Duke of Burgundy signed a six-year truce with Charles VII, further weakening his link with England.[184]

For the English, further adversity followed quickly. On 13 November 1432 Anne, wife of the Duke of Bedford, died in an epidemic in Paris, aged only 28. Not only a grievous personal loss to Bedford, she had also provided a positive political link with Philip of Burgundy, her brother. Bedford remarried five months later, into a family deeply distrusted by Philip, who was thus further alienated. In addition, the soldiers in the garrison at Calais mutinied for lack of pay. Still, the English leaders, Bedford, Gloucester and Henry Beaufort, failed to agree on a strategy for prosecuting the war in France.

The years 1435–36 saw multiple crises for the English, with serious implications for their control of the Channel. In the spring of 1435 most of the counties along the south coast were on the alert. The Isle of Wight was living in fear of a French invasion. In the summer that year Philip of Burgundy convened the equivalent of a peace conference at Arras, but the English failed to come to an agreement with the French. One week after that diplomatic failure, Bedford died in Rouen, in September 1435, and only a week later, Burgundy officially concluded peace with France, which left the English without allies.

In September 1435, Dieppe was lost to the French. Harfleur and the surrounding area followed in November. In January 1436 the English were faced with a popular uprising in Normandy. At Calais, the woollen exports piled up, having been subjected to a Flemish embargo. In July, a Burgundian siege of Calais failed only because of dissent within their own ranks.[185]

Against that background the young king Henry grew up, and it must have been increasingly obvious that he was the antithesis of his father. His interests and talents lay in directions very different from military matters or governmental control. He was a gentle, intelligent, peace-loving individual, who is now celebrated for founding and successfully influencing the early development of Eton College at Windsor and King's College, Cambridge. But, compassionate and caring, he was indiscriminately generous with his favours and lacked the ability to select good officers, advisors and confidants. He lacked political acumen. In short, he did not possess the credentials necessary for strong leadership in the fifteenth century.

In addition, during his adolescence Henry was caught between two bitterly opposed, argumentative uncles, each of whom sought to impose his own opinions on him. Not only that, he must also have witnessed, as a powerless spectator, the failures, military and diplomatic, of his representatives in France. How these experiences affected him is impossible to estimate, but it did not bode well for the peace which he so strongly favoured. In the next few years Henry supported moves towards a peaceful settlement with France, but that was a long time in coming. A commercial agreement was reached with Burgundy in 1439, but disagreements among the English participants postponed a peace agreement until 1444. In 1445 the king married Margaret of Anjou, a strong and, as it turned out, fiery character who vehemently refused to negotiate with anybody who opposed her husband, so did nothing to promote peace or conciliation. The couple became increasingly unpopular, and the government in England became increasingly divided and corrupt.

In France, meanwhile, Charles VII had been gathering strength, and on 31 July 1449 he seized his opportunity and declared war. His reconquest of Normandy took only thirteen months. It was the story of Henry V's conquest in reverse, and in mirror-image. Rouen, Caen, and Harfleur fell in quick succession and, last of all, Cherbourg capitulated on 12 August 1450. Once again, the Channel had become an international frontier.

The French then turned to Gascony, and on 17 July 1453 as the final *coup* they took Bordeaux, thus making it French for the first time in its history. The loss of that important, last, area of Aquitaine, which had been held in close economic and political association by England for the past three centuries, signalled the end of this chapter of history. It was also all too much for the sensitive Henry VI, who slipped into a coma that summer and remained unconscious for the following seventeen months.

During these twenty-four years in which the English were being forced to retreat, stage by stage, from Normandy, the English government was also becoming progressively weak at home. The national exchequer became increasingly impoverished, while at the same time the Church and some of the magnates were storing up massive fortunes for themselves. Defence of the coastline against raiders or invaders became a pressing issue, with mounting fear not only in the coastal communities themselves but also in government. But although the government was well aware of the need, no funds were available for defence. Law and order broke down, with corruption at all levels. This was the background, and the reason for, another intense period of uncontrolled piracy, which lasted until well after 1453.

This period was not only longer than others which have been discussed in this book, it was also more complex, as men found various devious ways to exploit situations and the law. The records are more complicated than ever before, and are therefore more difficult to interpret or to explain.

Enemy ships were legitimate prize so we are not concerned with them, but lengthy legal arguments were spun out concerning ships and cargoes of friendly countries. The statute of 1414 remained in force until 1435, although the merchants tried to get it repealed three times before that. They were chafing, complaining that it damaged English commerce. While their own hands were tied by it, foreign pirates were making off with English ships with impunity, without the possibility of retaliating with letters of marque.

In the meantime, while the English government resisted attempts to repeal the 1414 statute, they did take a rather different step in an attempt to regulate piracy. In 1426 a proclamation went out that when goods which had been captured at sea were brought into the ports, they were not to be disposed of until either the king's council, or the chancellor, or the admiral or his deputy, had decided whether they belonged to friends or enemies. This was probably an attempt to simplify procedures. But in effect, it placed responsibility in the hands of a local official, the admiral's deputy, giving excellent opportunities to the unscrupulous. The only recourse for wronged merchants was to complain to the chancellor, which is where we pick up their stories.[186]

During the first seven years of the new reign, however, as long as John, Duke of Bedford, still had control of the important continental ports, life in the Channel remained relatively quiet. But even then, some members of the families who had been well known for piracy in the time of Henry IV were already back, engaged in their old trade. And their methods were already remarkably involved and devious.

John Hawley III of Dartmouth was the only son of the famous John Hawley. Although he had started out assisting his father in the last few years of his life and carried on with piracy until 1413, no major complaints were made about his activities during the reign of Henry V. He kept relatively quiet. But in 1427 he showed up again, at sea in the Bay of Biscay. Near the harbour of Oleron, he captured a ship and her cargo valued at £220 which belonged to John Lovell, a merchant of Dundee. When a commission was issued for his own arrest, he went to Lovell and bargained with him, exonerating himself but suggesting that Lovell should obtain three more commissions in which he would accuse forty other pirates who had been, in fact, Hawley's accomplices. Hawley also agreed, using his position as a man of influence, to approach these men, to collect the money, with which he would make good all Lovell's losses. Equipped with the new commissions, Hawley collected the money from his one-time associates but then departed with it, ensuring that none of it reached Lovell. To make matters worse for the hapless Lovell, he was left in a position from which he could make no further claims for damages in this case. Hawley, on the other hand, was in an advantageous position: he had established his innocence in that particular case. He carried on in public service. In 1430, he was appointed a commissioner to arrest more pirates, and in 1436 he was a commissioner for array in Devonshire, intended to round up men and armaments for the defence of the realm, although as he died that May, he is unlikely to have taken that up.[187]

John Mixtow of Fowey, similarly from an old-established pirate family, appears in September 1430, in a very peculiar case involving an admiral's deputy. John Caryewe, master of the *Mary of Le Conquet*, who was sailing with a couple of other Breton vessels, had safely delivered a load of salt to Penzance. Soon after he had left for home with a quantity of cloth, he was captured 'in warlike manner' by a swarm of pirates from Marazion and other small local ports, contrary to the truce in force between England and Brittany. At that point John Mixtow and Harry Nanskaseke of Truro appeared on the scene, and persuaded the admiral's deputy, John Moure, to arrest the ship, invoking letters of marque which had been granted by the Duke of Brittany to Nanskaseke's father nineteen years previously. Using that as their excuse, they took possession of both the Breton ships and the cargo of cloth. We hear of that case because John Caryewe, complaining of great inconvenience, requested the chancellor to direct the Sheriff of Cornwall to ensure safe trading conditions for the Bretons. He also demanded that the chancellor should issue a writ of *subpoena* to John Moure, as well as Mixtow and Nanskaseke, to be examined in respect of the letters of marque they quoted. Unfortunately, there is no record of the outcome of this case but, more importantly, it is evidence that this official was very prepared to enter into collusion with the pirates.[188]

Mixtow was to be heard of again, slightly later. In July 1433 he was leader of a gang said to number 200, sailing in the great ship the *Edward* and a supporting balinger off Cape St Vincent, southern Portugal. 'Armed and arrayed for war', they captured a Genoese caravel (also described as a carrack), laden with woad, olive oil and *lye* destined for the port of Sandwich and eventually, no doubt, for London. The crew had offered no resistance. None the less, Mixtow abandoned them, destitute, on the coast of Portugal, wrongly accusing them of being 'Saracens'. Taken back to Fowey, her cargo was divided among the captors and was then distributed around Cornwall, Devon, Somerset and Wiltshire. Mixtow refused to accept the merchants' evidence of identification, the 'marks, charters and cockets' on their goods, no doubt playing for time, during which the goods could be further dispersed.[189]

Hawley and Mixtow were the forerunners of a new class of pirates, new men, who surfaced in the records from 1430 onwards (and it is remarkable that their appearance coincided exactly with the initial downturn of events in France). These were men who had never been employed by the Crown, as Eustace and John Crabbe had been. Nor were they, with one very short-term exception, sanctioned by the Crown as privateers, like the great John Hawley. They were not even, like the Alards or, again, John Hawley, leaders in society who would have ploughed some of their profits back into their communities. In contrast, they showed little or no allegiance to their roots. They were, to put it simply, full-time professional plunderers, whose sole objective was personal profit. The majority came from Devon and Cornwall, where they were well supported by men in high positions who in their turn stood to gain from their investment in the ships and the necessary victuals. But there were also others, from further east, who were playing the same game. Overall, these men were numerous, and particularly since their cases were very complex, it is only possible here to offer an insight into what was happening through the activities of a small representative sample.

They were as mobile as any of their forerunners, appearing wherever the prizes appealed. In the years up to 1436 their principal targets were the Breton ships sailing up the southern side of the Channel to Rouen and Dieppe, bringing the basic necessities to the English occupants of Normandy, and also to the Channel Islands. These amounted principally to food and

wine from La Rochelle, salt from the Bay, and linen cloth and cords from
Brittany, together with some commodities which had evidently come from
further south, such as iron, and resin for caulking their vessels. The individual claims for compensation for goods lost to them were noticeably small
in comparison to those of the previous century, which reflected the size of
the ships they were using. They were relatively small barges and balingers,
which had the advantage over the great long-distance ocean-going Italian
ships, in that they were able to work out from, and carry their prizes into,
the smaller harbours like Penzance and Teignmouth. But at the same time
they were apparently able to work long distances. They appeared in the Bay
of Biscay, and they also sold their goods at places all along the coast between
Cornwall and Portsmouth, including the Isle of Wight, which seems to have
been an important emporium, centred on Newport.

Some details illustrate how they received back-up support, and the nature
of the problems this caused. In the spring of 1432 two Breton merchants
complained specifically 'to show the chancellor how well protected the
wrong-doers on the sea-coasts of Devonshire were'. They said that those
captors were bribing the admiral's deputy to empanel juries made up for
the most part of their own relatives and friends, together with the victuallers and owners of the ship concerned. Those juries could be relied upon to
give false verdicts, for example stating that goods which had actually been
stolen from the king's friends had belonged instead to the king's enemies.
And, in return for a bribe of half the goods, the deputy could be relied
on to enrol that verdict, which rendered the king's commission ineffective.
The Bretons emphasised that as long as the deputy was in league with the
pirates, he was their guarantee that matters would be settled in their favour.
Importantly, a second commission dealing with the same event exposed
a complaint of extortion against John Baron, a merchant of Exeter, who
was one of the members of that commission. The results of an inquiry
into this case, which were enrolled four years later, revealed the extent of
Baron's extortion. In this case he had helped himself to a pipe of bastard
wine which belonged to the Bretons. As well as that, on the pretext of
the commission, he had taken one or two packs of cloth from every man
in the neighbourhood to whom he bore ill will. He had the stamp of an
exceptionally disagreeable and grasping individual. The upshot was that
nobody dared trade without first paying him a cut. The king thus lost his
customs and many people were wronged. In addition, it has emerged from
more recent research that Baron had a history of warrants out for his arrest.
These included one for stealing a ship which was under safe conduct direct
from a Breton harbour, possibly the *St Nunne,* which is described below.[190]

William Kydd was one of this new class of pirate. He rose from documentary obscurity in 1430 and subsequently flourished, travelling far and wide without much reference to his port of origin, Exmouth, at least before 1453. In October 1430 he was master of a balinger, *La Trinité of Exmouth*, which he had packed with other malefactors. They seized a ship as it was nearing Guernsey from Brittany with a cargo of food. The terms of the subsequent commission to the sheriff of Devon and others make it clear that the authorities were aware that the owners and victuallers of the ship were supporting the pirates because in the last resort, their goods and chattels were to be arrested. But, unfortunately for those merchants of Guernsey and for numerous others, this was a period when innumerable commissions were issued and very few indeed were acted upon. In other words, there was already unlimited immunity for the pirates.[191]

The following year, Kydd was among a group who, sailing with a flotilla of four barges 'armed and arraigned in the manner of war', captured four food ships on their way towards Rouen, took them back to Dartmouth, Fowey and Kingsbridge (on the Salcombe estuary) and sold the goods locally. Similar piracy continued intensively, and built up until, on 31 March 1436, Kydd led the large group of pirates who descended in a flotilla of eight barges and balingers on the harbour of St Paul de Lyon, south-east of Roscoff, and carried off the *Saint Nunne*, a ship sheltering in that harbour while waiting for a favourable wind to cross to England. They escorted that ship back to Plymouth, where she still lay in October six months later, together with goods worth 100*l* which included white wine of La Rochelle, two types of cloth, and 24 flychys of bacon which belonged to Thomas Horewood of Wells.[192]

In 1435, in order to respond to the crisis which was rapidly unfolding on the opposite shore of the Channel, the government had an acute need for ships. Some men concerned must have looked back regretfully to the time of Henry V, when royal or loyal hired vessels would have been used to cruise the Channel through the long summer season for the combined purposes of guarding against French ships leaving port, protecting English commerce and, if necessary, defending the south coast of England. But that was no longer an option. Even before Henry V died, those ships had become redundant and had started to decay. Back in 1423–24, the authorities, finding they were further decayed and maintenance would have been unjustifiable, and especially since there was then no pressing need for them, had sold off the ships which remained.[193]

Therefore, when crisis was looming in February 1436 the government took the only course open to it, and issued short-term (four-month) licences to certain individual shipowners to equip certain named ships at their own expense 'with a master, mariners, men at arms, archers, and other hibiliments of war, and victuals, to resist the king's enemies on the sea'. They were not to be paid, but all captured goods were to belong to the captors, except for the certain 'share' reserved for the admiral. Of the greatest significance, a proviso was included to exonerate those who made most of this piracy possible. It was stated that if any offence should be committed against the king's friends, the offender alone should answer for it: no responsibility was to fall on the owner or the victualler of the ship.

These commissions were mostly issued to men of east coast ports, but included one in the south-west, Thomas Gylle of Dartmouth. He was another of those who first appears in the records after 1430, although he was notable as a shipowner and merchant of some substance. He was six times MP for the town between 1433 and 1455, and one of the collectors of customs in Exeter and Dartmouth in 1439 and in 1453. Between 1431 and 1435 he had frequently served on commissions to arrest men, ships and goods brought into West Country ports. Now, in 1436, he was licensed to equip and arm two of his ships, l'Antony and Le Katerine, both of Dartmouth, together with two supporting balingers or barges. For this short time, at least, he was a fully accredited privateer. [194]

Gylle was heard of again in January 1440, in less dignified circumstances. His ship the Christopher of Dartmouth, 320 tons, was sailing home north to Dartmouth when, already in the lee of Start Point, she turned and, with full sail, a favourable wind and three well-harnessed men in the topcastle, rammed a much smaller ship which had been following some 3 miles behind her. She 'sliced in two' the George of Welles, 120 tons, and sank her. In his complaint to the chancellor, the owner, an Englishman born at Lancaster but then living in Drogheda, Ireland, prayed consideration for his great poverty, loss and delays and he took the opportunity to point out that while he was ignorant of Dartmouth, Gylle had 'great authority and power in that district'.[95]

Snapshots of the life of Hankyn Seelander illustrate the mobility, in more than one respect, of one of this new class of pirates. Both his address and even his name seem to have been readily adjustable. He is described variously as being of either Falmouth or Fowey, and it is also evident that he had valuable connections on the Isle of Wight.

In December 1433, as Hanquin Seland, he was accused of taking certain goods at sea from a ship of Bayonne. In 1439, a group of pirates in a balinger belonging to John Selander captured a Breton ship, the Saint Fiacre, sailing towards La Rochelle laden with goods belonging to John Loven. After Loven's letters of safe conduct had been thrown overboard, he was robbed of both the ship and the cargo. In the early summer of 1441 one Hankyn Hood, presumably the same man, was sailing as master of the *Marie* with John Fresshow of Falmouth, a frequent companion, somewhere south of Brittany. In company with several other Cornish vessels they captured a ship of Vannes, southern Brittany, which they took to sell her cargo in one of the ports in the Gironde.

And so he went on, being especially active and confident in 1443–44. Around midsummer 1443 Alphonso Mendes, a merchant of Portugal, sailing in a ship of Tavira (on the south coast of Portugal) lost certain goods, principally fruit and bastard wine, to pirates who were named as John Selander and Hankyn Loo, both of Fowey. Unfortunately the location of this piracy was not disclosed, but one wonders whether these two names stood for one and the same man. That September, he had stolen wine and other merchandise from another Breton ship, of which John Rous was master.

On the Sunday before Christmas 1443, a group of pirates in a barge named *Le Palmer of Fowey* owned by Hankyn Selander captured another English ship, *Le Mighell of Dartmouth*, as she was preparing to enter Plymouth harbour at the end of her voyage from Brittany. She was carrying 21 tuns of wine and 17 pieces of linen cloth for a joint group of English merchants from the Plymouth area operating in partnership, it seems, with two named men from Le Conquet, Brittany. The pirates diverted the ship with its cargo to Newport, Isle of Wight, where they 'did their will therof'. Although the goods may already have been sold, the commission which followed included the usual empty, unrealistic threat. He was to return the ship and the goods – or be committed to prison.[196]

Clays Stephen of Portsmouth was another similar individual. In the autumn of 1445 he joined Robert Wenyngton of Dartmouth and others who came from Kingswear, and captured a ship which had been sent by the Queen of France to bring a consignment of wine, iron and other merchandise to England. In spite of the ship having letters of safe conduct from the king and there being a truce between England and France, they brought it into Fowey. They disposed of the goods easily, and the merchants were severely beaten up and some were killed.

In about March 1448 Clays Stephen had travelled further in the opposite direction and was in the Thames estuary, where he was joined by William Kydd, who had come from even further west. They combined with others to attack a ship bringing goods for some London merchants from Arnemuiden near Middleburg in Zeeland to Queenborough near Sheerness. They took that ship first to Portsmouth and then disposed of the goods on the Isle of Wight.

That summer Clays Stephen, one of two pirates said to be staying at Sandwich, was busy in a flotilla out at sea 'between Dover and Calais', which encountered a small convoy on its way from La Rochelle to Sluys. He was the master of a balinger which took a similar ship, the *Saint Piere de Lavyon*, and relieved it of 39 tuns of wine belonging to a merchant of La Rochelle. At the same time another merchant lost 27 tuns of white wine from a second ship, the *Noel de Arninton*.

In the autumn of 1450 another small flotilla of English pirates captured a hulk (an old-fashioned term for a vessel which was probably a successor of the cog) named the *St George of Bruges*, which belonged to a group of merchants of that city and was on voyage home from Portugal. Clays Stephen was master of one of the pirate ships, *Le Carvell of Portsmouth*: others came from Southampton and Winchelsea.[197]

These are just a few examples of the culture of concentrated piracy which existed in the 1430s and 1440s. Numerous men were involved, and between Portugal and the North Sea no mariner can have felt safe from them.

In 1449 England was in a high state of uncertainty and insecurity, with the threat of French raids renewed because France had control of the opposing Channel ports. Then there was also a stream of refugees arriving from Normandy, many of them destitute, retreating after the collapse of Henry V's 'permanent' settlement. In April, the government appointed three senior officers to 'keep the seas', to cruise the Channel looking for trouble. Those officers included Robert Wenyngton of Dartmouth, where he had already served as bailiff in 1446 and as mayor two years later. A month after his appointment the government found itself with somewhat more than it had bargained for, the largest prize of the century.

On 23 May, when Wenyngton was cruising with his 'fellowship' in a small flotilla of small vessels, in the general area of mid-Channel between Guernsey and Portland, he came upon the entire Bay fleet, some 110 larger vessels, which were carrying to Flanders and the Baltic not only salt but also some more valuable commodities, cloth and wine. Since Wenyngton had somehow become separated from the other two senior officers, one wonders if this encounter was entirely accidental. However, in a show of bravado, and with the advantage of a following wind, after a short altercation in which their admiral rebuffed his challenge, rather than risk the damage which might result from a mid-Channel gunfight, the whole fleet surrendered to him and was ushered into Southampton Water. Dutch and Flemish ships were soon released, but enormous bills were presented to the English government by the Hanse on behalf of its merchants.[198]

In the penultimate month of our period, November 1453, Thomas Gylle of Dartmouth, merchant of substance who had a long history of apparent probity as an officer of the Crown, and who was the controller of customs in Exmouth that year seems, at last, to have been drawn into the web of corruption. He was working in collusion with William Kydd, the long-established pirate, in connection with a captured ship belonging to the Bishop of St Andrews which they brought into Exmouth. The ensuing documents stand out as being extraordinarily complicated and contorted, even by the standards of this period. Suffice it to say that they involved impersonation of the bishop's brother; obtaining a commission under false pretences; impounding another ship in Scotland by way of reprisal; death-threats to officers of the Crown who approached the ship when in Sandwich; and the eventual escape of the ship, after her name had been changed, for the second time, to the *Antony of Dartmouth*. By March 1456 she was carrying thirty pilgrims on their way south to the shrine of St James at Compostela in Galicia.[199]

All this time, piracy flourished, not only because of the usual reasons. The Crown was indeed weak, and deep-seated dynastic power struggles were taking place between excessively rich magnates. Law and order had certainly broken down in all levels of society. And, with the progressive loss of Normandy, the Channel became, once again, a dangerous frontier zone. In addition, and pervading all that, was corruption which reflected the under-lying loss of the checks and balances which had previously been provided by the feudal system.

The degree of corruption was such that administrators in the ports, wealthy landowners inland and high-level legal officers were all involved. Widespread plunder was being carried out by the men of the sea with the strong support, encouragement and participation of the whole establishment, particularly in Cornwall and Devon.

By way of an epilogue, it is a nice irony that when, after several years of civil war and political manoeuvring, the time came, on 26 June 1460, for the Earls of Warwick and Salisbury to escort the Duke of York and his teenage son Edward across the Channel from Calais to Sandwich, they did so in a ship recently stolen from the French. Within nine more tumultuous months Edward had taken over the throne as Edward IV.[200]

# 12

# Then and Now

n the early years of the twenty-first century, some 650 years after the medieval pirates were disrupting trade in the English Channel, pirates are active, in different ways, in several areas of the world. From 2007 until at least 2012, international attention has been focussed on an intense spate of piracy taking place off Somalia, East Africa. How different are these present-day pirates from their medieval predecessors? Who was involved then, and who is involved now? And how widely do the effects of piracy extend in each period, both commercially and politically?

In both these periods we see piracy being carried out by coastal communities, many of which have poor hinterlands and look to the sea for their living, originally depending entirely on fishing. In stark contrast to that modest existence, both communities also lie close to some of the busiest, richest shipping lanes of their day. In both places, the initial impetus for piracy seems to have come from the men of the coast themselves rather than from outside individuals or organisations, although an important difference is that in the medieval period the men came from organised port communities accustomed to trade, while the Somali communities have no commercial base. The discovery of $US 153,000 in cash on the body of a Somali pirate, who had drowned with four others when their skiff was wrecked returning home from what up till then had been a successful piratical expedition, strongly suggests that the share system operational in medieval times operates today in Somalia.[201] One small technological detail has persisted: in mounting their attacks, the pirates of today use metal grappling irons and hooks to maintain contact with their prey, much in the manner of their medieval predecessors. It also seems that on most occasions in both periods considerable care has been taken not to destroy either seaworthy ships or their cargoes, all of which are considered too valuable for wanton destruction.

In neither period is piracy static: it moves about over time and space, as opportunity presents itself. In medieval England it waxed and waned, generally becoming more intense as the control of affairs exercised by the government of the day, in effect the king, became weak. In Somalia it follows a similar pattern, the current spate of piracy beginning when effective government collapsed in 1991, and intensifying after 2005 when political conditions deteriorated still further. In England, during the two-and-a-half centuries considered here, the focus moved from one end of the Channel to the other, fluctuating from east to west. In Somalia what began near the coast, concentrating on the Gulf of Aden, soon spread out across the Indian Ocean. In other words, piracy crops up wherever, whenever, opportunity offers. There, however, similarity between the two periods ends.

Medieval ships were wooden, powered only by sail or oars. As far as possible they sailed close to land, because of the need to rely on landmarks for navigation, and in order to make frequent visits to harbours to collect water and other provisions. It was also necessary to be near port in case of storms. Even crossing the Channel was a perilous, although essential, undertaking. There was no guarantee that favourable winds would allow ship-masters to set out when they or their political leaders proposed. Or that, having set forth, they would reach their intended destination. Much was unpredictable, in the lap of the gods.

In contrast, modern seafaring appears, on the surface at least, infinitely more dependable. Nearly all modern ships are made of steel, with engines powered by heavy fuel oil or diesel. They use GPS, the space-based navigational system which gives their position and time in any part of the earth in all weathers, and they communicate with other ships or with land bases by satellite telephone. Because of this combination, vast modern ships are able to travel long distances, going anywhere in almost all weathers, except under the most extreme conditions. On that basis, it might be thought that modern man, with his technical resources and his huge specialised ships, could with confidence take almost unlimited cargoes anywhere across the oceans. But that would be reckoning without the intervention of the pirates.

The enormous increase in the size of cargo vessels, from the cogs on the Bordeaux route in the early fourteenth century, whose average capacity was less than 100 tons, to the smaller cargo ships of today with a capacity of 10,000 tonnes and the large tankers around 300,000, is very obvious. But changes in the design of the ships and the nature of their cargoes are more significant when it comes to facing pirates.

Medieval cogs had evolved to carry large cargoes. Because of that, they were tall vessels. Their sides rose high above the water level, and therefore they also provided a challenge, at least a deterrent, to boarding parties (see the cover illustration). With their castles rising even higher, those commercial vessels which doubled up as warships have well been described as 'floating fortresses'.[202] Very seldom did a lower-sided galley, although faster and easier to manoeuvre, successfully capture a cog. The expression 'taken by force of arms', which was frequently used when a medieval ship was captured, probably implied simply that the one with lower freeboard had submitted without a contest to a taller one.

Now, however, designs have moved on – or some might say backwards – in terms of self-defence. Vessels have become specialised, and the two functions neatly combined in medieval cogs have become separated, and ultimately further diversified. During the last 200 years, cargo ships have lost their element of self-defence. Commercial developments have given rise to specialised vessels which include oil tankers and container ships, both of which have particularly low freeboard, low sides designed for easy loading. Unfortunately, that low freeboard is also a gift playing into the hands of pirates intent on boarding, no matter the overall size of the ship. On the other hand, the development of fighting navies has given rise to frigates, submarines and aircraft carriers, examples designed to cope with the three principle spheres of action.

Against that background, present-day pirates operate in amazingly small craft. They use skiffs, tiny open boats powered by small petrol or diesel motors whose value lies in very high speed and easy manoeuvrability. The problem of frequent refuelling and limited range is overcome by working out from much larger 'mother ships', usually captured previously as pirate prizes, which carry the necessary supplies of fuel and other supplies, thus enabling the Somalis to range many hundreds of miles across the Indian Ocean.

Changes in both the nature of the cargoes and in the attitude to the value of human life have radically altered the purpose and culture of piracy. Medieval cargoes always consisted of a variety of different commodities. Anything which could be fitted in was carried. Some of the captured wine, the food-stuffs and other goods were doubtless useful in the home port of the pirates or its surrounding area. The rest, including materials for the cloth industry and, later, the consignments of iron, would have been sent on, along the accustomed trade routes, and the proceeds would have helped to maintain the ships and port facilities. The pirates and their wider communities thus had a direct interest in at least some of the goods they captured, and could make good commercial use of the rest. Since the cargoes were the property of a number of different merchants (or on certain occasions were carried by them on behalf of the king), when they were stolen the merchants' sole purpose was to retrieve their ships and their goods (often, apparently, a vain hope), or at least recover their value. At the same time, when life was uncertain and life expectancy was anyway short, only those relatively few captives who had commercial value or those mariners essential to sailing the captive ship could expect their lives to be spared, to be shipped home for free. The impression given, in both documents and illustrations, is that in the medieval period large numbers of other, useless, mariners were tipped overboard into the sea. Ransoms were certainly mentioned but were not a piratical priority. And the vast one, 3 million golden crowns, demanded for John II of France after he was captured at the Battle of Poitiers, proved impossible to collect.

In contrast to the medieval pirates, the Somalis have a very different objective, the direct acquisition of money, which they use to purchase ever more sophisticated equipment and arms. Most of the specialised vessels of today carry a vast bulk cargo of a single 'unitary' commodity, of no possible interest to the Somali fishermen. As an example, in November 2008 they captured the MV *Sirius Star*, a double-hulled tanker carrying 2 million barrels of crude oil, useless to them in itself, but valued at least at US$100 million. The ship was owned and operated by a subsidiary of the Saudi-Arabian state oil company.[203] All the modern pirates are armed with various kinds of AK47 rifles and the crew on board the captured ship became hostages whose lives were at risk in case of counter-attack.[204] National governments refuse to pay ransoms, but on the other hand, as national and international consortia are in business to keep their ships and cargoes moving as fast as possible, they elect to pay ransoms in a matter of weeks, after negotiation during which initial pirate demands are much reduced. In the case of the MV *Sirius Star*, a sum in excess of US$1 million is believed to have been dropped by parachute into the hands of the pirates waiting on deck, which ensured that the ship sailed on – but also guaranteed that piracy would continue. The international result was a rise in the price of crude oil on global markets.

How far-reaching were the effects of piracy? Piracy affects trade, puts up prices and causes shortages. Considering that both the south coast of England and Somalia lie close to some of the most important trade routes of their time, the disruption is felt as far away as the limits of those routes, in other words, effectively globally. Politically, however, we see a very significant difference between the two periods. In medieval times, piracy interfered with carefully negotiated international truces, agreements which facilitated trade. In the modern period, in contrast, the international community has united in condemning the curse of piracy, and has taken positive steps to combat the problem.

Why was piracy never controlled in the medieval period? The answer is that too many people in authority had an interest in the proceeds. The only exception, the man in a strong enough position to suppress it, was Henry V. But his success in combating piracy lasted less than ten years, during the time when he and his successors had control of all the Channel ports – except those of Brittany, whose mariners remained irrepressibly independent. There was no international cooperation. In the twenty-first century, on the other hand, national navies, sanctioned and encouraged by the UN, NATO and other international organisations, have reduced the incidence of piracy by preventing the skiffs from leaving their home bases. But even with modern means of detection they are unable to cover the whole ocean, and are powerless against armed pirates using hostages as human shields.

Pirates are essentially free, independent operators, flexible and adaptable. The success of all their activities depends on spontaneity, speed and unpredictability. As long as there are seaboard communities not dominated by a firm government, who can operate flexibly and adapt instantly as new opportunities open up, piracy will persist in one variation or another. It is most unlikely that the world will ever see the last of pirates.

# Appendix

## Fourteenth-Century Famine Relief

*On 15 December 1316 the result of an inquiry into the seizure of an Italian ship anchored off Sandwich, Kent was enrolled in the Patent Roll. This is of particular value because it includes, very unusually, a manifest of the component parts of the ship and everything carried in her. Following a précis of the main part of this document, the details, as listed in the roll, are printed here.*

At the height of the Great Famine of 1315–17 a dromond, a large antiquated vessel of a type which seldom ventured out of the Mediterranean, arrived under the king's safe conduct and anchored in The Downs, the roadstead outside Sandwich. The ship was the *St John of Genoa*, and her 'patron' (the owner and also acting master) was James de Roco, a merchant of Genoa. The cargo, however, is unlikely to have been taken on in Italy, but rather picked up in ports in Iberia or on the Atlantic coast of southern France. Summarised in the inquisition, it consisted of 'wheat, wine [*sic*], honey and other victuals', although in fact very little wine is listed in the manifest: the scribe may have entered that as a matter of habit. These supplies were probably intended either to feed the urban population of London, or to be trans-shipped to the starving garrison at Berwick. But they did not get to either of those places.

Reflecting the dire conditions and the intense competition for food at that time, on 20 May, Ascension Day, 1316 Berenger Blanc, Admiral of Calais, sailed across the Channel with a force of twenty-nine ships and carried off this ship, together with all its rigging, and the merchandise. Although the King of England made at least two demands of the King of France for the return of ship and goods, it seems most unlikely that his requests met a positive response.

The list, with minor annotations, is as follows:

| | | | |
|---|---|---|---|
| The hull of the ship, with mast, yard, rudder and 3 boats | of the price of | 300*l* | sterling. |
| Another spare mast | " | 10*l* | " |
| 2 new sails with bonnets | " | 70*l* | " |
| 2 coverings | " | 6*l* | " |
| 16 anchors | " | 50*l* | " |
| 13 great cables, new | " | 60*l* | " |
| 7 great cables, old | " | 22*l* | " |
| Many small ropes | " | 40*l* | " |
| 8 great cables of fibre *(de herb')* | " | 6*l* | " |
| 'Polleys' and 'crokes' of iron | " | 5*l* | " |
| 60 oars | " | 60*s* | " |
| 1 mast with sail for the boat | " | 65*s* | " |
| 2 little anchors and 60 planks for making bulwarks | " | 12*l* | " |
| 60 iron armours with 60 targets | " | 36*l* | " |
| 35 cross bows with as many strings ('bander') with 5 chests of quarrels, 35 dozen lances called 'darte' and 3 dozen long lances | " | 18*l* 10*s* | " |
| 10 swords | " | 60*s* | " |
| 5 empty casks, and 5 casks full of wine | " | 21*l* | " |
| 45 bacons, and 260 cheeses, and of 'biscoke' bread 300 cantels | " | 192*l* | " |
| 40 quarters of beans and peas and 14 sacks of flour, and oil, viz. 3 gallons ('joel') for the ship's stores | " | 110*l* | " |
| Tallow and candles, 36 quarters of salt, and salt-fish for the same stores | " | 32*l* | " |

| | | | |
|---|---|:---:|---|
| 11 quintals of rice, 5 quintals cloves (clav' magn'), and 6 parcels of figs (pec' coton') with other victuals | " | 21*l* | " |
| 160 hemp sacks and 10 hammers (martell'), 2 weights, 4 kettles (cacab') and 6 baners with divers iron instruments | " | 46*l* | " |
| A girdle of silk with silver cups and other jewels of the patron | " | 225*l* | " |
| 130 quarters of wheat of the goods of the patron and mariners (the price of a quarter 22*s* 6*d*) | " | 145*l* 10*s* | " |
| 14 sacks of wheat flour of the goods of the patron and mariners | " | 40*l* | " |
| Robes, beds, chests and necessaries of the mariners | " | 100*l* | " |
| Expenses of 45 mariners staying at Sandwich after the capture of the ship for 3 months, to each 3*d* a day while awaiting the delivery of the ship | " | 46*l* 5*s* | " |
| Expenses of the said 45 mariners returning to their own parts by land | " | 30*l* | " |

The foregoing were the goods of the patron and mariners and besides these the capture of the ship caused them a further loss of l,200*l* sterling, and also the expense of the patron bringing suit for the delivery of his ship as well in the King's Court as in France was 100*l* sterling.

There were also in the ship belonging to the merchants the following goods, viz.:

| | | | |
|---|---|:---:|---|
| 2,100 quarters of wheat, each quarter sale made at Sandwich of the price of | | 2362*l* 2*s* | sterling. |
| 6 cases of soap (savon') | " | 6*l* | " |
| 6 baskets of almonds | " | 12*l* | " |
| 2 bales of pelts | " | 6*l* | " |
| 30 hides of sable | " | 7*l* 10*s* | " |
| 2 casks of honey | " | 17*l* | " |
| 1 pipe of grease | " | 4*l* | " |
| 20 casks of oil | " | 120*l* | " |
| 9 saddles | " | 4*l* 10*s* | " |
| 6 sacks of flour | " | 24*l* | " |
| Loss to the merchants | " | 200*l* | " |

# Notes

## 1. A Lawless Domain

1 Rodger, *The Safeguard*, 79, a complaint by (Great) Yarmouth in 1386

2 Power, *Wool Trade*, 59; CPR 1266–72, 567; CCR 1272–1279, pp. 124–5

3 The names Castile and Spain are used interchangeably here, following academic practice

4 Childs, *Anglo-Castilian Trade*, p. 11

5 Ruddock, *Italian Merchants*, p. 81. See also Briys and Didier, p. 1

6 Sylvester, *Winchelsea*, pp. 230–1, 259–60, refers to old-established custom on the east, south-east and Cornish coasts of England; Gardiner, Early Chancery Proceedings, xiv; Kowaleski, M. South-west Fisheries EcHR 2000; pp. 443, 445–6 Fn 60,62

7 Platt, *Southampton*, pp. 54–66

8 Sumption, III, pp. 153–5

9 Nicholas, II, p. 350

10 James, *Medieval Wine*, pp. 120

11 Evans, *Unconquered Knight*, *passim*

12 Gardiner, *Chancery Proceedings*, xiv

13 Marsden, *Prize Jurisdiction*, pp. 675–86; also Gardiner, *Chancery Proceedings*, pp. ix-xii

14 Marsden, *Law and Custom*, pp. i, 2; Allmand, *Henry V*, p. 67

## 2. THE PASSING TRADE

15 Power, *Wool Trade*, pp. 63–85

16 Power, pp. 16–17, 33; Carus-Wilson and Coleman, *Export Trade*, pp. 1–4: Blair and Ramsay, *Medieval Industries*, p. xxxi. Note: in 2006 the office of Lord Chancellor was split. It is now the Lord Speaker who sits on the woolsack

17 Carus-Wilson, *Twelfth and Thirteenth Centuries*

18 Power, pp. 13–16, 53–5; Ruddock, *Italian Merchants*, p. 44

19 Ruddock, pp. 90–1

20 Salzman, *English Trade*, p. 376

21 Carus-Wilson, *Merchant Venturers*, p. 29

22 Salzman, pp. 376–405; James, *Medieval Wine*, pp. 1–31, 119–50; Platt, *Southampton*, pp. 13, 70–1

23 See below, chapter 8

24 Ruddock, pp. 76–7, 81. Carus Wilson, *Merchant Venturers*, p. 216; Childs, p. 107

25 Ruddock, pp. 81–2. Briys and Didier, 2006, I. The Gulf of Smyrna is now better known as the Gulf of Izmir

26 Childs, pp. 12–14

27 Childs, p. 19

28 Margaret Sparks, historian of Canterbury Cathedral, personal communication

29 Salzman, *English Trade*, p. 409: CPR 1354–58, p. 546

30 James, p. 201

31 Bridbury, *Salt Trade*, pp. xv–xviii, 36–7, 41, 66–9, 76–8

32 Ruddock, pp. 72–93; Platt, pp. 153–4

## 3. SHIPS, SHIPPING AND TRADE ROUTES

33 General references for this chapter: Anderson, *Sailing Ship*, pp. 58–120; Friel, *Good Ship*; Gardiner, *Cogs, Caravels*

34 e.g. CPR 1292–1301, p. 328; 1321–24, p. 413

35   Anderson, *Sailing Ship*, pp. 98–9, 107, 110

36   Ruddock, *Italian Merchants*, pp. 20–1

37   Fryde, *Trade and Finance*, XIV, p. 297

38   Rodger, *Safeguard*, pp. 66, 82

39   Anderson, p. 120

40   CPR 1429–36, p. 355

41   CPR 1446–52, 442 describes goods being stolen from small vessels while being transferred from Genoese carracks to the shore at Southampton

42   e.g. CPR 1454, p. 169

43   James, *Wine*, pp. 16,18, 24–6, 44, 126–33

44   Nicholas, *History* I, p. 199. The third reissue of Magna Carta can be seen in the Online Library of Liberty

45   Platt, *Southampton*, p. 76. Salzman, *English Trade*, p. 249. Childs, *Anglo-Castilian*, p. 163–72 gives a wider, more detailed, account of the management and crewing of commercial shipping

## 4. The English Channel: A New Frontier

46   Eddison, *Romney Marsh*, pp. 77–82

47   Platt, *Southampton*, pp. 107–8

48   Nicholas I, pp. 170–82; Cannon, *Battle of Sandwich*, pp. 650–1; Brooks, *English Naval Forces*, pp. 204–7

49   Nicholas I, p. 168

50   Cannon, p. 654, quoting Wendover, *Flores Historiarum*

51   Dates from Carpenter, *Minority*

52   Carpenter, *Minority*, p. 27

53   Cannon, *Battle, passim*; also Carpenter, *Minority*; Nicholas I, pp. 174–80

## 5. The Cinque Ports

54   Murray, *Constitutional History*, p. 41

55   Saul, *Herring Industry*, pp. 33–4

56   Rodger, *Safeguard*, p. 49

57   Rodger, *Naval Service*, p. 649–50

58   Murray, p. 19

59  Nicholas, *Royal Navy* 1, pp. 175–83; Rodger, Naval Service, p. 638–9; Murray, p. 35–6

60  Nicholas 1, p. 233; Salzman, *Family of Alard*, pp. 126–41; Childs, *Anglo-Castilian Trade*, pp. 12–13

61  Nicholas 1, 224–9; Salzman, *Family of Alard*, p. 28; CPR 1232–47, pp. 270, 305

62  Childs, *Anglo-Castilian*, pp. 12–13; Salzman, *Family of Alard*, pp. 129, 130

63  Nicholas, I, pp. 200, 241; Murray, p. 33

64  Vale, *Origins*, pp. 59–63

65  Murray, pp. 28–31, 226–30

66  Gervase, ii, pp. 214, 218

67  Nicholas I, p. 213

68  CPR 1258–66, pp. 651, 655

69  Murray, pp. 37–40; CPR 1258–66; Nicholas I, p. 233

70  CPR 1258–66, 573, 1 April 1266; 1266–72, 142, 3 June 1267

71  Eddison, *Romney Marsh*, pp. 96–7

72  Nicholas, I, p. 299

73  Murray, 32–3 and Cheyette, *The Sovereign*, pp. 56–8, both following Marsden, Law and Custom, 50 ff.

74  CPR 1292–1301, pp. 20, 22

75  Nicholas, I, pp. 273–4

76  Brooks, *Cinque Ports Feud*, pp. 44–5

77  Murray, 3

## 6. INSOLVENCY AND FAMINE

78  Vale, *Origins*, p. 176; Childs, *Anglo Castilian Trade*, pp. 12–15

79  Rodger, *Safeguard*, p. 82; Rousson, p. 354

80  Eddison, *Catastrophic Changes*, p. 70; Nicholas 1, p. 270

81  Prestwich, *Edward I*, p. 378; Vale, *Origins*, p. 209

82  Prestwich, p. 372

83  CCR 1302–07, pp. 3, 8, 48; Nightingale, *Mercantile Community*, p. 92

84  CPR 1301–07, pp. 144, 375. Ruddock, *Italian Merchants*, p. 21, gives their name as Spinola

85  CCR 1302–07, p. 34; CPR 1301–07, p. 245

86   CCR 1302–07, pp. 38–9

87   CPR 1301–07, p. 286

88   CCR 1296–1302, p. 499; CPR 1301–07, p. 358

89   CCR 1302–07, p. 196; CPR 1301–07, pp. 208, 237

90   Prestwich, p. 401

91   CPR 1307–13, pp. 364–8

92   CPR 1313–1317, p. 144

93   CPR 1307–13, p. 418

94   Power, *Wool Trade*, p. 59; CCR 1313–18, pp. 73,93

95   CPR 1313–17, pp. 234–5, 585

96   Kershaw, *Great Famine*; Jordan, *Great Famine*, chapter 2

97   CCR 1313–18, pp. 291, 341, 425; CPR 1313–17 501–02, pp. 571–2

98   CCR 1313–18, pp. 385, 457, 563

99   CCR 1313–18, pp. 385, 456–7; 1313–18, pp. 168, 259

100  CCR 1313–18, pp. 461, 594, 593

101  CPR 1313–17, pp. 545–6 ; CCR 1313–18, pp. 315, 553; 1318–23, p. 13.
     All refer to *La Petite Bayard*, except the first, which refers to earlier
     piracy at Margate

102  CPR 1313–17, *passim*, e.g. pp. 514, 583; 1317–21, 167, 180, 601–2
     (at Craudon, Brittany, possibly Crozon, south of Brest)

103  CPR 1317–21, p. 557

104  CCR 1318–23, p. 486; Platt, *Southampton*, p. 107

105  CPR 1321–24, pp. 160, 385

106  Hamilton, *DNB: Tuck, Crown and Nobility*, p. 77

## 7. PORTRAIT OF A PIRATE: JOHN CRABBE (*C.* 1290–1352)

107  This chapter owes a considerable debt to Lucas, John Crabbe

108  CCR 1307–1313, pp. 57–1. For identification of *Crasden*, Brittany, see
     previous chapter, note 25

109  CIM II, p. 89

110  CCR 1313–18, pp. 387, 536

111  The dates here follow the ERS, rather than Lucas

112  Lucas, p. 345

113 CCR 1339–41,pp. 11,139,146, 223–4

114 Sumption, I, p. 264

115 For a detailed account of the Battle of Sluys, see Sumption I, pp. 324–8

## 8. Raids, Devastation and Fear 1337–1389

116 CPR 1338–40, p. 70

117 Nicholas ii, p. 27: Sumption I, pp. 225–7

118 Searle and Burghart, p. 371

119 Ruddock, pp. 32–3; Platt, Southampton, p. 111; CCR 1339–41, p. 74

120 CFR 1337–47, p. 97; Platt, pp. 110, 252

121 Platt, pp. 111–15; Searle and Burghart, p. 374

122 Nicholas, ii, 39; Sumption I, p. 249, II, p. 503

123 VCH Sussex, I, p. 509; Searle and Burghart, p. 373; Nicholas ii, pp. 41–2

124 Sumption I, p. 265, 321. The account of this second raid on Boulogne in 'the winter' looks suspiciously like that reported it the previous year. It is possible that the records became duplicated. For a detailed account of the Battle of Sluys, see Sumption, I, pp. 324–8

125 Searle and Burghart, pp. 374–5

126 Sumption, I, p. 348

127 Sumption, I, p. 346–7

128 Sumption, I, 582

129 Sumption, I, pp. 536–8, 576–83; CPR 1345–48, pp. 562–8. For details of Roger Norman, see Platt, p. 253

130 Fowler, p. 101; Sumption II, pp. 66–7

131 Nicholas ii, p. 99; CCR 1354–60, pp. 268–9

132 CCR 1360–64, p. 101; VCH Sussex ix, p. 67; Martin, p. 101

133 Sumption, ii, pp. 437, 445. Leure was the original port on the north bank at the mouth of the Seine. That area has totally disappeared under Le Havre, which was founded in 1517 by Francis I. The fifteenth-century waterfront and old town of Harfleur have, however, survived, though as the result of silting and modern industrial development, the channel of the Seine is now a good mile to the south

134 Nightingale, p. 236; Rodger, Safeguard, p. 110

135 Searle and Burghart, pp. 380–2: Saul, Richard II, pp. 33; Sumption, III, pp. 280–8, 325. I am indebted to Christopher Whittick of ESRO, for the information about prisoners detained in France

136  CPR 1381–85, pp. 425–6

137  *VCH Sussex*, i, pp. 509–12; ii, pp. 139–41; CPR 1381–85, p. 588;
Rodger, *Safeguard*, p. 113

## 9. PRIVATEEERS OF THE WEST COUNTRY

138  Kowalesci, *Port Towns of Fourteenth-Century Devon*, pp. 62–71;
Hatcher, *Tin*, p. 22,25

139  For Hawley, see Watkin, *Dartmouth*; Gardiner, *John Hawley of
Dartmouth*; Pistono, *Henry IV and the English Privateers*, *Henry IV and
John Hawley*

140  The dam is still there in the landscape of today, forming the foundation
of Foss Street

141  Gardiner, pp. 178 et seq., especially 180

142  CPR 1389–92, p. 156 ; CPR 1385–89, pp. 428, 499

143  Watkin, pp. 183–4, 272; CPR 1389–92, pp. 338, 519

144  Watkin, pp. ix–x. The site is marked by a blue plaque

145  Pistono, *Henry IV and the English Privateers*; CPR 1399–1401, p. 271
locates Richard Spicer in Plymouth but this must have been a clerical
error. On that occasion it was said that his armed barge had seized a
ship freighted in Spain in the Downs, off Sandwich

146  CPR 1399–1401, p. 271

147  Pistono, *Henry IV and John Hawley*, pp. 149 Fn 32

148  Ford, *Piracy*, pp. 66,72

149  CCR 1402–05, pp. 24, 27, 57–8, 76

150  CPR 1401–05, pp. 276; CCR 1402–05, p. 57; *Henry IV and John Hawley*,
p. 152

151  CPR 1401–05, pp. 276, 279, 424–5; 1405–08, pp. 228. Guérande
is near St Nazaire in the extreme south of Brittany. The last of these
three had on board bastard wine, and *Lepes*, a wine from the area of
Lepes, a port west of Huelva in the south-west of Spain, which was
well-regarded in England

152  CPR 1401–05, p. 298

153  CPR 1401–05, pp. 360–1, 363, 426–8; CIM 141. The place name
*Plesancia* is problematical. These records suggest it was a port on the
coast of northern Castile, but the only present-day place of that name
is far from the sea in Extremadura, an inland province of Spain west
of Madrid

154 Watkin, p. 378

155 CPR 1401–05, pp. 357,361,364; CCR 1402–05, p. 203, Marsden, *Law and Custom*, p. 112; Rodger, *Safeguard*, p. 114

156 Evans, pp. 115–30, 154–88. Gijon is nearly 100 miles west of Santander, and Finisterre a further 200 miles west

157 CPR 1405–08, pp. 228–9; CPR 1413–16, pp. 36; CPR 1405–09, p. 166

158 Wylie, *Henry IV*, iii, pp. 80–2; Nicholas, ii, p. 463, for the payment for this trip to Paris; Wylie, *Henry V* i, pp. 40 fn1, shows Pay as Water Bailiff of Calais

159 See, for example, Watkin, *Dartmouth*, pp. 381–7

## 10. HENRY V: PIRATES SUPPRESSED

160 Wylie, *Henry IV*, iii, pp. 52–67 *passim*

161 Fernandez-Armesto, *The myth of Henry V. British History in-depth*, Online

162 Allmand, *Henry V*, p. 69

163 Allmand, pp. 222–31; Platt, *Southampton*, pp. 149–50, 257–8; Richmond, *War at Sea*, pp. 112–15; Rose, *Navy*, pp. 247–52; Beaumont Jones, Oxford DNB, William Soper. It is very difficult to establish a precise number for Henry's ships. At any one time, some were decaying and side-lined, while others were still being built

164 Wylie, *Henry V*, i, p. 329; Gardiner, *West Country Shipping*, p. 17; Watkin, *Dartmouth*, pp. 386–7

165 Gardiner, pp. xiv; Wylie, *Henry V*, i, p. 331

166 Gardiner, pp. xv; CPR 1413–16, pp. 110, 344, 410

167 Wylie, *Henry V*, i, p. 449

168 Wylie and Waugh, ii, p. 62

169 Nicholas ii, p. 415

170 Newhall, *English Conquest*, pp. 22–6

171 Nicholas ii, p. 419; Newhall, pp. 29–30

172 Ruddock, *Italian Merchants*, pp. 57–61

173 Newhall, p. 55

174 Newhall, p. 114

175 Newhall, pp. 196e99; CPR 1416–22, pp. 145, 148, 197, 181–2, 201

176 Newhall, pp. 196–201; Barker, *Conquest*, pp. 34–5

177   Newhall, p. 286

178   CCR 1413–19, pp. 525–6; CPR 1416–22, pp. 209 et seq.; Ruddock, p. 60

179   Allmand, pp. 140–4

## 11. HENRY VI: RESURGENCE OF PIRACY

180   Griffiths, *Henry VI*, chapter 1

181   Griffiths, pp. 19–22

182   Newhall, *English Conquest*, p. 292; Barker, *Conquest*, pp. 85–6

183   Barker, *Conquest*, pp. 85–6

184   Griffiths, p. 93

185   Griffiths, pp. 207, 223; Richmond, *Keeping of the Seas*, p. 283; Stratford, John of Bedford, DNB online; Harriss, Henry Beaufort, DNB online

186   Gardiner, xvi

187   Kingsford, pp. 85–7; Gardiner, Chancery Proceedings ## 9, 11,14a–c, 15,16, 24, 25. This book, exceptionally, is referenced according to the numbering of the commissions

188   Gardiner #26; Kingsford, pp. 86–7

189   Gardiner #33; Kingsford, pp. 88–9

190   CPR 1429–36, pp. 218, 221, Gardiner, Chancery Proceedings #28

191   CPR 1429–36, p. 128

192   CPR 1429–36, pp. 128, 202, 608

193   Richmond, *Keeping of the Seas*, pp. 285–9

194   CPR 1429–36, 509, 1436–41, p. 1; Gardiner #39, note

195   Gardiner #45a

196   CPR 1429–36, p. 352; 1436–41, pp. 373, 575–6; 1441–46, p. 246. CCR 1441–47, p. 148

197   CPR 1441–46, pp. 420–1; 1446–52, pp. 186, 189, 190, 432, 435

198   Bridbury, *Salt Trade*, pp. 90–1

199   Kingswood, pp. 89–90

200   Tuck, p. 313

## 12. T<small>HEN AND</small> N<small>OW</small>

201 *Associated Press*, 28 November 2008; *Times of India*, 3 December 2008

202 Runyan 1994, *The Cog*, p. 49

203 BBC News Channel online, 2 November 2009, 9.30 GMT

204 The risk to life has been demonstrated several times when counter-attacks failed. For example, two of a ship's crew were murdered on 26 January 2011 when an attempt was made to rescue hostages, BBC News online, 10 February 2011; and four American hostages were shot on board their yacht in similar circumstances, Associated Press release, 27 April 2012

# Bibliography

ABBREVIATIONS

CCR   Calendar of the Close Rolls

CFR   Calendar of the Fine Rolls

CIM   Calendar of Inquisitions Miscellaneous

CPR   Calendar of the Patent Rolls

DNB   Oxford Dictionary of Biography, online version

       Library of Liberty, online version

EcHR   Economic History Review

EHR   English Historical Review

ERS   Exchequer Rolls of Scotland

TRHS  Transactions of the Royal Historical Society

VCH   Victoria County History, Sussex, vols i, ii, ix


Gervase of Canterbury, Rolls Series 73, 2 vols, 1879, 1880, London,
   Longmans, ed. W. Stubbs
Matthew Paris, *Chronica Majora*, Rolls Series vols ii, iii, 1874, 1876,
   ed. H.R. Luard

Allmand, Christopher, *Henry V* (Methuen, 1992)

Anderson, R. and R.C., *The Sailing Ship* (2nd Edn) (Harrap, 1948)

Barker, J., *Conquest, the English Kingdom of France* (Abacus, 2009) (paperback edition, 2010)

Beaumont Jones, Tom, William Soper (d.1459) DNB (2004)

Blair, J. and Ramsay, N. (eds), *English Medieval Industries* (Hambledon, 1991)

Bridbury, A.R., *England and the Salt Trade in the Later Middle Ages* (Oxford, 1955)

Briys, Eric and Didier, Joos de ter Beerst, 'The Zaccaria Deal'. Draft of paper, *XIV International Economic History Conference* (Helsinki, 2006)

Brooks, F.W., *The English Naval Forces, 1199–1272* (London, 1962)

Brooks, F.W., 'The Cinque Ports Feud with Yarmouth in the Thirteenth Century', *Mariners Mirror* (1933), pp. 19, 27–51

Cannon, H.L., 'The Battle of Sandwich and Eustace the Monk', *EHR* xxvii (1912), pp. 649–70

Carpenter, D.A., *The Minority of Henry III* (Methuen, 1990)

Carus-Wilson, E.M., 'The English Cloth Industry in the late Twelfth and Early Thirteenth Centuries', *EcHR* (Ser.1) (1944), pp. xiv, 32–50

Carus-Wilson, E.M., *Medieval Merchant Venturers* (Methuen, 1954)

Carus-Wilson, E.M. and Coleman, O., *England's Export Trade 1275–1547* (Oxford, 1963)

Cheyette, F.L., 'The Sovereign and the Pirates 1332', *Speculum* 45 (1970), pp. 40–60

Childs, W.R., *Anglo Castilian Trade* (Manchester, 1978)

Eddison, J., 'Catastrophic Changes: Evolution of the Barrier Beaches of Rye Bay', in *Romney Marsh, Environmental Change*, (ed. Eddison, J., Gardiner, M. & Long, A.), OUCA monograph (1998), pp. 46, 65–88

Eddison, J. *Romney Marsh; Survival on a Frontier* (Tempus, 2000)

Evans, J. (ed. and trans.) *Diaz de Gamez, Gutierre, 1431–1449. The Unconquered Knight: A Chronicle of the Deeds of Don Pero Nino* (1928, Republished Boydell, 2004)

Fernandez-Armesto, Felipe, 'The Myth of Henry V', British History in-depth, Online (2009)

Ford, C.J., 'Piracy or Policy: The Crisis in the Channel, 1400–1403', *TRHS* 5th ser. (1979), pp. 29, 63–78

Fowler, K (ed.), *The Hundred Years War* (Macmillan, 1971)

Friel, I., 'The Carrack: The Advent of the Full Rigged Ship', in *Cogs, Caravels and Galleons,* ed R. Gardiner (1994), pp. 77–90

Friel, I., *The Good Ship, 1200–1520* (British Museum, 1995)

Fryde, E.B., *Studies in Medieval Trade and Finance* (Hambledon, 1983)

Gardiner, D., *Historic Haven: The Story of Sandwich* (Pilgrim Press, Derby, 1954)

Gardiner, D., 'John Hawley of Dartmouth', Devonshire Association for the Advancement of Science, Literature and Art., Rep. and Trans. (1966), pp. 98, 173–205

Gardiner, D. (ed. and intro.), *A Calendar of Early Chancery Proceedings relating to West Country Shipping 1388–1493* (Devon and Cornwall Record Society, NS, 21) (1976)

Gardiner, R. (ed.), *Cogs, Caravels and Galleons 1000–1650* (Conway Maritime Press, 1994)

Griffiths, R.A., *The Reign of King Henry VI* (Sutton, 1998)

Hamilton, J.S., 'Hugh Despenser the Younger' (2004), Oxford DNB online edn, 2008

Harriss, G.L., 'Henry Beaufort (1375?–1447)' (2004), Oxford DNB online edn, 2010

Hatcher, John, *English Tin Production and Trade before 1550* (Oxford, 1973)

Homer, R.F. (ed. Blair, J. and Ramsay, N.), 'Tin, Lead and Pewter' in *English Medieval Industries* (1991), pp. 57–80

James, Margery K. (ed. Veale, E.M.) *Studies in the Medieval Wine Trade* (Oxford, 1971)

Jordan, W.C., *The Great Famine: Northern Europe in the Early Fourteenth Century* (Princeton, 1996)

Kershaw, Ian, 'The Great Famine and Agrarian Crisis in England, 1315–1322', *Past and Present* (1973), pp. 59, 3–50

Kingsford, C.L., 'West Country Piracy: The School of English Seamen' in *Prejudice and Promise* (Oxford, 1925), pp. 78–106

Kowaleski, M., 'The Expansion of the South-Western Fisheries in late Medieval England', *Ec.H.R.* 53(3) (2000), pp. 429–54

Kowaleski, M. (ed. London, Duffy) 'The Port Towns of Fourteenth-Century Devon', in *The New Maritime History of Devon*, 1 (1992)

Lucas, Henry S., 'John Crabbe: Flemish Pirate, Merchant and Adventurer', *Speculum* 20 (1945), pp. 334–350

Marsden, R.G. (ed.), 'Documents Relating to the Law and Custom of the Sea', *Navy Records Soc.* (1915), p. 49

Marsden, R.G., 'Early Prize Jurisdiction and Prize Law in England', *EcHR* (1909), pp. xxiv, 675–97

Martin, D. and B., *New Winchelsea, Sussex: A Medieval Port Town* (English Heritage, 2004)

Murray, K.M.E., *The Constitutional History of the Cinque Ports* (Manchester, 1935)

Newhall, R.A., *The English Conquest of Normandy 1416–1424* (Yale, 1924)

Nicholas, N.H., *A History of the Royal Navy from the Earliest Times to 1422* 2 vols. (1847, Second Edn, The Scholars' Bookshelf, Cranbury, NJ, USA, 2005)

Nightingale, Pamela, *A Medieval Mercantile Community: The Grocers Company 1000–1485* (Yale, 1995)

Pistono, Stephen, 'Henry IV and the English Privateers', *EcHR* (1975), pp. 90, pp. 322–30

Pistono, Stephen, 'Henry IV and John Hawley, Privateer, 1399–1408', *Devon Ass. Advmt Sci* (1979), pp. 111, 145–63

Platt, Colin, *Medieval Southampton* (Routledge, 1973)

Power, Eileen, *The Wool Trade in English Medieval History* (Oxford, 1941)

Prestwich, M., *Edward I* (Guild Publishing, with Methuen, 1988)

Richmond, C.F., 'The Keeping of the Seas during the Hundred Years War, 1422–1440', *History*, NS 49 (1964), pp. 283–98

Rodger, N.A.M, 'The Naval Service of the Cinque Ports', *EHR* (1996), pp. 636–51

Rodger, N.A.M. *The Safeguard of the Sea: A Naval History of Britain*, I (HarperCollins, 1997)

Rose, S. 'Accounts and Inventories of William Soper, 1422–1427', Navy Records Soc. (1982)

Ruddock, Alwyn A., *Italian Merchants and Shipping in Southampton, 1270–1600* (Southampton, 1951)

Runyan, T.J. (ed. Gardiner, R.), 'The Cog as Warship' in *Cogs, Caravels and Galleons* (1994), pp. 47–58

Salzman, L.F., *English Trade in the Middle Ages* (Oxford, 1931)

Salzman, L.F., 'Some Notes on the Family of Alard', *Sussex Arch. Coll.* LXI (1920), pp. 126–41

Saul, A., 'The Herring Industry at Great Yarmouth c.1280–c.1400', *Norfolk Archaeology* 38 (1983), pp. 33–41

Saul, Nigel, *Richard II* (Yale, 1997)

Searle, E. and Burghart, R., 'The Defense of England and the Peasants Revolt', *Viator* 3 (1972), pp. 365–88

Stratford, J., *John Duke of Bedford, 1389–1435* (2004) Oxford DNB online edn, 2011

Sumption, J., *The Hundred Years War: i Trial by Battle* (1990); *ii Trial by Fire* (1999); *iii Divided Houses* (2009) (Faber and Faber)

Tuck, A., *Crown and Nobility 1272–1461* (Blackwell, 1985)

Tuck, A., 'Richard II (1367–1400)' (2004) in Oxford DNB online edn, 2009

Vale, M., *The Origins of the Hundred Years War* (Clarendon, Oxford, 1996)

Vos, P.C. and Van Heeringen (ed. Fishcher, M.M.), 'Holocene Geology and Occupation History of Zeeland' i, Nethersland Inst. Applied Geoscience (1996)

Watkin, H.R., *Dartmouth* (Devonshire Association, 1935)

Wylie, J.H., *History of England under Henry the Fourth* (4 vols) (London, 1984–98)

Wylie, J.H. (and W. Templeman Waugh), *The Reign of Henry V* (3 vols) (Cambridge, 1914–29)

Unpublished DPhil thesis:

Sylvester, David, 'Maritime Communities in pre-plague England. Winchelsea and the Cinque Ports' (Fordham University, 1999)

# Index